Fifty-Two Years in the Cockpit

VOLUME ONE

by
Sqn Ldr KR (Jacko) Jackson
M.B.E. A.F.C. R.A.F. (Ret)

First Published in Great Britain in 2006 by Tucann Books
Text © Sqn Ldr KR Jackson
All rights reserved
Design © TUCANN*design&print*

ISBN N° 1 873257 69 4

Produced by: TUCANN*design&print*, 19 High Street, Heighington Lincoln LN4 1RG
Tel & Fax: 01522 790009
www.tucann.co.uk

CONTENTS

CHAPTER 1
Early Days

It seems to be something of a cliche that all aviators when they eventually get around to writing their memoirs state that becoming a pilot was all that they had ever dreamt about in their youth. In my case I can, with hand on heart, state that was absolutely true, but I must add that there were two particularly good reasons why it should have been so in my case. Firstly, my mother's only brother, Henry Brockbank, had served in WWI as an RFC pilot. He had started out as a despatch rider due, it seems, to the fact that in pre-1914 times he was the proud owner of a motor bike- one of the few so to speak. He eventually transferred to the RFC and completed his pilot training at an airfield called Rendcombe, near Cirencester, which is still in use today, both as an airfield and wartime museum. It is based on the concept of an operational RFC airfield, with one or two of the original buildings still in use. It is home to the "Crunchie" aerobatic team, amongst others and well worth a visit.

The second influence on my decision to aim for a life in aviation was that my home town of Southport, Lancashire was well to the fore when it came to aviation. However, I had better start at the very beginning.

I was born on the 5th September 1923, the second son of Charles and Violet Jackson. My father, who served throughout WWI in one of the 'pals' regiments, was a born and bred Sandgrounder. That is a nickname given to people from Marshside, a village to the north of Southport whose main industry was shrimping. This was done by horse and cart in the shallow waters off the very flat coastline. The name lived on in that Southport Football Club, my second passion in life, have ever since formation been referred to as the Sandgrounders. On my mother's side, the Brockbank family had been in the cotton industry in Bolton. Due to my Grandfather's suffering severe health problems from industrial pollution, they had been told that his only chance was to move to a seaside resort, or even migrate to a better climate, so they moved to sunny Southport. Henry Brockbank senior lived to a ripe old age! He often talked of seeing a German airship over Bolton during WWI and when for the first time he saw an aeroplane in flight during a visit to Blackpool. It was flown by a Claude Grahame-White. The Guinness book of air facts and feats records that Grahame-White, on 10th August 1910, attempted the very first unofficial mail carriage by air in the UK. He had taken off from Squires Gate, Blackpool with the intention of landing at Southport, but was forced down by bad weather. That book also records that he was flying a Bleriot monoplane, as per the first Channel crossing. When one considers that the Wright brothers only took to the skies in 1903, 1910 was very early days indeed. The Guinness book also records another first for Southport. It states that the first regular civil air service in England was started there by A V Roe and Co on 10th May 1919, and was discontinued on 30th September 1919. Using three seat Avro aircraft, services were flown from Alexander Park airstrip, Manchester to Southport and also to Blackpool. One hundred and ninety four scheduled flights were made during that period. The cost of a one way flight was four guineas. What with the cost and the unpredictable sea fogs that sometimes sweep in from the Irish Sea to affect the Lancashire shore line at times, plus the fact that both towns had direct rail links with Manchester, it was not surprising that it was such a short lived venture.

My own first recollection of aeroplanes was standing on the sand dunes watching a pleasure flight taking off and landing on Southport beach, just across the road from the town's Pleasure Land. The aircraft in use initially were Avro 504s, soon to be replaced by D H Moths which could accommodate four passengers in a cabin, with the pilot in an open cockpit to the rear. I seem to remember that the cost was about five shillings for once around the town. Twenty five pence in today's money. The operation was owned and operated by an ex-RFC friend of my uncle, named Girox, a French Canadian who had decided the UK was the place to be after WWI. Needless to say, Alan Cobham's flying circus was an annual summer event. Not only aerobatics, but also parachute descents from an aircraft when two parachutists would position themselves, one on each side of the twin engined bi-plane, clinging to the outer struts at take off. Another item I recall was a "flying flea", A type which was eventually grounded, after a number of structural failures resulting in fatalities.

Then there was a chap called "The Birdman: who would jump from an aircraft with fabric wings attached to his wrists and ankles and swoop around like a bat before pulling the rip cord of his chest type parachute after folding his wings. It was to be sixty years later before I was given an account of his sad death during one of his descents. I was told that he usually fitted his chest type parachute himself after donning his harness because being left handed he always fitted the chute with the release handle to his left side for obvious reasons. On the fateful day a lady 'helper' put it on for a right handed person. The rest is history as they say.

The mid 1930s to the start of WWII in 1939 was pure vintage from an aviation point of view in Southport. We had two firsts during that time, both by the same pilot, Captain Dick Merrill, a legend in his own life time if ever there was one. Basically, Dick Merrill was the first pilot to complete a round trip of the Atlantic after he took off from the hard packed Southport sands to make the return flight with Harry Rickman, a well known entertainer in those days, as his co-pilot. The aircraft used was a Vultee single engined monoplane, named 'Lady Peace'. The only remaining example of that type can be seen in the Shannon air museum. Great play was made in the press about the aircraft carrying 40,000 ping pong balls to keep the aircraft afloat in the event of a ditching which, in the event, very nearly occurred when the co-pilot released a lot of fuel over the Atlantic, due to a monumental misunderstanding between the two pilots. However, they managed to make a landing of sorts on a peat bog in Newfoundland. Because of the prevailing westerly winds over the North Atlantic a lot more fuel was to be carried on this second leg, which brought the total weight to over twice that recommended by the aircraft makers. Although the authorities at both Croydon Airport, runway length 3,600', and Liverpool Airport, runway length 6,000', tried desperately hard to induce Dick Merrill to take off from their airfields, Dick decided that Southport, with 10 miles of sand, was the answer. Take off time on the 14th September 1936 was scheduled for about 4 o'clock in the morning and my grandfather, who was almost as keen as myself to witness this historic event, drove the entire family down to the beach in his Lanchester car. This car was rather unique for it's time having a fluid fly wheel pre-selector engine which I was allowed to drive, both during and after WWII. Watching the night take off from a position on top of the tallest sand dune we could find at about the mid point of the three mile run was quite something. I have often noted over the years that aeroplanes always look so much larger at night when one can only see the wing tip navigation lights of green and red, representing starboard and port respectively. This was no exception, particularly so, as it was my very first view of a night take off. The "Lady Peace" looked gigantic for those days, and the take off run seemed to go on forever. Although Dick thought he had taken off in about a mile, a daylight inspection later indicated that from the tyre imprints in the sand it was nearer a mile and a half. Dick had been proved right, perhaps the Guinness record book should have recorded this as the longest runway ever in the UK. Dick Merrill was back again at Southport sands well within the year to complete another double crossing of the Atlantic.

This time it was the first ever commercial double crossing in that he flew pictures of the Hindenburg airship disaster eastbound, and those of the 1937 Coronation westbound. This time Dick's co-pilot was a professional pilot called Jack Lambie who, like Dick, was employed by Eastern Airlines. The Mayor of Southport promised a five mile prepared strip this time for the flight, which was flown on the 13th May 1937 in a Lockheed twin engined aircraft named "Daily Express". This type was an early Electra, which later led on to Hudsons, Lodestars, etc The full detail of Dick Merrill's flying life during which he amassed 45,000 flying hours, can be found in a book entitled "Wings of man". A snippet from that book came as a complete surprise- the use of ping pong balls by Dick Merrill in his Vulta aeroplane was not a first, Handley Page having already used them some time before in one of their larger aircraft. It was ironic that the weather in the London area delayed the aircraft bringing the Coronation pictures to Southport to the extent that Dick had to keep delaying his departure until last light, when he eventually took off at about 8.30pm. The twin Lockheed was still in view heading west as the inbound aircraft from London landed. Other 'first day' items aboard the Electra still made it the first commercial double crossing of the Atlantic.

The Southport sands were also used for motor bike racing as well as world land speed record attempts by the late Malcolm Campbell in his car called "Bluebird". One man well to the fore, as his trophy cabinet indicated at the time, was my ex-RFC uncle who used to ride for both the "Cotton" and "Norton" teams, plus some light car racing. "Brockie", as my uncle Harry was known throughout the racing world, was also an Isle of Man TT rider and managed a second place one year. It was my grandfather's wish to see his only son actually race in the TT that led to my first aeroplane flight. Due to advancing years he made some inquiries and established that it could all be done in one short day, and so it was that the family car was used to drive the two of us to Liverpool Speke airport. My boyish enthusiasm, I was only 12 years old at the time, knew no bounds as we were led out to a beautiful looking, twin engined bi-plane. It was a D H Rapide of Railway Air Services that was to take us across the Irish Sea to Ronaldsway. However, the day was to improve. My grandfather was looking very pleased indeed each time my uncle whizzed by. I was to find out later that on the equivalent day, some years before, he had seen a news vendor, with his billboard stating- Local rider in TT crash. Yes, it was Brockie, but my grandfather, after losing no time in buying a copy, had read, "the rider was seriously injured". What had actually been printed was "the rider was not seriously injured". He had been too distressed to r-read the article before quickly departing for home. After the race we duly reported back at Ronaldsway to find not only a change of aircraft type, but route as well. I could hardly believe my eyes when we trooped out to a four engined aircraft bi-plane, a D H 86 in fact. We had been told that there would be an intermediate stop at Squires Gate Blackpool before Liverpool. They could have stopped at ten intermediates for all I cared. What a day!

Other aerial activity that kept my interest in aviation on a high came thick and fast. With the prospect of another war with Germany looking ever more likely towards the end of the thirties, the army had called upon a civilian aircraft firm to provide aircraft as targets for searchlight practice for the defenders of Liverpool. When the searchlights did pick up their target, which did not seem all that often, the illuminated aircraft looked lovely against the black skies, until sudden turns by the pilot usually managed to effect an escape for a while.

Between 1935 and the start of WWII a vast expansion programme of the RAF had started in earnest and as part of the propaganda to attract new recruits there appeared a poster entitled "See life from a new angle". It depicted a pilot's view from the cockpit of a Miles Magister aircraft, in a very steep turn looking earthwards. By far the most evocative poster that any service ever produced before or since.

On April 1st 1939, the RAF's twenty first birthday, the Air Secretary, Sir Kingsley Wood, announced that 50 RAF squadrons would be twinned with various tows and cities in the UK. Southport was one of them and became affiliated to No. 58 based at Linton-on-Ouse, Yorkshire. At that time they flew large Armstrong Whitley Bombers and one was sent to not only give a fly past over Southport but actually land on the beach! Another memorable day.

One unscheduled aviation event was an aircraft trailing white smoke, sign writing "Persil" in the sky. This was performed above our village of Ainsdale, population all of 1500 in those days, and I expect that this was a map reading error of an unbelievable magnitude. Persil would, no doubt, have preferred their name over the city of Liverpool to get their moneys worth. This type of sign writing was achieved by injecting a fluid into the aircraft's engine exhaust at the push of a button and, unlike vapour trails made by high flying aircraft, can be carried out at any level.

The last of my aviation recollections of those days was an item appearing in the local press that a passenger flying boat was shortly to fly over significant seaside resorts around the UK, and that Southport would be included on this goodwill flight. The Royal Navy would, of course, have called it showing the flag. A plus or minus time was given, which led to a lot of chit chat amongst my friends. We could not all play hookey on the same day or the game would be up. One of our brighter lads suddenly worked out that on that particular day we had our monthly swimming lesson at the Victoria Baths on Southport promenade, right behind the Southport pier which would, we reasoned, be the focal point for the aircraft. Although we were normally in high spirits when we collected our bus tokens for the unsupervised ride into town, the lady teacher handing them out did make the point that we all seemed to be on a high, even by our standards, when getting away from school for the morning. The plus or minus time for the Short "C" class Flying Boat meant that if it arrived early we might all miss seeing it by a whisker. The next person to show some disbelief was the baths supervisor, who normally had some difficulty in getting us out of the pool at the appointed time of mid day. By that time he had run out of customers as one by one we had all slunk off and after getting changed in double quick time started to form a group on the prom roadside all looking skyward. The aircraft was, in the event, spot on time. It was one of the largest aircraft of it's day and left an indelible impression on my mind, not least of all when I boarded one on the River Nile in Cairo for a two day passage to Karachi which I will cover later. The aircraft looked so elegant and completely in it's element. If only I could have been up there and would I, one day, become a pilot? Events were to prove stranger than fiction in the context of four engined aircraft over that part of Southport 40 years later, almost to the day.

It was about 1937 that I decided to throw everything into joining the RAF through the Aircraft Apprentice Scheme when one or two of our senior boys returned to our school to tell us about it, or was it to show off their brand new RAF uniforms? A bit of both I suspect. However, meeting other boys who had actually sat the entrance exam proved very useful indeed. Obviously, some of us needed extra tuition in technical subjects and so it was that the headmaster decided to change the syllabus for the five or six boys who wanted to join the RAF, Royal Navy, or in two cases the Mercantile Marine. I can still remember all the names of our little group (Jimmy Hesketh, Les Blunt, Ken Clarke, Ken Scrambler, and Billy Wynne), not least because our headmaster, a Mr Watkins, organised a real voyage of discovery which all our group of six went on. I had better explain that before WWII all military movements to foreign parts, mainly the Middle and Far East, was carried out by troopships such as the Somersetshire. However, due to the fact the vast majority of these movements consisted of entire army units who, naturally, wanted the movement over a short time scale and once there might spend up to 7 or 8 years before returning, meant that these ships were not exactly over employed at times. In fact, there were two specific periods in each year called trooping seasons, Spring and Autumn. This left quite a lot of slack, so the ship owners offered up these troopers for the use of school children to see parts of the world. In our case it was a voyage of 10 days along the Norwegian coast beyond the Arctic Circle and back, and all for the princely sum of £5. Some ports visited included Bergen, Stavanger, Trondheim, Tromso, and a village called Hell! Our ship was called the Navasa and life aboard was as for it's normal role; i.e. sleeping in hammocks, food delivered to each mess table and served by each of us in turn according to a rota. The crew by and large were Taskas from Northern India with British Officers. The cruise started and ended at Tilbury and what would be unthinkable nowadays was that we made our own way to the ship and back to Southport unescorted. This trip left me well prepared for a wartime voyage to South Africa, to say nothing of a zest for foreign travel.

On our return it was back to the 'grindstone' with a vengeance to prepare ourselves for the entrance exams. The thought process behind hoping to join the Royal Air Force as a boy apprentice was that it was well known that in those days the only way to become a service pilot was either as an officer via a university, particularly so from universities that had their own air squadron (UAS) or as a Sergeant Pilot, taken invariably from those already serving. In both cases they were for only four to six years flying.

The entrance exams for boys was held twice a year, in the Spring and Autumn, with the successful applicants joining the following August or February respectively. Ken Clarke and myself both took and passed the exam in the spring of 1939. I still remember my father rushing upstairs to tell me the good news after the first post arrived. I don't think my mother was all that pleased however! I still have the large brown envelope sent by the Air Ministry giving details of successful candidates. We had been asked to write out our own address on envelopes at the time of the exam and I can still recognise my own youthful writing on it.

So it was that I was to join the 40th entry of Halton Aircraft Apprentices Our entry was to be the largest yet, due to the expansion scheme of the RAF which was then in full swing. This meant that induction dates, always on a Tuesday, would still start in late August but in our case drift into the first week of September. It was to be the 5th September, my birthday, just two days after the start of World War II, when I was to report to RAF Halton. Would they still want us with the prospect of a three year training course ahead? However my joining instructions arrived in a later post along with my rail warrant. I was to report to Baker Street Station, London where I was to meet an RAF corporal, who would be in uniform, on platform something or other. Sherlock Holmes! Baker Street, what next? Well later that week, I was sworn in with the number 577221. I know it was only by chance after all, but it still made my day 221 Baker Street.

My father had walked with me to our local station on the Southport to Liverpool line to see me on my way. He carried my suitcase, which had been donated to me by my mothers unmarried twin sister, Lilly Brockbank, to mark my entering the RAF. Sadly she died 18 months later. (I still have that suitcase as a reminder.) Nearing the Liverpool Exchange Station I was taken aback to see Barrage Balloons flying over the city-quite a forboding sight. I walked to Lime St. Station to catch the London Euston train and then on to Baker St.

CHAPTER 2
A Trenchard Brat - Halton

After reporting to the RAF Corporal at Baker St. Station, and seeing my name ticked off his list, there followed a longish wait as other boys arrived in dribs and drabs from all corners of the UK. Eventually a special train pulled in to the platform and the corporal told us that it was to take us to a place called Wendover, which turned out to be a lovely little village in the Buckinghamshire countryside, and remains so to this day. After alighting, the Corporal, plus quite a few reinforcements of a similar rank from Halton Camp, soon rounded us up in squads of fifty or so and marched us off in four abreast. Four abreast was the norm until 1940 when it was reduced to three. The march of about 2 miles up the hill to Paine barracks took us right down the main street of Wendover, and even as boys we could not help but notice the interest the locals took in our progress. I must admit that all of us being just out of school that summer term of 1939, and one or two still in short trousers, must have presented quite a spectacle. We found out the real reason for the locals' intense interest later when we discovered that we were the first boy recruits to Halton to have been seen marching in civilian clothes. The unedifying scene was due to the usual 3 ton RAF lorries being otherwise engaged on more important duties, and/or civilian coaches were not available.

On arrival at No 3 Wing in Payne Barracks, we were allocated beds in 3 story barrack blocks in alphabetical order, twenty per room. We were told that we need not start making friends just yet because later in the week we would be re-located, depending on what trade we had been selected for. A Leading Apprentice from a senior entry was on hand in each room to give us instruction in bed making and no one could have got by without it. The beds were called Macdonald's and made completely out of cast iron. They split into two distinct halves so that the foot end could be pushed back under the headrest end to give more floor space during the day.

After pulling out the underpart of the Macdonald to it's full length three identical pieces of square mattress were placed on the rigid structure, these were always referred to as biscuits. The first of four blankets was used to wrap around the biscuits to try and keep them in a compact unit, then followed two sheets and the three remaining blankets. This meant that all beds had to be completely made up each morning and re-laid in the evening. Quite a task in itself because all sheets and blankets had to be folded and left in a specific order ready for a daily inspection. In a steel locker near each bed a knife, fork and spoon plus a drinking mug had already been pre-laid for use. The leading apprentice in charge then led us off to the cookhouse for our first RAF meal. After being fed and watered it was a pleasure to try our hand at bed making Macdonald style. During this first hit and miss attempt it became very obvious that one or two had never made a bed in their lives, unlike the majority of us who had been on a Scout camp. Fifty plus years later, to mark the ending of the Aircraft Apprentice scheme, which had lasted from inception in 1922 to it's demise in 1993, the RAF Museum at Hendon laid on a special exhibition to highlight it's achievements. I lost no time in thinking of a good excuse to visit London after it's opening and, of course, the museum. I found it fascinating to look over all the exhibits and memorabilia on display. The last notice I read, however, gave rise to a wry smile and, no doubt, to all others of pre-1946 RAF Halton vintage who read it. It stated that the museum was very keen to trace a Macdonald bed to add to this collection. Fat chance! No doubt all had been snapped up by scrap dealers years ago.

The rest of the week was all go and included a stiff medical, issue of uniforms and the swearing in, which in our case took place in the reading room in the NAAFI. It was during the issuing of uniforms that an amusing incident occurred. One of our entry in the queue, near me, was on the short or 'minimum' size. After eventually receiving his slacks and tunic from a stock pile, well towards the very back of the stores he held them up for inspection. His tunic looked about the right size, but the look of horror on his face when he held up his slacks was something to behold. They should have been destroyed some three years before when pantaloon trousers, worn with puttees and choke neck tunics, were consigned to the RAF's dustbin of history. We discovered later that was also the time that public beatings for serious crime came to an end for aircraft apprentices. Folk law had it that this barbaric punishment was helped on it's way out by some Officers feeling that the F/Sgt policeman who administered these beatings was more heavy handed than he needed to be. He also appeared to take sadistic pleasure in dishing it out. All generations of apprentices had, up until WWII, the option of buying themselves out in the first three months of service, although it seems very few did. In our case, joining just as WWII broke out, all of the fortieth entry had the option of returning home immediately without penalty- not one did so.

The allocation of trades also took place in this first week. I was to become a Fitter IIA, that is to say a Fitter Airframes. I was a little disappointed to say the least because I had hoped for Fitter IIE, that was a Fitter Engines. My childish rationale was that the importance of fitter airframes, or riggers as they were still called in those days, would diminish with the demise of fabric covered bi-planes, which needed constant checking and craftsmanship, being replaced with metal stressed skin monoplanes which would require far less attention and expertise. The expertise required by engine fitters also took a nose dive when jet engines for aircraft became the norm.

It was in the 1920s that Frank Whittle had managed to become an aircraft apprentice at his third attempt. The first time he tried to enlist he was rejected for being too small, at his second attempt, which was after growing 3 inches in no time at all after taking special exercises recommended by an RAF Corporal, he was again rejected because he had been rejected once before! In today's parlance he became economical with the truth in that he forgot to record these two failed attempts on his third application! Bingo, the inventor of the jet engine was eventually allowed to join the RAF as an Aircraft Apprentice, after which he was specially selected for a Cranwell cadetship and later still a technical university course. Overlapping all of this activity he was working hard on the concept of pure jet propulsion to power aircraft and actually registered his patent in 1936, although it was not until 1941 that a jet aircraft flew in England for the first time, appropriately enough, from RAF Cranwell, where the late Air Commodore Frank Whittle had gained his RAF wings. The jet engine was in nearly all respects to simplify the world of the aircraft aero engine technician.

To return to my own time at RAF Halton, the pace was frantic, first of all we had to re-locate as forewarned. All Fitter Airframes were to stay in No 3 Wing, which was a bonus because we just walked from one barrack block to another and, in any event, the second one was closer to the cookhouse and NAAFI. Trades other than Fitter IIA moved to other wings and for electrical trades other Stations. Two of our more popular drill and physical training instructors (PTIs) both volunteered to become air gunners and left at the same time in 1940 to start aircrew training. The names of Corporals Scott and Welch were easy to remember and I have often wondered over the years if either survived the war. The odds seem stacked against both being alive by 1945.

We soon received lectures on customs of the service and one of importance to us all was pay and leave arrangements. The pay was to be 1 shilling per day and paid every fortnight. However, 3 days pay per week was to be withheld to pay for any barrack damage that might occur. This withheld money would be released at each of the three times per year leave points; Christmas, Easter and Summer. This left 4 shillings per week to squander! In today's money that is 33p. It did not work out too badly in the event due to the fact that time to spend money was very scarce indeed as we were working $5^1/2$ days per week plus a church parade on Sunday mornings. Also, we were not allowed to smoke, drink alcohol or even try and make our mark with females. Leaving the camp was only allowed after duty on Saturdays and Sundays. The bright side was that the camp cinema charged only three pence for admission (about $1^1/2$ new pennies) and sausage and chips in the NAAFI (6 pence (3 new pennies)).

We soon settled down in our new dorm to make friendships that in some cases have lasted for close on sixty years. It was unusual to meet more than a handful of ex-room mates after leaving Halton and entering the big big world of man's service with well over 1,000 stations worldwide in those days but one or two still turn up at Halton's Triennial reunions.

A lecture on air raid precautions brought some ribald comments when we were told that in the event of an air raid warning being sounded during the night hours, we should all take cover under our Macdonald beds! The safest place in the world, we all concurred! The routine from then on was strict and demanding. reveille was sounded at 06:30 hrs by the duty bugler, when we had 'gunfire' which consisted of a cup of coffee and biscuits, then followed the eternal cry of "get fell in' ready to march to the workshops for technical training or Kermode Hall for general studies. At midday it was back up the hill for lunch before returning again to our place of work until 17:00 hrs. During all this toing and froing we were marching behind our own respective wing bands. Although these bands consisted of pipes, bugles and drums, they were always referred to as the drums and consisted of volunteer aircraft apprentices, many of whom had never played anything in their lives before except truant. These marches of about a mile or so were, obviously, under the strict supervision of drill instructors. We marched double ranking, that is in eight abreast until mid 1940, and then six abreast thereafter. In both cases it caused a bit of a nuisance to civilian traffic for the two hundred or so yards that we were on the main Wendover to Tring road. For safety reasons, storm lanterns had to be carried at the rear of the last column for the 17:00 march in Winter. A mighty cheer went up on the rare occasions that the band threw caution to the wind and struck up a tune that had been specifically banned. These proscribed tunes, I understand, had something to do with the Black and Tans in Northern Ireland and the troubles in Scotland of years long ago.

One day that the drums would never have dared to transgress was on a particular Sunday, after church parade, when the Air Officer Commanding (AOC), AVM Sir Oliver Swann CB CBE, had decided that all Wings would march past a dais placed outside the old workshops where he would personally take the salute. When the order "eyes right" was given to our Squadron we all concluded later it was, as 15/16 year olds, a great shock to see our Commander for the first time. He looked so old and ancient. However, when one considers that he was born all of 25 years before an aeroplane ever flew, and that he had reached the dizzy heights of a Captain in the Royal Navy during the first world war, he would look old, wouldn't he? In fact, he had been born in 1878 and had been the first pilot to take off from salt water in England, although the landing was something of a disaster. He had been called out of retirement to command Halton for the first year of WWII. Sir Oliver had been born, like the Royal family, with a Germanic name. Both thought it prudent, during WWI to change surnames. In the case of our AOC it was from Schwann to Swan. He passed away in 1948, 8 years after leaving Halton.

It was not long after we arrived that the most senior course disappeared, literally overnight, about three months short of their normal 3 year point. This pattern was to continue and the 40th entry course came to be the shortest ever at 20 months. However, with reduced periods of leave, less drill and longer working hours, the syllabus was fully covered. This included basic metal work down to millionths of an inch, heat treatment of metals, fabric work, riveting, making control cables to exact lengths by splicing, welding, rigging of the biggest bi-plane the RAF had ever operated (the Sidestrand). The all important airfield stage, and periods in the new workshops, working on modern aircraft, such as the Spitfire, Battle, Hurricane and Lysander followed. This last stage consisted of dismantling and re-fitting of major parts such as mainplanes and tail units, plus metal repairs to fuselages. We also worked on Oleo legs and wheels. It was whilst working on a Lysander that I was more than surprised to find printed on the fuel tank, in bold letters, the name and address of the manufacturer. Not only was it the Vulcan works in my home town of Southport, but it was also the factory that my father was employed, doing his bit for the war effort. Surprise, surprise, during a German night raid on Liverpool a Luftwaffe bomber, in 1941, selected the works for special attention. Direct hits were scored, but my father, who was on duty that night escaped unhurt.

Many events come to mind of my time at Halton, none more so than that of my first flight in an RAF aircraft. The aircraft was a Miles Magister and during the first turn after take off I was immediately reminded of the evocative pre-war poster saying "see life from a new angle"- I certainly was. The pilot was one of our own flight commanders who was one of many on a ground tour at Halton, although what they did with themselves during the day, apart from these odd air experience flights, was something of a mystery. I picked up courage and asked if it was possible to experience a loop the loop. The pilot seemed quite pleased to oblige, although it meant climbing to a higher level than the norm. He not only looped many times, but also threw in one or two rolls. This increased the flight time by about 50% or so, which threw a small spanner in the works for that mornings roster. Apart from my pure delight about the flight it also allayed some fears I secretly held about the possibility of airsickness.

The aerodrome course of about four weeks, which in our case came in the summer of 1940, was the highlight of any aircraft apprentice's time at

Halton. We actually swung propellers to start engines, and generally learnt the strict self discipline required when working on any active airfield. The extra marching distance to the airfield was of no consequence compared with the freedom from the workshops for those few short weeks. It was during our course that we spotted two very interesting aircraft in flight. The first was the magnificent Handley Page 42. A 4 engined bi-plane, operated initially by Imperial Airways. It was making it's stately, slow progress across the Chilterns towards London. An impressive sight by any standards, with both wings and all four engines above the passenger cabin, it was without doubt the Orient Express of the skies. The second aircraft sighting was far more sinister. During an afternoon tea break one of our party suddenly shouted, "Look at that". It was without a shadow of a doubt a JU88 German twin engined bomber, flying at very high speed, for those days at least, and very low level indeed across the far end of the field from West to East. Although there were one or two anti-aircraft machine gun nests around the camp, none had time to fire, nor we to take cover for that matter, it was all over in seconds.

It was during 1940 that I received news from home that my brother, Harry, had been called up and would be joining the Army. It seemed a very short period indeed before he contacted me to arrange a meeting in Wendover one Sunday afternoon. It turned out that he was by then a fully trained member of the Royal Artillery and on very active service in that he was manning ack-ack guns at Maidenhead, in the defence of London. Shortly after our, all too brief, meeting he was posted to the Middle East and we were not to meet again for another three years, and that was under very unusual circumstances.

The final memory recall of Halton days was the high activity required to prepare the old workshops for a royal visit. On the big day I was at my usual bench position, which was not only one of those nearest the central gangway, but also facing the approaching royal party. My only other sight of royalty had been at junior school in Ainsdale when all staff and children of St John's Church had turned out to wave flags at Edward VIII, who in the event sped by and was gone in the blink of an eye. He was on his way to play a round of golf on our world famous Southport and Ainsdale course (The S & A). This time, however, the royal entourage of the Duke of Kent was making very slow progress indeed, down the central aisle. Although he did not speak, he certainly seemed to be taking a keen interest in our attempts at hand filing cubes of metal, with constant referrals to micrometers to check for size. I was later shocked to hear of his death in a Sunderland Flying Boat accident in Scotland , when he was in transit to Iceland to boost morale in RAF Anti-submarine squadrons based on that island. There was one survivor, the rear gunner, of that tragic accident, one of the unsolved mysteries of the air category.

The big day came at long last when we were to leave that great institution of the RAF, Halton. No longer would we be merely Trenchard Brats, we would be known as ex-Brats and take great pride in it to the end of our days- long or short. And for those who became Flight Engineers in Bomber Command it was in many cases all too short. It was policy at the time to try and arrange initial postings for the start of our mans service to Stations nearest to our home towns with maintenance units having highest priority. It was normally for about six months and from then on it was a case of anywhere and everywhere. With Liverpool and Manchester having high population levels, about 20 of the fortieth entry found ourselves on our way to No 30 Maintenance Unit at RAF Sealand near Chester.

CHAPTER 3
Aircraft Fitter, RAF Sealand

We found it very strange indeed that the RAF should think it necessary to provide a Sergeant as an escort to Sealand. After all, on first joining we had all found our way to Baker Street by ourselves and on leave periods also. One or two cynics in our party suggested that as some of us had not reached the magic age of $17^1/_2$ when mans pay became due, he had been sent along to explain the intricacies of boy's pay to the local accounts department so that no overpayment would occur. Others thought that apprentices travelling on leave in units of one or two was one thing, but the thought of twenty in one railway carriage was another, especially on day one of being let loose from Halton. Yet another recalled, as if we ever needed to be reminded, that during the return to Halton by a special train of about 400 members of our entry who had been sent to RAF Cosford for their first year of our course, an object had been hurled from a train window, which had seriously injured a track repair worker, and no chance of a repetition was being taken. Whatever the reason we were stuck with him, which meant no high jinks this time. Most of our route was by now getting very familiar. Embark at Tring railway station, pity it was not Wendover for a last look, change at Crewe for Chester and then after another change we disembarked at Sealand. A very pleasant surprise followed when we found that the rail station was right in the middle of Sealand camp. Only a few hundred yards to lug our bulging kitbags remained. So ended the first chapter in my life in the Royal Air Force which was to span 44 years to the very day.

There was a set procedure on arriving or departing any RAF station in those days, and might well still be so to this day. It consisted of traipsing around the camp collecting signatures on a piece of paper at the more important sections. Some aircrew actually carried a replica around when they were not arriving, nor departing! It saved answering unwanted questions when they were on the scive. It was only a matter of time when quite a few of our party of twenty met up at the same place and time, doing the rounds. I recall it was a WAAF corporal in her thirty somethings in accounts who seemed to be under pressure sorting out a group of five or six as to who were over $17^1/_2$ years old for mans pay, and those under that age who would remain on boys pay, when one of the Station padres arrived on the scene: they always seemed to have that knack. After having a quick look around to take in the situation he, no doubt, concluded that the Royal Air Force had been reduced to cradle snatching to boost numbers. In a very religious voice he implored the WAAF corporal to "look after them, mother them a bit, they would probably be homesick" and then departed so quickly that the poor girl did not have time to reply. The look on her face, however, told all. She had, no doubt, dealt with ex-brats before and heard all about the antics that went on down at Halton. She probably felt that if anybody needed looking after it would be the young girls under her care with yet another 20 monsters on the Station.

Before starting work each morning at Sealand a full turn out took place on the station parade ground at 08:00, despite the fact that the war had been on for nearly two years. On operational stations, open 24 hours a day, a 3 shift system meant that such parades were not only out of the question, but on those built during the war, physically impossible, war or no war, due to the fact that the building of parade grounds was considered a luxury that the nation could well do without nor afford. At Sealand, the Discipline F/Sgt loved his moment of glory but could not help showing his aversion to ex-brats. Perhaps he had good reason, he might even have been on the staff at Halton in years gone by. He was still in full cry when I returned to Sealand 18 months later and did a double take when he spotted me and, no doubt, noted that this time round I was wearing a white flash in my glengarry to denote I was on a flying course, and beyond his control.

My six months, at No 30 MU was split into two distinct parts. One was pure metal work in the workshops on the main camp site, which was to the east of the main Birkenhead to North Wales road. Only one task remains in my mind that was of any real importance and that was helping to make gun mountings from scratch, that is from blueprints and not copies of mountings already in existence. The importance of that particular task was highlighted when a signal was received stating that the Catalina aircraft which had first re-located the German Battleship Bismacrk off Greenland was fitted with gun mountings recently made at

No 30 MU. For the few who do not know about the Catalina, it was an American amphibian with two engines and first sold or lease/lent to the RAF without any defensive armaments. This was before the USA had entered the war of course. The Bismarck was eventually dispatched to the deep by gunfire, after being crippled by torpedoes dropped by Swordfish aircraft operating off a Royal Navy carrier, but not, unfortunately, before the Bismarck had sunk the British Battleship HMS Hood. It was the sinking of the Hood that led to one of Winston Churchill's most famous orders; "Sink the Bismarck".

One other event, albeit of a very frivolous nature, occurred in those early days of ladies in uniform. I think it had been visualised that the girls would, in the main, be employed on admin duties and that skirts and not slacks would be the order of the day. that was all to change, of course, and they eventually found their way into virtually every ground trade. However, slacks had still not been issued to all of them when ten or so WAAFs appeared to work alongside us chaps. Improvisation being very much to the fore, meant that in no time at all a wooden hut had been positioned outside the workshops so that the girls could change into and out of their working overhauls after discarding their skirts. This shed was, needless to say, kept firmly locked during working hours, but the day came, of course, when the girl with the key had gone off to the dentist or whatever, and expected to be back before the end of work time. It was a very hot summer's day, and some small windows at the top of the main window frames had been left open to keep the temperature down. In no time at all, one enterprising girl had, with a bit of loose wire, got a main window open. In she jumped and was soon handing out skirts for those outside to sort out. All items of uniform, by the way, had the owners individual service number sewn on at the time of issue. The WAAFs then started to do the almost unthinkable and it was almost certainly a case of 'let's all be girls together' when they all started to take their overalls off in full public view. I, of course, turned the other way and pretended not to notice. Not so in the case of an ever increasing number of interested male spectators. Interested, that is, until one of the more senior girls gave one of the most ear bending rebukes that I had ever heard. Any self respecting drill instructor would have been proud of it. From my own point of view, I now knew at first hand what the WAAFs in the Red Shield Club had occasionally been tittering (if that's the right word" about when mentioning passion killers and blackouts. Both apt descriptions I now thought.

Sealand was, like RAF Cranwell, a very rare Station in having two distinct airfields. Both of these airfields at Sealand were to the west of the main road and although the road traffic was nothing to write home about it had been seen fit to build a full road bridge across it. When marching to and from work in the hangars across this bridge we had a magnificent view of aircraft taking off and landing. This was, on occasions, very distracting, not least when I saw for my very last time, an Avro 504 in flight. A very rare bird indeed by 1941.

Work in the hangars was both interesting and exciting. It also blew one of my previous theories sky high. I had thought at Halton during rigging sessions on Harts and the dear old Overstrand, that with each passing day I was getting less and less likely to put to use this hard earned expertise. But here at Sealand we were actually working on Hinds, Harts, Audax and even the old Walrus amphibian. All, of course, strut rigged bi-planes. I set my heart on being aboard a Walrus come it's eventual air test, because it was known that during air tests on that type that a sea landing was always a requirement. It was not to be, although most of us did manage a flight in Wellington bombers later on, which we had often completely recovered in fabric after major repairs. It was in the Wellington hangar that security was suddenly tightened. This had absolutely nothing to do with the 'Wimpy', but everything to do with the sudden arrival of many Bristol Beaufighters, straight off production lines, which had been fitted with highly secret radar for night fighter duties. In double quick time, 24 hour working days had hit one small part of RAF Sealand with a vengeance.

Very soon after arriving at No. 30 MU I had volunteered for pilot training but fell at the first fence. My first, and only, interview was with our own technical Warrant Officer who had been recalled to the colours from retirement. He had started by asking me did I realise how many of our bombers had been lost over Germany the previous night? No problem with that one, I listened to the radio each morning like most other people in the UK. The next thing was the old chestnut that ex-apprentices were just as important as aircrew and the RAF wanted some return on their investment. I left his office not best pleased and thinking 'pig's ear' to the concept of even ex-Brats being on a par with Pilots, and surely at my age I would have been a fighter pilot if I ever made it, and not on bombers. But who knows what might have happened if he had given me the ok in mid 1941. Would I be writing about my time in aviation right now? Probably not. It was to be another six months before I made my second, and successful, attempt at being selected for aircrew training. By that time, however, a pilots course had been gradually increased from about twelve months to nearly two years and the waiting list had also increased by about six months to one year.

Two interesting events concerning the Airborne Forces occurred during my time on the airfield side of Sealand. The first was the selection of Sealand for a practice airborne assault on an airfield target by paratroopers operating out of RAF Ringway (the Paras first training depot and now Manchester International Airport). The aircraft used were Armstrong Whitleys which disgorged quite a few parachutists each from an aperture under the aircraft, made originally for a ventral gun position. The second event was also a practice assault, but this time it was by one glider only, which had been towed overhead by, yet again, a Whitley bomber. After the Hotspur glider, had safely landed about 8 Army types exited rapidly and charged around with their rifles in typical infantry fashion.

Needless to say, it was not all work and no play. For starters, with now being on normal pay for the rank held we could afford the odd drink once or twice a week in local taverns, and even venture into Chester which is, in my opinion, one of the most delightful cities in England. It was nearly always on the upper level of Chester's famous shopping arcade that we first made for. Up there, well above street level was a famous watering hole called Barlow's bar. We knew that without fail that in that bar we would almost certainly bump into one or more Air Transport Auxiliary Pilots from the ferry pool at nearby RAF Harwarden. These pilots ferried almost every known type of RAF land plane in service from airfield to airfield as and when required. They would talk quite freely about the good and bad points of various aircraft types. This was of immense interest, especially when technical failings got a mention. These pilots even included us in their conversations on occasions, which always boosted our morale. If Barlow's bar had been frequented by RAF officers instead of ATA pilots it would, without doubt, have been put off limits to other ranks like so many were in wartime England. The only other bar that we saw fit to drink in was the Spit and Sawdust department of a delightful hotel called the Blossoms. It was Blossoms Hotel that I and the rest of my crew were allocated to after landing at Hawarden airfield for a night stop over 35 years later. That revived so many memories of my youth and RAF Sealand. The trip I was on in the 1970s had quite a twist to it, but more of that later.

Only one lad from the fortieth entry Halton who had been in the same barrack room as myself was posted to Sealand and that was because he came from the Liverpool area like myself. Stan Molinyoux was to solve one of our mutual transport problems, for the summer of 1941 at least, which concerned weekend leave when we both needed to get to Birkenhead as starters, then we would be spoilt for choice. Take the ferry across the river Mersey, transit to Liverpool by the underground rail link or try and cadge a lift from one of the few motorists or even lorries using the road tunnel. After that it would be plain sailing. Stan by bus and myself by the electric line that connected Liverpool to Southport. The real problem was the first leg- getting to Birkenhead. The return on Monday mornings was no problem with one of the very few buses that passed Sealand leaving Birkenhead at an optimum time, from our point of view at least, of 07: 00. The problem of getting away from Sealand was that the midday end of work on Saturdays was not set in concrete and if we missed one bus it could be about three to four hours or so before the next one which pushed back our time of arrival at home to such a late hour that it was hardly worth it. Stan's answer was that perhaps his old tandem bicycle could be brought out of retirement. It could be useful around the local area in the evening, if nothing else. I knew from family trips to North Wales that the ferries had stopped taking cars on our route when the Mersey road tunnel had first opened in the 1930s so perhaps they had put a stop to bicycles at the same time? Stan said he would look into it. The news was even better than expected. The road tunnel accepted bicycles, so it was that we set off on our many trips while the Summer lasted. Using a bike on road tunnels such as the Mersey would be unthinkable in today's traffic. It was during this up and down performance to Birkenhead that Stan and I noticed quite a large increase in the number of very big wooden crates parked on the roadsides for a number of miles to the north of Sealand. For those in the know it meant that our sister MU on the South Airfield at Sealand must have been working overtime in a big way. There job in life was to receive aircraft arriving by air and, after dismantling same, crate them up for shipment out of Liverpool Docks to all foreign parts. Russia, Canada, the Middle and Far East, South Africa you name it. Stan later on, after leaving Sealand, was posted to South Africa where he noticed a number of Harts which we had both worked on. They bore a little plaque stating reconditioned by No 30 MU Sealand, a nice touch.

Stan must also have vivid memories of those days because when our 40th Entry reunions allowed ladies to attend in the 1980s, Stan first mentioned these bike rides to my dear wife, Betty. Come to think of it, he mentioned them quite a few times over the years. It started with Stan saying that he thought Jacko on the back of his tandem never seemed to have peddled as hard as he had up front, to eventually saying he didn't think Jacko had peddled at all and was only along for the ride. I think he was most likely right on the last version. Your past does tend to catch up with you sooner or later, but surely not 50 odd years later!

About the only activity in the evenings was visits to the NAAFI or Red Shield Club. I think the later was preferred by most of us. Little cliques tended to develop, and one or two of the WAAFs from our workplace often joined us. In fact they always seemed to be there from opening time to last orders. It turned out it was the warmth and not the male company that was the attraction. We airmen, from the centrally heated barrack blocks were soon told that it was all very well for the men but the WAAFs had all to live in married quarters that had been vacated for the duration. The only form of heating in those houses was by way of a very small ration of coal per house per week, which during cold spells could quite easily run out on days 3 or 4. In fact, they went on to say, that during a very cold spell during the previous winter, girls in one house had, in desperation, started to chop up staircase handrails as firewood. Word soon spread and in no time at all any trace of wooden bannisters would have been hard to find in the entire patch. With eyes popping in disbelief, a friend of mine, no doubt thinking of our Halton days, asked the obvious question: what about daily inspections? "What daily inspections?" came the reply, the only men allowed anywhere near the quarters were those that delivered the coal. It also turned out that the odd WAAF officer and Sergeant based at Sealand left the girls very much to their own devices.

It was only in recent times that a Sunday lunchtime drinking partner of mine Ken Rix, also an ex-apprentice, but about four years before my time, started to recall his early Halton days. His second posting after leaving Halton was to a Squadron sent to France after the start of the German offensive in the Spring of 1940. His time in France, of course, did not last all that long before the evacuation. It was shortly after arriving back in England that he was posted overseas yet again. This time it was to South Africa and one of his first jobs out there was to help with the unpacking of Hart trainers for use by the Commonwealth Air Training plan. Ex-Sealand no doubt. In South Africa, he fell in love and married a young South African girl, called Pam, who had joined their Air Force. Ken, on return to the UK some years later was first posted to the famous 617 Dambuster squadron based in Woodhall Spa and immediately, like myself, came under the Woodhall Spa spell. Pam eventually managed a passage to the UK in a troopship, just before the end of hostilities in Europe. After finding lodging, it seemed no time at all before Ken was on the move again. This time it was to RAF Sealand. He was told that due to the rapid run down at the station he stood a very good chance of moving straight into married quarters that the WAAFs were soon to vacate. Both the works and bricks man and the barrack warden told Ken at the marching in that he wouldn't believe the amount of work that had been involved in bringing them back to habitation standard. No doubt Ken wouldn't believe it, but I could.

The only form of entertainment on base at Sealand during my time there was a station cinema, luckily for those of us on the airfield technical side, run almost single handedly by a WAAF corporal who was, during the working day, in charge of our technical stores. On many occasions she had given the nod at the pay in point when she saw her young lads, as she liked to call us ex-brats, approaching -provided, of course, that no one else was around. We made sure of that by discreet positioning for most of the time. On my second time at Sealand I made a point of going to the cinema to see if she was still there, which she was, but by now a little tired and worn out and very much looking forward to a return to civvy street. We never did find out what her expectations for the future were, nor how fate had treated her in the past.

My six months of a "Near Home" posting were now coming towards an end. When news of my next move did arrive I thought it would be via our Flight Sergeant and not by a phone call from an airman in Station HQ. I thought that he had said I would be going to Persia, as Iran was called in those days. I was telling all and sundry that I was going overseas to Persia when one of the older airmen started to say in a slow voice that he came from Wyre Pipple near Worcester and I should check to see if it was by any chance RAF Pershore that I was posted to because there was an airfield of that name in the next village to his.

When he had first started to drawl on I had thought what on earth had Wyre Piddle got to do with anything in particular. In fact I was posted to no 23 Operation Training Unit, RAF Pershore and not the Middle East.

CHAPTER 4
No 23 OCU, RAF Pershore

The location was idyllic, being almost dead centre of the Vale of Evesham. It had taken some time at Sealand, gradually getting used to working with men of all ages and not exclusively with youths, all still in their teens. Many of the older types had been recalled from the reserve and seemed to be particularly pleased to be back in the RAF. Some of the conscripts, however, with the upper age limit up to 42 for joining, could not in many cases come to terms with the service life. However, when there was a specific job to do they always got stuck in and invariably worked just as hard, if not harder, than the rest of us. It had been a useful experience and helped no end in settling in on this new station and all that followed.

The dedicated task for No 23 OCU was the training of Bomber crews for front line squadrons and was equipped at first with Vickers Wellington bombers, powered by two Bristol Pegasus engines, later superceded by Wellington IIIs, powered by the Bristol Hercules engine. The Hercules engines powered many of the aircraft that I was subsequently to fly right up to the end of 1977- an engine second to none in the piston world. All Wellington fuselages were of georetic construction, covered with fabric, the brainchild of Barnes Wallace of Bouncing Bomb fame. Being a Fitter II, and not a Flight Mechanic meant that with this higher grading I would be working on second line duties in the main hangar and not out on the airfield with the flying flights. This normally meant working fixed hours on an 8 till 5 basis but, unlike Sealand, seven days per week with just one day off per fortnight. The second line was the place that all inspections on aircraft, other than the daily checks, were carried out. These inspections were called minors or majors and came up on flying hours. For most RAF aircraft. It was 30 hours and 300 hours respectively. In both cases there was also a time limit of 3 months or one year but this was rarely reached in wartime, of course.

RAF Pershore was to be my first, but certainly not last, experience of living on a camp built during WWII. The good news first was that without a parade ground we just walked to and from the work, so even marching was out, for now at least. The bad news was the wooden huts that we had for sleeping in, about 25 to each hut, were all heated by one centrally placed coke fired stove. The washing, bathing and WC area was in another building catering for quite a few huts and some 50 yards away. A very cold journey at times, and with the airfield only recently completed, over very soggy ground at times. A new Station Commander cured this last problem when he called a halt to flying for half a day and managed to provide a spade for each and every airman. One morning's digging of all ground on the domestic site not occupied by buildings produced a minor miracle. The water puddles disappeared forever.

To keep some semblance of cleanliness, one member of each hut was detailed to be room orderly for one week at a time. He was given each morning off work during his week of duty to sweep, polish and generally tidy up the hut. He also had to clean out the boiler and make it ready for a ritual fire-up in the evenings by laying paper, wood and a small amount of coal. The evening fire lighting was not easily achieved by any means and often depended on the inventiveness of the room orderly. One night we got within a whisker of burning our hut down, along with all our belongings due to one smart alec trying aviation petrol as an accelerant. Two members of our hut were told that their normal work was so important to general morale that they could not be spared for other duties such as room orderly. These very special duties? Well these two gents used to tour the various aircraft dispersal areas around the perimeter of the aerodrome and clean out the very basic WCs. As is so often the case, these two chaps took great pride in their work. Airmen can do without running water for a time at dispersal points provided, that is, that the NAAFI van arrives on time and a WC is available, no matter how primitive. Nature waiteth for no man at times.

The new Station Commander was to be well remembered for two reasons over a very short space of time. The first was that having noticed, like everybody else for miles around, that for several nights running German bombers had been droning overhead to and from targets in the Midlands, he became utterly convinced that one night soon a German transport plane would be in the stream and drop stormtroopers on his aerodrome, who would wipe out most of 23 OTU's Wellingtons. Naturally, not many others thought so. This led to many hours on the rifle range and, under the tuition of the recently formed RAF Regiment, to actually hurl live Mills bombs, with the safety pin out, from slit trenches. I have never met anyone since in the RAF who has thrown a Mills Bomb for real. Another of his ideas, which he managed to push through in the context of airfield defence, was that despite a shortage of rifles in the Home Guard and other places, he persuaded the powers that be that there should be enough rifles to arm all technical airmen on his station come the night of the para drop. My final recollection is that he scared the living daylights out of a friend of mine one morning. I had better start by saying that there was a duty called Key Orderly, loathed by all because this meant drawing keys each morning from the Guard Room, about one hour before the normal start of work time, and unlocking all doors and offices just before the rest of the workers arrived. It was also his job to activate the mains electrical master switch in the hangar. The reverse routine was followed in the evening, of course. This chore was particularly disliked because keys could go missing, somebody or other had to work late on special duties, plus various other reasons, which could make it a very long day indeed at times. My friend was on duty one morning at a time of the year when it was still pitch black as he opened the main hangar door. It was whilst groping around, making his way towards the main electric switch, falling over bits of equipment that had been left around at ankle level that the beam of his torch suddenly lit up the rear turret of one of our Wellingtons. Sitting there was the life like figure of an airman in flying overalls, helmet on, strapped in and staring into space. My friend shouted "Bloody Hell, A ghost!", and inadvertently dropped his torch whilst trying to extricate himself from the hangar in total darkness. His panic was not helped one little bit when a voice boomed out "Don't worry airman, I'm not really a ghost". Hangar acoustics being what they are gave a frightening tone to this utterance which convinced him that it definitely was a message from the other side. It was none other than our Station Commander, who did have a torch, that eventually exited the aircraft. He then made his way to the open door and outside told my still shaking friend that he knew damn well that he was not too old at 45. He then snapped out "Get on with it man, you're all right. Open up fully and then get on to MT and tell them to have my car down here pronto- understand?". "Yes, Sir", was the squeaky reply. The story, needless to say, spread like wildfire to such an extent that one of our technical officers thought he had better explain the situation to us lower ranks. It turned out that the Station Commander was determined to go on an impending bombing raid over Germany which even OTU aircraft got involved in on occasions. He had been fobbed off with the excuse that he had not flown a Wellington for quite some time and in any event he was getting on a bit. Stuff and nonsense was more or less his riposte. Even if he hadn't flown a Wimpey for yonks he would go as a rear-gunner. Ah yes, the aviators countered but have you ever thought about what it would be like to be cooped up in a rear turret for up to eight hours or so at your age, sir? And so it came to pass that the CO had gone down to our hangar at the end of the working day the previous evening and told the duty key orderly, who was already in the process of locking up for the night, to report back to the hangar at 10 o'clock and lock him in. The bemused airman meekly said, "Of course, sir". At the appointed time the Station Commander arrived and said "Good lad", and added as an afterthought, "And don't forget to tell the guard room to warn tomorrow's key orderly what to expect". Of course, the best laid plans of mice and men, etc.

It might be a good time to mention age in relation to aviation as it was then and now. During WWII you were definitely over the hill for training as a fighter pilot after the age of 23 and unlikely to be accepted for pilot training full stop if over 29. There were just one or two exceptions in both cases of course. Another ten years on and the Americans found out after a lot of research during the Korean war that the best results by their fighter pilots against Russian built MIGs were achieved by those pilots at about the age of 38. It has since been proved that all pilots can retain there skills up to and beyond the age of 60, providing that they continue to maintain exacting medical standards. I myself was to fly continuously with the RAF up to the age of 60 and then on to 72 with a civilian flying club as a full time Chief Flying Instructor.

A story about flying WWII type fighter aircraft might underline the strange attitudes prevailing at the time of the big change over from bi-planes to Hurricanes and Spitfires. No 19 Squadron was the first RAF fighter unit to receive Spitfires, and that was just 13 months before the onset of war with Germany. Eager to show off these latest, state of the art, machines to their less fortunate contemporaries, who were still flying Gladiators etc meant that visitors to No 19 Squadron mess at RAF Duxford were always most welcome and positively encouraged. Those that stayed over for the night returned to their own Stations with a very strange tale indeed. All 19 Squadron pilots had given up drinking because they had been told that alcohol and flying aircraft with speeds up to 400 mph was just not on.

Another facet of our life in second line servicing was that we were called upon to take care of some tasks that did not justify full time manning. One was to look after transiting aircraft using our field. Some arrivals were pre-booked, others due to weather diversions and in one case due to battle damage. This was a Lancaster with a fair amount of one elevator shot away. The repairs were obviously going to take some time so we managed to fit it into one of our hangars and, of course, I had a good look inside the cockpit on a number of occasions later.

Two other incidents when I was detailed to look after visiting aircraft remain in my mind to this day. After marshalling aircraft into their alloted parking slots I had developed the habit of jumping up on the wings of the single engined types and asking the pilot if I could assist in the harness unstrapping procedure which was to take the shoulder straps when released and place one hanging out of each side of the cockpit. On occasions some pilots were glad to offer up their flying helmets and gloves, etc for safe keeping, whilst they gathered up their maps, etc. I, needless to say, had a good look around the cockpits, particularly those of aircraft that I had not seen before. I got a shock one day when I asked an ATA pilot who arrived in a Hurricane if I could be of any help. "Certainly old boy!", came the reply and I instantly thought, 'well this one is not ex-RAF like some of the older ones are. I was soon to discover why he was so glad of my offer when looking inside the cockpit. All was revealed as they say. The lower part of his left arm, that is the throttle control arm, was missing and his attached hook was still locked around the throttle lever. This 'Captain Hook' was definitely not one of those ATA pilots that I had met in Barlow's Bar in Chester. I would have remembered him, wouldn't I?

On the second occasion it was a lady ATA pilot flying a Royal Navy Barracuda that gave a very terse "No thankyou very much" in reply to my offer of help. One's mind could go into overdrive when considering what had given rise to her attitude. Had some airman at another station...? I think we will leave it there, one will never know of course.

One little empire within our big one was virtually a one man band. We had one T2 hangar that was never used, except to provide overhead cover for a Westland Lysander which had been converted for target towing. One of the very few drogue operators was left in charge of this hangar and had to be on call for most of the day because weather was a big factor in when, or when not, it was possible to allow Air Gunners to fire at the drogues from their turrets. Another reason for somebody being on duty most of the time was the fact that this recently erected hangar was still awaiting it's massive sliding doors to make it secure. This chap in charge, whose name does not come to mind after all these years, had just begun to make a name for himself on the stage when the war started and had immediately volunteered for aircrew duties but failed the medical. After arriving at Pershore, when it first opened, he had jumped at the chance of becoming a drogue operator for the Lysander. Not only would he be flying many times a week, without needing an aircrew medical, but also get extra pay for the privilege, about one shilling and six pence per day in fact. When one considers that Sergeant Pilots fighting in the Battle of Britain were only on 12s 6d a day it is clear it was a nice little earner.

This drogue operator, trying to keep the elements at bay, particularly the cold in Winter, without the protection of doors, took the law into his own hands and built a small tin shack inside his hangar and acquired, if that is the right word, a nightwatchman's stove from somewhere or other. During our mid morning breaks, a select few of us used to slope off to this hangar to sit around his stove and have a brew up. My contribution was via a WAAF I had met in the one and only nearby pub, called the 'Coach and Horses'. It turned out that this WAAF, having been born in York, had left home to work in service for a cotton baron in my home town of Southport before joining up. Her job at Pershore was working as a cook in the airman's mess so the ingredients for a few cups of tea per week were never missed, nor the odd extra sausage for myself at breakfast time when she was manning the servery. History was to repeat itself in two short months at Pershore when one of our group, yet again, threw a little petrol on the fire in the hangar shack to speed things up. Although it was indeed a small amount of petrol this time, the effect was quite dramatic, all four or five of us instinctively shied away backwards from the sudden 'whoosh' and flames, to the extent that our combined backwards pressure forced out all three sides of the shack- the fourth being a side of the hangar- closely followed by the roof falling in. No serious injuries, thank God, it would certainly have taken some explaining away.

One morning all 12 sliding doors duly arrived by lorry with a team of about five men from the contracting firm that had originally built the airfield. With ropes, pulleys and gantries, etc and with the help of an RAF crane the first section of twelve, six per hangar end, was duly lifted to the vertical, but try as they may it was going to take more than their team of men to control the swinging section steady long enough to complete the lowering of the wheels into the door runners. Our little band had been watching with intense interest during our tea break when their foreman approached with a plea for help. I was about to say "No trouble", when our chief Drouge operator said, "Now let's see, it would cost no end of time and money to call for extra men to be sent down here by your firm, wouldn't it?". "Well, yes, I suppose so" spluttered the foreman in disbelief. "I tell you what", our leader went on, "we'll only charge you one shilling per man per door". So, a deal was struck, 12 shillings for each of the five of us. That was about double what the RAF gave us per day. I thought the Drouge operator would make a better trade union leader than going back to acting come the end of the war. However, for the four of us from the main hangar it was not long before our absence was noted and we had only managed two doors when, in the distance, we saw the unmistakable figure of our very own F/Sgt Bishop, who had probably been tipped off about our mid-morning routine, approaching. However, instead of giving us a right earful he was all smiles. "When do you think you will have it finished, we've been waiting for this hangar long enough", was his only comment. A seal of approval indeed. It was, of course, the end of an era now that the hangar was fully complete and could be secured. The lone Lysander was soon to be joined by Wellingtons. No more stove fires and morning brew ups.

I came across the Chieffy just once more in the RAF and that was 11 years later when he was a crew chief on B29s and I was flying Ansons. We were stuck at RAF Odiham for about three weeks for the coronation Royal Review of the RAF in 1953. Yes, he did remember most of the incidents at RAF Pershore, good and bad, of the mid-war years.

I had, of course, re-applied for pilot training after arriving on this new station and this time it was so different. The first interview was with a commissioned officer, in fact our own senior technical officer, holding the rank of Sqdn Leader, although he looked so young even to me, still in my teens. This time round it went like clockwork he only wished that he, too, could apply for aircrew but a medical problem prevented this. In fact, he died of natural causes within a year. On this station, at least, interviews even reached Station Commander level, and for the first time, but not the last, I noted that when it came to the inevitable question of educational level, a mention of having passed the Halton Entrance Exam came under the heading of enough said. On leaving the Station Commander's office

I was under the distinct impression that I probably knew as much about his past as anyone else on the Station. At least half of the time he had talked about life of years gone by on the Frontier. I must admit that in later life I was to notice that service in India before WWII had certainly left it's mark on those who had been out there, which always seemed to be beneficial to their outlook on service matters.

It was about another two months before I went before an Aircrew Selection Board, and this was, of course, the big make or break time. In fact, I was quite impressed that it was a university in Oxford that I was to report to and I only wish that I had put the name of that university in my memory bank, then in future years I would be in a position to say, yes I was up at, whatever it was, Oxford, only as a joke of course. On entering the interview room I was confronted by a Group Captain and at least two other officers. Spread out on the table before them were models of just about every aircraft that the RAF was operating at that time. One must remember that about 95% of applicants for aircrew training were civilians so there was a certain rationale in testing candidates interest in the RAF when asking the first question: How many of these models can you put a name to? I had no trouble in naming them all, having worked on many of the types represented. A good start, and although I cannot remember a great deal more about the proceedings it seemed to go pretty well. Two weeks later I got a letter saying that I had been accepted for the PNB scheme, Pilot, Navigator or Bomb aimer depending on the results of 12 hours of flying at a grading school. It was at this point that I was supposed to sport a white flash in my RAF glengarry side hat. I chose not to because I did not want to worry my mother earlier than I needed to and, secondly, I felt that somehow it would be like sailing under false colours. Surely the white flash should only be worn by those actually under flying training and certainly not by those just waiting to start an aircrew course.

I have already mentioned that second line technicians could be called out to deal with any situation that was outside normal routine and we should not have been as surprised as in fact we were when our Flight Sergeant came around our hut at about 10 o'clock one night and told ten of us to don heavy duty clothing and report to the MT section. He went on to say that we would be on guard duty at an off station site until about 9 o'clock the next morning. It was very obvious that the old had not been selected, old to us lads meant any over 30 in those days. A coach, normally used to take crews to and from aircraft, was already waiting for us and our only stop before the Malvern Hills was to pick up a tea urn and sandwiches from the cookhouse. We were to guard the crash site of one of our Wellingtons which had impacted up in the hills. Nothing was left of the front half of the aircraft but the last third was relatively intact thanks to Barnes Wallis's Geodetic construction.

The rear turret was beam on, which was the norm for some gunners when the aircraft was taking off or landing. This was so a quick exit could be made in the event of a crash on take-off or landing so perhaps the aircraft was positioning to land at RAF Defford, the relief landing ground for Pershore at that time. The rear gunner was obviously dead after such a crash but he looked so peaceful sitting there, not a mark on his face. This was my first site of a dead body and it was a terrible thought looking at his shoulder flash, indicating that he was Canadian, that it would take some time to relay news of this tragic accident to his next of kin, and all other loved ones so far away on another continent. Although I never found out, it was more than likely that the rest of the crew would be Canadians as well, because the vast majority of trainees at Pershore came from that Country, although we also had a few Australians and British crews passing through at times.

They say it never rains but it pours, and it was so in this case because a team of the young and fit were called out yet again. This time it was not so frantic in that we knew in the late afternoon of the day before what the task was to be on the morrow. An Anson aircraft had put down in a field near Worcester for non-technical reasons and it was the opinion of the pilot that the field was long enough for the plane to be flown out of again, apart from one small snag, it had settled in some soft ground but could be got out of there with the two engines under a fair amount of power, and our gang of five or six pushing from behind the back of the two wheel struts per side. It seemed that was just beginning to happen when the accident occurred. It was the slight movement forward that caused the airman pushing on the same wheel mounting as myself to lose his footing and lurch forward. He tried to topple to his right away from the rotating propeller but got caught on his left shoulder blade area. He ran off screaming for ten or twenty yards before coming to a halt. The pilot, luckily, had seen the incident and seemed to be on the scene within seconds with his aircraft's first aid kit, after having stopped the engines first. Although memory can play tricks, I think he gave the poor man a morphine injection. As usual, we were never told why the Anson had landed in that field in the first place, but surmised that he had got lost, which all aircrew prefer to call 'temporarily unsure of position'.

There was precious little to do in the evenings on the camp so on one or two evenings a week it was down to the Coach and Horses, which became very crowded at times, or the three mile hike each way into Pershore village. In addition to a number of pubs, the village hall had been turned into a forces canteen which anyone in uniform, including the ladies of the Land Army of course, could use in the evenings. Every one got on particularly well with each other apart from one little group of WAAFs. These particular ladies kept themselves very much to themselves and looked, acted and talked as if they were superior beings and no way were they going to mix with the 'plebs'. We soon found out that they came from a ground radar site on higher ground, just north of the village. Advanced technology can only be operated by people of high intelligence of course, or that was the operators' opinion anyway. Two of our favourite watering holes were the "Brandy Cask" and the spit and sawdust department of the "Angel Hotel", the saloon and cocktail bars both being off limits to other ranks. All was not lost however, because the young daughter of the house made it plain to all that she much preferred chatting up airmen than officers. The 'Brandy Cask' was an unpretentious pub that went down in Pershore history for the wrong reasons. I had better start by saying that Vickers Armstrong had their own airfield hangar and a civilian staff for special work, such as extensive Wellington modifications. The manager and his female secretary were very popular on the Station, at all levels. It was very sad news indeed that I learnt some time after leaving Pershore that both the manager and his secretary had gone on a Wellington Air Test and that it had crashed into the Brandy Cask pub with the loss of all aboard. Why Pershore village? Why the Brandy Cask pub? I have often asked myself over the years. Perhaps there is someone out there still who knows the answer.

I made two particularly good friends during my time at RAF Pershore but the chances of any of us three getting the same day off together on our ration of one day free per fortnight seemed very remote indeed. The only real options for our individual away days were Evesham or Worcester, both having lovely river walks, etc. Worcester just had the edge with an all day forces canteen next to a church, where we met up with other RAF types to catch up on the latest gossip or gen as it was called in the RAF in those days (Pukka gen and duff gen). The army was also represented in the canteen and around the city with a large number of them wearing the 'Crossed Keys', a badge I was next to see in India towards the end of the war. The enlarged male population of Evesham, on the other hand, was largely made up of civilians working for the BBC who, we understood, had been evacuated from London.

The first of my two friends was called 'Darkey', who got his nickname from his Mediterranean looks and colour. Although he was on the small side I felt he could have taken care of himself if the need had ever arisen. In today's parlance, he was certainly streetwise, but when it came to our place of work in the main hangar he was, at times, a walking disaster. His first effort was asking me as an ex-brat if I could help out on a job that had obviously gone wrong. It turned out that the corporal normally in charge of his team had gone on leave and left "Darkey' in charge for a week. The team had re-fitted elevators to a Wellington, after taking them off so as to insert new control runners. They had then spent more than a full working day trying to adjust the new runners to fit around the elevators without any luck at all. As is so often the case, an outsider- an ex-brat or not- can sometimes spot the problem at first glance. 'Darkey' and his men had managed to fit the port elevator to the starboard side and vice versa. If anyone thinks that is impossible just ponder about it. Tip an elevator upside down and it would fit the other side nicely. However, most aircraft have only a trim tab on the port or starboard side and that is what should have been spotted when re-fitting.

Darkey's next effort nearly did me a permanent injury, or worse. A sense of urgency had been building up for a number of days to get aircraft back on line to the extent that leave and days off had been cancelled. Also long periods of overtime had become the norm and aircraft on minor or major inspections were targeted for early completion and return to the flying flights by employing more than one team on those aircraft nearest to returning to full flying status. So it turned out that 'Darkey' and myself found ourselves working side by side, literally. It was May 29th 1942, a date that has stuck in my mind ever since because, unbeknown to us at the time, it was the day before the world's first ever 1,000 bomber raid. A message from one of the flying flights requested that, if possible, de-icing paste should be applied to the leading edges of the main planes (wings) and tailplanes of two particular aircraft because they would, if serviceable, be flown on an important mission the following night. That would only be possible if we took on the extra chore, they must have also asked the armourers to take on an extra job as well, as it turned out.

'Darkey' and I had been applying de-icing paste to one of the Wellington wings, working from wing tip towards the engines and the cockpit area when 'Darkey', who was on the inside of me, tried to apply paste with his screwdriver to a part of the wing behind a protrusion. There was a God almighty bang and the blade of his screwdriver whistled past my nose having been severed by a loaded balloon cable cutter, invented to deal with German barrage balloons and not unsuspecting RAF ground crew. Nobody ever found out who was responsible for the cable cutters on that particular aircraft being armed. It was, of course, writ large that no explosives of any kind should be allowed in the servicing hangar. This very loud report which echoed around the hangar was a real show stopper, now not a sound could be heard, but needless to say the silence was short lived and soon everyone of any importance whatsoever arrived on the scene to hold an impromptu inquest.

The next morning quite a few instructor air gunners, all supposed to be on rest tours after completing 30 missions on operational bomber squadrons, appeared in our hangar and made for individual aircraft which they had obviously been allocated to for the big one, and started to clean the perspex on their rear turrets. At first we were a little poked because we thought that having cleaned them ourselves that should have been sufficient. However, after they had finished we had to admit, grudgingly, that they had made a far better job of it than we had. No self respecting DIY person would disagree with the concept that when one is working for one's self it results in a much better outcome at the end of the day. We had noted that all of the staff gunners had been in particularly gung ho spirits and raring to go, despite already having 30 raids under their belts.

Having produced every available aircraft that was ever likely to fly within the next few days, quite a few of our team were drafted to the flying flights to reinforce the hard pressed ground staff at the cutting edge of 23 OTU. They had not, for instance, completed the de-icing paste task on all aircraft. It should be pointed out, however, that this was an extra burden because OTU Bombers, flying on training sorties around the UK, did not normally fly at the higher altitudes that operational bombers on missions over Germany used and therefore did not require this treatment on a day to day basis. We were still working around the dispersal areas as required right up to chocks away time on the world's first ever 1,000 bomber raid on the night of 30th May 1942, which was against Cologne. Two nights later, on 1st June, the second 1,000 bomber raid took place, this time the target was Essen and once again our Wellingtons were heavily involved. The book 'Bomber Command Losses 1942' by W R Chorley records the Pershore losses as follows: Cologne. One aircraft lost; Captain RCAF, other 3 RAAF and one UK crew member.

Essen. Two aircraft lost; first, Captain RAAF, 3 RCAF and 1 UK crew member. Second aircraft, all UK crew members with ranks and decorations indicating all instructors.

The 15 crew members from Pershore all recorded lost in action.

I was stationed at RAF Pershore throughout 1942 and Mr Chorley's book records that aircraft losses from all causes during that year as 9 Wellingtons lost in action, 23 in training and 1 on the ground. The one ground loss indicates it was damaged beyond repair when not being used on flying duties. The total loss of 33 aircraft in one year at Pershore is somewhat alarming, but it was on a par with the other 29 bomber OTUs.

After the two 1,000 bomber raids it was back to the steady OTU routine of training bomber crews, mainly Canadians, which meant that they would probably be posted to Yorkshire, via heavy conversion units, to fly Halifax four engined aircraft, although this was not always the case.

To return to "Darkey's" knack of getting things wrong on matters mechanical. On minor inspections, aircraft tended to be in and out in double quick time unless, of course, a serious defect was found. Major inspections, on the other hand, were taken far more seriously with every nook and cranny put under the microscope which included removing all cowlings and fabric inspection covers so that a good 'look see', by using a torch and a long rod with a mirror attached, could be made. It was also a good time to remove all dirt and grime that tended to accumulate in the fabric squares formed by the Geodetic construction. We found a good way of disposing of the grime and grit was by way of a vacuum cleaner after rubbing around the area with a stiff brush. Unbeknown to the rest of his team, 'Darkey' had got in the habit of using petrol to loosen the unwanted dirt, and after waiting for the petrol to evaporate, set too with the electric cleaners. It was an accident waiting to happen, of course, and it duly did. 'Darkey' mistimed the drying out time and after switching on the cleaner, up she went in flames! I was working on another aircraft nearby when it all happened. Darkey was in an ambulance within minutes and away to the station sick quarters. F/Sgts Bishop and Ramsey were real stars, having all other aircraft out of the hangar in double quick time before it became a major disaster, although 'Darkey's' aircraft was never to fly again. After work that night I made my way to the medical centre to ask what chances 'Darkey' had and was pleasantly surprised when the WAAF nurse said I could have a chat with him. Apart from all fingers and thumbs being bandaged, and eyebrows singed he seemed to be in good working order. We had a chat about what he would say at the future inquiry but as no disciplinary action was taken against him I think the old adage of "truth will out" did not apply on this occasion.

My very next shock to the system was provided unintentionally by our hangar team of WAAFs who we always called "Fabric bashers" because their main job in life was to make running repairs to the fabric skin of the Wellington after damage by enemy action, but more often than not by carelessness on the ground. They also re-sealed inspection panels after we had completed our various jobs. The fabric was held in position by a liberal application of dope which also tightened the fabric. In todays world they would have had to wear face masks and work limited hours. However, the only concession to our ladies was a plentiful supply of free coffee collected from the cookhouse twice a day but it is very doubtful indeed if that kept the effects of the obnoxious dope fumes at bay. On the day in question I was working in the cockpit with all the side windows open when the girl who had been down to the cookhouse arrived back. It was a shout of "I suppose the effing coffee is cold again" that stunned me. I had never heard a female use that word before. I suppose some of the old hands would have taken it in their stride, but I had led a very sheltered life before Halton. A Methodist upbringing which meant church three times on Sundays, no drinking, no gambling, no Sunday papers plus a very important reason for putting all females, up to that point at least, on a pedestal.

It was about mid-summer when the second good friend I made at Pershore arrived on the scene. He was known to all as Mac, and all I can remember 60 odd years on was that he came from Macclesfield, and was one of the most modest men that I ever met. One night in the NAAFI canteen having a coffee with Mac and Darkey, we were joined by a much older Airman who had just returned from an overseas tour of seven years in India. He gave us the pros and cons of the tour and said he would jump at the chance of going out east again because he was having difficulty in coming to terms with life in the RAF now compared with pre-war days in the UK. Darkey quickly indicated that he would hate the idea of going overseas, as for myself it would be a foregone conclusion that, if and when, I gained a pilot's course I would be going to Canada, America or Southern Africa. Darkey then asked for Mac's thoughts about it. Eventually he said he was very unsure of his position, because he had done an overseas tour of sorts, it had, however been for a short time and perhaps that didn't count. Ah, France we all thought, plenty of booze, etc until the last few weeks before Dunkirk. No, not France, but by convoy to and from Murmansk in Northern Russia with the RAF's 151 Wing who flew Hurricanes. The most dangerous waters in the entire world at that time. If that didn't count as an overseas tour it should have.

During the steady plod towards the end of 1942 we still had one or two moments to remember. On one occasion after a full days work we had just returned to our billets when we were urgently recalled. A Wellington had come to grief just short of the main runway with one landing leg collapsed in softish ground. Chieffy Bishop again led the charge, but it was to be a long drawn out battle. We got off to a good start when I was to see for the first time the use of air bags for lifting a wing, but otherwise it was a long hard slog which ended about mid-morning of the next day, about 26 hours after first start of work the previous day. We all remembered the serial number of that particular Wellington, of course, and noted that after a long repair job it was soon to become a complete write off in yet another accident. A bit of panic set in with the station's Works and Brick department, as it was known to all throughout the service for years to come. It was a small civilian organisation set up on all stations to maintain not only structural integrity of buildings but also to check the standards of new additions. It turned out that at one newly built RAF Station in the north a random check had revealed a shortfall on the depth of concrete on all taxi ways and runways. It was almost unthinkable that any contractor would make extra money this way in wartime and also risk the break up of operational runways, but there it was. I suppose they might well have lasted a few years, until the end of the war. The works and bricks department soon returned to normal after Pershore passed an independent inspection with flying colours. Our runways, however, did suffer a very curious, to us at least, fate along with many others on various stations throughout our area, and probably in other places as well. It was the affixation of wood chippings to our runways. That mystified all and sundry, particularly those of us graded as riggers/ fitter airframes when we were told that it was to prolong tyre life. As far as we were concerned tyres would be changed after a certain number of landings regardless. I cannot remember the magic number for Wellingtons but 200 sticks in my mind for Spitfires when operating off Tarmac. I think the real reason for the use of the wood chippings was first revealed to me about five years later when I first flew at night over the UK and noticed how well runways stuck out, particularly after rain on moonlit nights. Mystery solved.

I was on my final few furlongs of the predicted 12 months wait for aircrew training so I thought I had better use up some of my annual leave allowance and travel north to Southport and see the family. Quite a few shocks ensued. On the electric line from Liverpool to Southport I noticed, passing Formby, that what had been their golf course was now a full blown RAF airfield, made for the defence of Liverpool and the North West, including a large part of the Irish Sea. The night raids on Liverpool had petered out the previous year but German JU88 bombers operating from the Brest peninsula could make an uninterrupted low level sea crossing, via the St George's Channel, to the Liverpool bay area and further north, well below radar cover for the most part. They posed not only an instant threat to shipping but more importantly, an incalculable danger when on information gathering operations as regards shipping movements. For example, even one large ship leaving the Mersey estuary area probably meant that a convoy was forming up at Gourock, near Glasgow or, as in my case sometime later, Belfast Loch. I also noted that even our Ainsdale Beach Lido on the foreshore was now in the hands of the Royal Navy who used the site to train ack ack gunners who fired at aircraft towed drogues just out to sea. My mother had taken one or two of the young Wrens at this establishment under her wing via her work in a forces tea shop set up in our very small village. One Wren wrote to her long after the war had ended which pleased my mother greatly. The sheds used during WWI, and later by our local pleasure flight company, to the north of the town had been re-activated as an aircraft packing centre by the RAF. On this occasion the aircraft arrived by road as opposed to being flown in during WWI. One thing that I did not understand, then or since, was why our magnificent beach used for famous flights, as already recorded, and by both myself and later Batty for learning to drive on, had been deemed by some unthinking person or organisation to be just the place that the Germans might use for an airborne landing, so it was littered with 20' high concrete poles to prevent this most unlikely event taking place. If the Germans had ever thought that was possible, even in their wildest dreams, the war would have already been a lost cause. These posts were not pulled up after VE day but left for nature to take it's course which took 20 or so years in the event.

Another very obvious change was the Palace Hotel, the largest in town, and well known to generations of wealthy Lancastrians, had been taken over by the USA Army Air Corps, as it was known at the time, for rest and recuperation (RR). Most seemed to enjoy their short break by the seaside, but one or two groups wandered up and down Lord St, thought by many to be the best shopping street in the UK, pre war, looking like lost souls. Perhaps they were complete B17 Flying Fortress crews whose mind was on the future when they returned to squadron life, or pondering on the fate of fellow crews during their absence? It was certainly food for thought at the time hearing about their loss rate which was to become in the last three years of the war more than Bomber Command had suffered in nearly six years, and that had been bad enough. In round figures the Eighth Air Force lost 80,000 KIA against Bomber Command's 55,000 KIA during WWII.

This leave was the first one I had taken from Worcestershire and I completely mis-timed my return in that the last train out of Worcester, stopping at Pershore village, had already left by the time I arrived. However, it was to prove to be an interesting night before the Milk Train was due to pull out. What is a Milk Train some young readers might well ask? Although I was by now well familiar with the forces canteen in the town centre I never realised that a smaller version on one of the station platforms was an all night affair, to cater for such unfortunates as myself. Soon, a Sergeant arrived looking particularly young to be wearing three stripes. After discarding his greatcoat I noted with more than passing interest that he was wearing a Pilot's brevet, not only that, he actually came over and sat at the same table for a chat. No, he was not from RAF Pershore but on his way to join his first squadron, a Spitfire squadron in fact. I was glad to have missed my train by now, but it was most unlikely he was by the time I eventually left on the milk run. It had been a long question and answer night, virtually all of the questions asked by myself were all about flying a Spitfire, my ultimate ambition.

Sometime during the last few weeks leading up to the Christmas of 1942 I received quite a shock, I was posted to RAF Warmwell, near Weymouth Naval Base. It was known to be a day fighter station so perhaps I would at least be working on Spitfire's even if not yet flying them. However, No. 257 (Burma) Squadron had converted to Typhoons, one of the few RAF aircraft I had not actually yet seen. Still not wearing a white flash in my RAF hat, I thought it prudent to inform my superiors that it might all be a waste of time being posted at that juncture due to my impending transfer to aircrew. I got a coded message, that even I could understand, which was basically; 'Yes, they knew I would be lost to them sooner or later so I might as well be one of the two airframe fitters urgently required down there for a special job. I thought it all petty minded but if I was to work on a front line squadron at long last, so be it. The really good news was that Mac was the other 'specially selected' airman, but why Mac, we both pondered. His medical category ruled him out for aircrew so what had they got up their sleeve for him, if anything. We kept in touch for a while after I left Warmwell to start my aircrew training and it turned out he too had been on some list or other that would mean his time at Pershore did not have long to run either. Although remaining in the RAF, he was eventually sent to work on one of the Hawker aircraft production lines turning out Hurricanes. He lived and worked as if a civilian, digs having been provided. It was put around at the time that aircraft production was failing to meet targets due to lack of manpower. History books on the RAF tell another story. Technical training had reached such a pitch that the RAF was rapidly reaching an overmanning in technical trades approaching 50,000. The RAF insisted that they could have used all these engineers if only aircraft production had been up to expectations. It is unthinkable that the UK could have supported many more airfields, even if needed, after the arrival of the US Army Air Corps in 1942. I think it was Winston Churchill who said that the UK was a gigantic aircraft carrier anchored off mainland Europe. The "Action Stations" series of books, records that at least two aircraft storage stations had 1000 aircraft apiece on hold towards the end of WWII. Many taps should have been turned down, if not off, somewhere along the line. I often thought about Mac working in civvies and hoped nobody would ever give him a white feather with two arctic convoys under his belt. He was not the type to have reacted, but what thoughts would have gone through his mind is another matter. It turned out that Mac was somewhat lucky to be still working on aircraft because many other surplus to requirements RAF chaps found themselves transferred to the army, working down coal mines and even employed as stokers on steam trains.

CHAPTER 5
Warmwell

The very important task at Warmwell that had warranted more airframe fitters was already half completed by the time Mac and I arrived on the scene. It caused astonishment to us both, and no doubt to all others before us who had been called upon to work on this project, which was to rivet strengtheners at given intervals around the outside of the entire rear fuselage, on all the Typhoons of 257 Squadron. We were soon to learn that there had been a number of structural failures from the earliest days of this new Hawker product and that it also suffered many engine failures as well, with the still to be proven Sabre engine. It must have given food for thought to the Typhoon pilots that both the fuselage and engine failures had led to fatal accidents at the start of this type's flying life. However, it all came good later when it not only became the only allied aircraft capable of dealing with FW190 hit and run raiders along the South coast, due to it's speed of over 400 mph at sea level, but also when armed with bombs and rockets it became the most effective ground attack aircraft during the Normandy landings and the allied advance through Western Europe. It had a short, but sweet, life before being phased out in favour of it's successor, the Hawker Tempest. before the end of 1945.

The havoc caused by the Typhoons and other ground attack types against German tanks, road and rail traffic and many other military targets such as radar sites and military headquarters was immense, and undoubtedly the turning point in many engagements, particularly during the Normandy breakouts from the bridgeheads. The price paid, however, was on a par with that suffered during the Battle of Britain, if not higher on some squadrons. On one particular squadron there was only one survivor from those on strength on D-day by the end of the war in Europe. A lesson that had to be re-learned during the Gulf war was that attacking pin point targets such as airfields, and armoured convoys at low level was a very dangerous undertaking at the best of times. This was because during low level operations the attacking aircraft, after releasing it's weapons would invariably fly over it's target before the pilot had any chance to pull away from it's flight path in time. Both Russia and Germany had perfected very rapid firing anti aircraft guns which when pointing vertically upwards stood a very good chance of securing hits on attacking aircraft as they passed overhead. RAF anti-shipping strike squadrons had already suffered severely for the same reason. Stand off weapons are the only alternative as the Americans, at least, employed during the Gulf War.

To return to RAF Warmwell itself, it was situated in the idyllic Dorset countryside, just a short distance from the famous Lulworth Cove, in the area that the US Army was later to lose 800 lives during a D-day practice assault. It had been a pre-war armaments practice camp, but little of the original buildings were left after numerous German bombing attacks, For obvious reasons, newly built accommodation had been well scattered and our barrack hut was inside a wooded area as were aircraft dispersals whenever possible. One irritant was that although we worked on No. 257 Squadron's aircraft, officially we had actually been posted to a "Servicing Echelon" whose number I never put in my memory bank. One Battle of Britain pilot who rose to Air rank later in life wrote in his memoirs that in his war time experience it was one of the worst blunders the RAF ever committed in inventing these echelons. It had destroyed the Squadron spirit, and front line aircraft had not always been ready when required as they had been during the fateful days of 1940. I could not agree more, and I always - in those days- referred to myself as being on 257 Squadron.

Also based at Warmwell when we arrived was No 263 Squadron flying the twin engined Westland Whirlwind which only equipped one other squadron. At that time No 263 Squadron was commanded by Sqdn Leader Wykham-Barnes who was 20 years later the Air Commander of the Far Eastern Air Force during my time out there. However he then went under the name of Air Marshal Wykham, at some point during the twenty year period he had met and married a daughter of J B Priestley. A third unit was No 302 Polish Spitfire Squadron who were always raring to go. The odd autogyro also operated out of the field but no one seemed to know what it was up to and it was long after the war was over that I learnt it had been on radar calibration duties. Some secrets can be kept it seems.

It was during a tea break, which in those days was only available from a NAAFI van or the Salvation Army twice per day, and always a good chance to gaze across the airfield to see what was going on, that a most unfortunate accident occurred. We all saw the flare that shot up from the watch office, as air traffic control was then called, which was the signal for the stand by fighters to take off immediately. If the wind was within limits they would depart straight across the field from their static positions and not waste time in conforming with the 'Runway in use' direction. The theory was that aircraft preparing to land would see the flare and hold off for a time. It did not work out like that on this occasion because the aircraft taking off collided with another on it's landing run, one of the two pilots involved was killed instantly. I think he was a F/Sgt or Flight Lieutenant, a very sad day indeed, and a particularly unfortunate ending for a Battle of Britain pilot.

A twist of fate befell me more than 40 years later when, after leaving the RAF at long last, I took up the position of Chief Flying Instructor at Sherburn Aero Club in Yorkshire. I had often flown with a chap from Harrogate who had spent the 40 years immediately following the end of WWII in Sweden. Came the day when flying was definitely off due to bad weather, so we both took to the coffee bar for a chat about this and that. It would be interesting to hear about his life and times in a Nordic country. When he said he had actually been born in Dorset and not Harrogate my interest quickened. "Anywhere near Warmwell?" was my obvious question. "Well, yes", was his reply, and that had started his interest in becoming a pilot, seeing aircraft taking off and landing there from his home. In fact he often cycled down to the airfield as a school boy to look through the hedgerow to get a better view. One day he had seen a terrible accident when two aircraft collided. But for the bad weather that day I would never have heard his story, but as they say what a small world.

At Warmwell, it was not all work and no play. We had a lovely pub near our local railway station which was well within walking distance where the locals still talked about Lawrence of Arabia coming to grief just up the road when serving in the tank corps at Bovingdon. That was of more than passing interest to anyone serving in the RAF due to Lawrence having joined and left the service twice since WWI before finally re-joining the Army.

With Warmwell being so close to the Channel shore line a German Commando type raid was still considered a remote possibility so we all had to take our turn with the armed sentry guard to Squadron aircraft lined up on the grass during the night hours. It was on rare occasions that anyone in authority checked on our alertness, they may have thought it unwise to do so when you come to think about it, loaded rifles and all that. However, a very keen young orderly officer tried it out one night when I was on guard. I heard a car in the distance which caught my immediate attention. Although the driver turned the engine off when still a long way away but any fool should have known that on a still clear night in the wide open spaces of an airfield noise can travel vast distances. I immediately took up position behind the fuselage at the end of the line nearest the noise emission and steadied my unloaded rifle. Eventually a ghostly figure appeared to be tip toeing towards me. Trying to slip the ammo magazine into my rifle's insert position caused more noise than I had anticipated. Panic ensued from the approaching figure and before I could shout the eternal cry of "Who goes there?, Friend or foe?", the Orderly Officer, as he turned out to be, stole my thunder by shouting "Don't shoot, don't shoot, it's the Orderly Officer". Sanity returned when I said, "Ok sir, advance and be recognised". He had the grace to complement me on my alertness so it ended in a no score draw. Recording that incident reminds me of a story doing the rounds in the 1970s when the OC of RAF Akrotiri in Cyprus, one dark night sneaked up on the sentry on the main camp entrance and threw a rock at the poor chap who instantly presented arms. The OC, beside himself with rage, shouted "What on earth are you doing man, I'm a terrorist". "No you're not sir, you're the Station Commander", replied the airman. Game, set and match, I thought.

Back to Warmwell. With the remote possibility of a seaborne raiding party still with us, we were in our wooden sleeping hut one dark night, with it's wartime subdued lighting, and were taken aback when the entrance door was suddenly thrown open with some vigour and a voice rang out, "I'm the General". The chap's uniform was certainly difficult to discern in the dim light and from a distance, my first thought was 'bloody hell, they've sent some eyeties over' however it was a Salvation Army General in fact, who commenced to give us a real old pep talk. Not exactly a morale booster, but we heard him out. Perhaps he should have brought some of us his young girls in their funny little hats with him, that would really have livened things up no end. To be serious for a moment, I must say the Salvation Army did a magnificent job throughout the UK and beyond. Always happy and smiling with canteens second to none, circumstances permitting.

I don't know if our superiors had begun to regard Mac and I as the terrible twins but quite often we were detailed as a team of two for odd jobs in addition to our normal work. We did not object, however, when we were offered two places for a three day break at a leave centre that had opened in Bournemouth. It was run entirely by the RAF but we noted a large number of Canadian airmen taking advantage of the facility as well. It had obviously been one of the resort's main hotels pre-war, and now doing it's job as a morale booster. Unfortunately, it later suffered bomb damage, along with a local hospital, from a FW190 tip and run raider. In these circumstances people tend to blame the pilots for such diabolical behaviour. However, when flying in from the sea at very low level, with speeds of up to 300 mph it is virtually impossible to identify targets with any accuracy. The name of "nuisance raids" was very apt indeed. Defending aircraft arrived on the scene to find an empty sky, and work on the ground was brought to a standstill for miles around. If the raiders did not drop bombs they would eventually be ignored In peace time I have always been sceptical when reports of air disasters always seem to heap praise on the pilot's valiant attempts at trying to avoid some building or other, invariably a school or hospital, to save lives. Apart from some light single engined flying club types of aircraft, the pilots do not usually have much control of the impact point if disaster is unavoidable.

Mac and I thought we had been buttered up when we arrived back from our very pleasant three day sojourn in down town Bournemouth. The news was, yet again, we had been specially selected for a task in North Wales. It turned out to be at RAF Valley on the island of Anglesey that our presence was required. The job to be undertaken was not stated but, unusually, our travel arrangements were very specific. All by train but with a one night stop over in London at an RAF run hostel near Euston Station, and then by the first train to Holyhead out of London the next morning. The details were unusual in that the RAF did not normally care if you had to spend a night on some deserted station or other on postings. The mail train run up to North Wales was pleasant enough and particularly interesting to me as we passed the Chester area and came within spitting distance of Sealand where fate was to send me to again in the near future. Another unusual feature of this journey was that there was actually a driver and transport waiting when we disembarked at a station just short of Holyhead. The WAAF driver took a look at Mac and I and asked "are you two cousins?". One or other of us said "No, not cousins, just good drinking mates". Obviously she was not amused and said, "Are you cousins, you know, Operation Cousins?". The penny finally dropped and we explained that we did not have the slightest idea why we had come to Valley. She then said, "You'll be Cousins all right, jump aboard". During the very short journey to Valley we both tried a bit of charm and gradually got the information we now badly needed. It turned out that "Operation Cousins" was so named because we would be working alongside our American cousins who were to form their No 414 Beaufighter squadron. To start with it was virtually all RAF groundcrews and the reverse for aircrews. It was the first and last time that I worked on first line only duties, all the aircraft were virtually brand new and nowhere near to second line inspection time.

From the flying side I only recall one incident during my short stay in Wales and that was when a pilot lost an engine at about 1,000 after take off and manage to turn the Beau through 180° and land back on the duty runway. Later in life I was to learn that was just not on in any type of aircraft let alone the Bristol beaufighter which had a certain reputation in the RAF as regards asymmetric flying.

There is no doubt that North Wales is one of the top beauty spots in the whole of the United Kingdom and looking across the Menai straits towards Snowdonia was a sight to behold and, in my case, brought back many happy memories of family holidays in those parts before the outbreak of war. However, a sour note was soon struck which, rightly or wrongly, has remained with me ever since. This sad business started when Mac and myself first visited a local public house when the locals, who had all been happily chattering away in English suddenly stopped all conversations for a while and then recommenced their conflabs in Welsh. It was obvious that we were often the topic of their conversations by the looks we received and this happened on every occasion that we walked in, so eventually we took our limited custom elsewhere, but surprise, surprise, we got exactly the same reaction, so it became NAAFI only, during the rest of our stay.

CHAPTER 6
From ground to air

It was certainly blessed relief when I was recalled to Warmwell as my aircrew training was about to begin at long last and I now found myself at the great crossroads in life as far as aviation was concerned. From ground to air, but with the satisfaction of once an ex-brat, always an ex-brat, the accolade that all ex-apprentices glory in, regardless of whatever rank they eventually achieve. My first check in point for my future career, be it long or short, was once again dear old London town. Not Baker St this time but then again not a million miles away either, just up the road in fact it was to a place called Abbey Lodge, part and parcel of Regents Park that I was to report to. Our sleeping quarters were quite salubrious, compared with any hitherto. They had been very high class flats before the war and, needless to say, the contents had been put into storage for the duration of hostilities and RAF furniture installed. Nevertheless, we got a fair impression of how the other half had lived before the onset of WWII. Although there were several such buildings commandeered by the RAF, ours was Viceroy Court. The corporal in charge of our particular group related that there had been several hit and run raids by German fighter bombers recently, and that the only thing to do, because it was all over within minutes of the sirens sounding, was to get under the beds immediately. Where had I heard that one before, the dear old Macdonald bed would have been a far better bet, was the thought going through my mind. He then went on to say that all rank badges worn by serving airmen, like myself and just a few others, had to be taken down as, henceforth, we were plain cadets and all on an equal footing. Having reached the dizzy heights of Leading Aircraftman, which meant I was wearing a badge on each arm depicting a two bladed propeller, this order was of no importance whatsoever. One or two corporals took it rather badly now that the dreaded day had arrived, although we all knew that it was part of the deal well before we had transferred to aircrew. Although he said nothing himself, we felt particularly sorry for a Sergeant Air Gunner in our palatial room in Viceroy who had actually completed a full tour of bomber operations. His three stripes had gone, but no one could order the removal of his flying brevet. His only reference to his bomber raids was when he proudly showed us a shirt that he had been wearing when he suffered slight shrapnel wounds, a kindly nurse had made sure that he retained it as a keepsake. I never met him after ACRC (Aircrew Reception Centre) but I do hope he made good his great ambition of becoming a pilot.

During our standard three weeks in London we always seemed to be on the move, marching around in groups of about 50 or so. It was particularly strange the first week because the vast majority of our squad were still in civilian clothes, and it showed. Obviously, not many had marched at all before. I think the RAF's theory was 'why give them uniforms until they have passed the medical?' .

The medicals took place at Lords Cricket Ground and some WAAF medical orderlies have since been quoted as saying that the Long Room lived up to it's name in more ways than one. The Aircrew Medical was just about the same as that at Halton with perhaps more emphasis placed on eyesight and colour blindness, probably due to our age band there were surprisingly few failures. Issuing of uniforms also took place at Lords, after the medicals, but we serving airmen also had to go along as well because the issue of flying clothing took place at the same time. We now felt that we were really getting somewhere with our flying helmets, goggles, flying overalls, etc. A big surprise for our small band of serving airmen was the issue of civilian type shoes, it was boots or nothing for RAF other ranks at that time. I felt then, and have ever since for that matter, that the flying hand gauntlets dished out would hinder, rather than help when piloting an aeroplane. No doubt they would help keep the cold out for bomber crews operating over Germany, but for fighter pilots and the many who spent the rest of the war in foreign parts they were just an extra item to carry around and never to be worn. A few days before the issue of uniforms a mass gathering of all those who had joined on the same day had been held at the Seymour Baths, which doubled as a lecture hall and a swimming proficiency test centre. A mass lecture ensued by a Group Captain who, in addition to stating that if we made it to brevet standard we would find it was not to be all beer and skittles, and the brylcream image of the dashing fighter pilot was pure myth. He was now in full cry and embarrassed those of us already in uniform, which was 5% or less of those present, by saying "have a good look around you at those in uniform, they are serving airmen who could see the war out without being presented with a white feather, but they have chosen to become aircrew. They know what the score is, most have worked on aircraft that failed to return, seen injured and dead crew members being removed from badly damaged planes", and so on. Quite a performance, but what was it really all about, we in uniform pondered, was he trying to test the resolve of any waverers? We never found out.

The next Officer centre stage left us in no doubt whatsoever. He was a Medical Officer who after the usual guff about the benefits of personal hygiene to general good health, when overseas always remember the drinking water is suspect and to close the WC lid after use, before going on to the real reason for his presence, what might happen to anyone who went with any of the ladies of the night in London. Going blind by 40, etc. It was at this point that about three of the lads still in civvies took funny turns, perhaps the message was too late for them, those of us in uniform had heard it all before of course. As regards the MO's remarks about closing WC lids, I was to find out later that overseas they were very rare birds indeed, even on RAF stations in the Middle and Far East. Off base, a hole in the ground was often the norm and on trains in Egypt a hole in the floorboards had to suffice.

Our next visit to Seymour Baths was for the swimming tests. Rumour control had it that poor swimmers, and especially non-swimmers, would definitely be posted to ITWs (Initial Training Wings), based in seaside resorts that all had ample swimming facilities of one kind or other. For good swimmers it was just possible they could end up at Stratford-upon-Avon, or even Buxton, which was well off the map for us bird brained airmen of tender years. So it was that those of us who thought we were in the know floundered around the pool and duly had our names recorded, it might all have been true, I wound up in Scarborough, so nothing was lost at the end of the day.

The catering arrangements for those of us in the de-luxe flats already mentioned were very unique, even by RAF standards. The cookhouse was a makeshift affair in one of the world's most famous zoos. I refer, of course, to Regents Park Zoo which was just across the road from Viceroy Court. The vast numbers of would be pilots etc, meant that at meal times the queue would often stretch well outside the dining area towards a public right of way. Sometimes, in the early Spring weather, groups of civilians would gather and gawk at us through the perimeter railings. Invariably, it was the high spirited, just out of school lads, that occasionally reacted, or over reacted perhaps, to this perceived intrusion, by jumping up and down on two feet, scratching under their arms and making Chimp like facial expressions with grunting noises thrown in. The onlookers for their part thought it was hilarious. A damn good job nobody in authority saw those antics, the more sober of us thought.

As already mentioned during the acceptance medical at Lords that general eye and colour blind tests required a very high standard from candidates to gain a pass for aircrew training, although small defects might well lead to service in ground branches. After the Night Fighter force was equipped with air to air radar, their operators, in theory, could vector pilots to visual range of enemy aircraft at night for the kill and visual contact rates seemed to indicate that some pilots must have better night vision than others, although all had passed the normal day time eye tests to the same standard. History books tell us it was the skill of the rear crew radar operator that was the deciding factor and when a pilot found one with exceptional skills he clung on to him. However it came to pass that a dedicated night vision testing centre was set up in Abbey Lodge and was a bit of a performance. About ten at a time sat around a rather large round table and each had a wire clip on device attached to our rear tunic collars so that it was impossible to move forward from a rigid upright sitting position so as to better read letters under varying degrees of darkness. When everything was ready for the off the WAAF officer in charge plunged the room into total darkness before very gradually increasing the illumination on reading cards. Each candidate had then to read out aloud what was on his individual card if possible. It was the first, and last, time that I had been subjected to a night vision test during my 44 years of service in the RAF. I understand that nowadays even initial medicals for RAF aircrew do not include this type of examination. Older readers might well remember that during the last war, one of the top nightfighter pilots was given the name of "Cats eyes Cunningham" because of his supposed extraordinary night vision accounting for his ever increasing number of night victims. The papers even suggested that it was due to the fact that he ate raw carrots! After the war it was revealed that it was a piece of propaganda to try and hide the fact from the Germans that we had airborne radar. There was no way in the world that it could have been kept secret for any length of time. Perhaps this night test at Abbey Lodge had been part and parcel of the theory that some people had better night vision than others. I have always been led to believe it had more to do with age than anything else.

As always, we soon formed small groups and in the evenings made off for a pint or two, a pub to our liking was soon found, it was in a quiet back street behind Viceroy Court it would have long ago been lost to memory in the mists of time but for a chance meeting. One night a member of our gang recognised one of the two officers standing at the bar, they looked to be in the depths of despair, long faces, not even speaking to each other. Eye contact was eventually made and the officer came over and introductions were made all round. When I addressed this officer as Sir, he said you can forget about all that, I won't be one by the end of the week. Yes, he was what had been whispered about over the recent past as LMF. This stood for Lack of Moral Fibre, meaning that enough was enough and that the nerves could not take any more. In today's parlance, he would have been assessed as being a victim of post traumatic stress and sent for counselling, and might even have rated compensation. Both officers had passed the twenty bomber operation mark and I have always thought that a far better system of dealing with such situations could have been devised. They deserved better than being reduced to the ranks and, in some cases, transferred to the Army, as private soldiers.

Some situations can get under anyone's skin in time and it was a corporal on the staff at ACRe who had a minor freak out. For more than a year he had been responsible for sending out groups of thirty or so cadets to the numerous ITWs around the country. It really hit the fan when having several hundred cadets to dispose of he targeted all those with the surnames of Smith, Jones and Brown and sent them all to one particular ITW. Luckily the ITW in question was in a resort that housed another two ITWs so unscrambling was possible to a certain extent, it was, of course, the end of his career at Regents Park. I often wondered what posting he got, Aden perhaps, or even worse.

Those of us posted to 17 ITW in Scarborough considered ourselves particularly fortunate. It was a very compact seaside resort with everything within walking or for the most part, marching distance. Two of the three ITWs located there were based in the town's two largest hotels on the sea front that had been taken over for the duration. No 17 ITW, however, operated from what had been, pre-war, Scarborough College. This College had been built to house two distinct departments, male and female, with a vast playing area dividing the two. The cadets occupied the half nearest to the town which was at the top of a steepish hill to the south on the Bridlington Road. I'm not sure who actually lived in the other section, but I do recall that it contained an indoor swimming pool which each of the three ITWs could use on one specific night per week. Another night was for the use of WAAFs only and no doubt the staff only evenings took care of the rest. One RAF cadet during our three month course at Scarborough claimed he became totally confused about who used the baths on what nights and blundered in on a WAAFs only night and, before being ejected, recalled that he couldn't help noticing that some of the WAAFs preferred to swim in the altogether. "Perhaps they had grown out of their costumes", one of the many disbelievers observed rather dryly.

The ground training course in Meteorology, Navigation and other related subjects proved to be first class. Our tutors were almost invariably school teachers called to the colours, with many from top grade institutions. The lecture rooms had been improvised in the town's outdoor swimming pool with one exception which was learning Morse Code and that took place in a smallish pre-war hotel just across the road from the pool. This was run by an ex-GPO engineer who had volunteered to come out of retirement to take these classes as a civilian, being too old for uniformed service. A super chap who had the extra chore of also trying to teach us the art of sending and receiving messages by the Aldis Lamp which had become standard fit in bombers and maritime aircraft. This last bit was a real challenge, reading the lamp signals and writing the message down at the same time. Being all convinced that we would be Spitfire pilots at the end of the day we did not put as much effort into lamp reading as we should have and it showed in our results until one magic day. During the Aldis reading sessions our instructor would position himself on one cliff top and our class on another across the bay. The honour system prevailed, of course, and there was no comparing of notes before handing in our pathetic attempts for marking. None of us thought it was really cheating when one morning a couple of Wrens appeared and stood behind us to rattle off the messages word perfect. The instructor at the de-brief just gave a very deep sigh and said "those Wrens again". It was thus obvious that it was not the first time that one of his outdoor lessons had been sabotaged and no doubt he realised that it was most unlikely to be the last.

One very memorable day during our course was when ground tuition was suspended for the day. All three ITWs had to provide a full turn out of cadets for a "Wings for Victory" day march through the delightful market town of Malton, which was about 20 miles inland, on the main rail line to York. Boarding our train shortly after mid-day we were more than pleased to observe that the WAAFs were also providing a flight for the parade, the event itself was well received, with a large crowd who thronged the Market Square shouting and clapping with approval. Even if I say so myself, the marching was spot on, but that was largely due to following behind a first class brass band, It was ever thus, it's so much easier to keep in step and look proud when martial music is available. Back in Scarborough it was just about opening time and a few of the WAAFs seemed quite pleased to join us in a jar or two. It was in another local pub one night when I was on a solo run ashore that one of the regulars, looking at my white flash, did not beat around the bush when he asked me "which one are you from then?". "Up the hill at Scarborough College", I thought was more descriptive than just 17 ITW. "Scarborough College, eh!", was his immediate riposte, "them there girls up there before they packed 'em off for the war, St Trinians had nothing on that lot, I'll tell you".

It was well into my second career in Aviation, which was civilian flying in Yorkshire, when I was in a position to indulge my dear wife Betty in one of her interests which was visiting stately piles. We had already covered Harewood House when the film 'Brideshead Revisited' spurred on her desire to visit Castle Howard. It was while trailing around, following the main group of visitors, that the rather superior sounding lady guide awakened my interest by saying. "Now we come to the scene of a most unfortunate accident when this part of the building was set on fire. The occupants at the time were girl evacuees from Scarborough College". A year later the BBC put on a two part series dealing exclusively with lady evacuees from Scarborough College who had lived in Castle Howard during WWII. There were close ups and group pictures of now very mature, staid, expensively dressed ladies looking as if butter would not melt in their mouths. Scarborough College had obviously left it's mark in the long term.

About the mid point of the ITW course I was called before my Flight Commander. He was a kindly officer who even sported a World War One medal which placed him in the late 40s age group bracket, at least. When he asked me to take a seat I thought, 'My God, has anything happened to my brother, last heard of in the Western desert". It turned out that he had been tasked with interviewing any cadet with an engineering background and point out that they could become operational sooner if they transferred to Flight Engineer duties on four engined aircraft. He said he could well understand that for anyone reaching this stage in the PNB scheme changing horses now was most unlikely and as any aircrew position was for volunteers only, compulsion was out of the question. The particular shortage in the Flight Engineer grade was partly due to the fact that the RAF had to train them not only for our service but also for the Canadians, Australians and others who flew British aircraft. I decided to stick with my one aim in life however if after grading school, I had been assessed as fit for Navigator Bomb Aimer duties only and not Pilot, I would ask to change over. I kept these thoughts to myself for obvious reasons.

One cadet had a service friend who was half way thorough a bomber tour on Halifaxes at RAF Lissett, which was not all that far away, he thought it might be a good idea if we met up one night when his friend was not on ops, the night duly arrived and we had quite a party. He had brought a member of his crew with him and they seemed to be quite serious when they agreed it might be possible to take both of us on a bombing mission. From my observations at RAF Pershore I concluded that it was the beer talking. We had all heard about the odd dog going on board, and even a WAAF friend of a crew member on one occasion, but two aircrew cadets from a non-flying station was quite out of the question. The repercussions for all concerned, if the worst happened, did not bare thinking about, perhaps they were just trying it on to see our reaction.

We were quite used to engine noises in those parts, but one night walking along the prom two of us heard an aircraft that seemed to be going flat out for some reason or other. As we gazed into the night sky in it's general direction, we suddenly saw a blaze of tracer fire streak out, the noise arriving a second or so later sounded more like cannon fire than the .303, or even .5, machine gun reports. Was it a Beaufighter night fighter firing at a German bomber or, being just off the coastline a pilot testing his guns? It certainly gave us something to talk about for the rest of our trek back to camp.

The end of our course was rapidly approaching so it was the dreaded exams at last, whatever day of the week they were taken, the results were known within 48 hours. A big surprise to most of us was that we had as a group attained the highest marks for quite some time. The next big question was which grading school were we going to, there were about 15 of them in total stretching from Perth in Scotland to the South Midlands. I was absolutely delighted when the list was read out, I was going back to dear old Sealand, with it's many memories.

CHAPTER 7
Return to Sealand, No 24 EFTS
and then Heaton Park

Leaving Scarborough was rather emotional, we had just completed a particularly well run course under dedicated tutors and staff and in delightful surroundings, what more could one ask for. Only three of our course were allocated to 24 EFTS, RAF Sealand. The rail journey was straight forward enough, change at York, Nottingham and Chester and then de-train at the now very familiar station in the centre of Sealand camp. The big difference this time was that I now had two kitbags to lug around and not just the one of two years ago, the second contained the as yet brand new flying clothing. One surprise was that aircrew cadets had taken over the barrack block that I had lived in on posting from Halton, the messing arrangements, however, couldn't have been different. No cookhouse this time around, in fact, all catering for cadets was carried out by Short Bros. of Belfast who operated their own mess hall on the airfield site. They also ran the entire grading operation, including the technical side of the Tiger Moth fleet, and even had their own transport aircraft in the form of a Short Scion, this was a twin engined, high winged monoplane. Due to the fact that only eleven were ever made I wonder if the one undergoing re-build right now at Southend Airport could have been the Sealand Scion. Many other things at Sealand remained just the same, including the Discip F/Sgt still revelling in his morning parades,. With our Barrack block being on the edge of the parade square it was just a matter of time before eye contact was made, when he carried out the original double take. If there had been a bubble caption above his head, I am sure it would have read something like: "Bloody Hell, him becoming aircrew, things must be getting really bad". I just gave him the best smile I could muster and passed on my way under my own steam.

Now to the airfield side. As already mentioned, our favourite WAAF

Corporal was still in full charge of the camp cinema, and still giving the nod to her young lads, a lovely lady indeed. The RAF decided that it was a waste of materials to provide us with flying log books because by the very nature of a grading scheme there would be many failures at the first hurdle, Navigators and Bomb Aimers had also to be found as well as Pilots. It has always been a regret, over the years, that I have no record of when and whom I flew with at the very beginning of my 52 years in the cockpit. Many situations contrived to make the 12 hours Tiger Flying under my belt a protracted affair. It was to take six full weeks starting at the end of August 1943, and continued into the first week of October with the last two weeks being hit by bad weather, mostly in the form of high winds. This made control of the tailwheel bi-planes, without brakes, virtually impossible. Although the Tiger Moth has always been highly regarded by experienced pilots I have always thought it a touch too demanding for training. Another drawback to good instruction was that communication between instructor and student was by way of a speaking tube, always referred to as the Gosport tube, no matter what aircraft it was fitted to. The lack of radio was not a problem in the Sealand area, at least with the River Dee estuary being a good anchor point, like almost all other pilots before me, I found the take-off and all upper air work no problem at all after a few lessons. However again, like all others, the landing of an aircraft required a lot of practice and an art that could never be taken for granted, constant vigilance was the order of the day no matter how many flying hours one might have on type.

The social life was almost predictable, a couple of pubs known to me in Queensferry and, needless to say, visits to Barlow's bar in Chester-which proved very popular, especially to first timers. Yes, the ATA pilots were still in good form and all too ready to have a chat, especially with pilots on the first rung of the ladder. It was nearly goodbye time to RAF Sealand, yet again, although I was to re-appear as a display pilot of the Persival Prentice at the Battle of Britain Air Day of 1949. Before leaving I did the rounds, which included a farewell to my ex NCO boss in my "Rigger" days, he loved to call himself our charge hand, but to us lesser mortals he was Corporal Jake. As we had been under the direct control of Short Bros. we had been spared the tedious chore of going around the Station with arrival and departure forms, so I never did find out if the old battleaxe of a WAAF Corporal was still in the accounts department, but she probably was.

It was now off to RAF Heaton Park to await our fate, that is the announcement of who was to become a U/T Pilot, Navigator or Bomb aimer. This ritual, as we had already heard from some of our instructors, was carried out by an NCO standing on the pre-war bandstand reading off surnames, with the accolade coming last, quite a nerve racking experience resulting in mixed emotions from all the assembled. I was literally, over the moon when it was announced: 'Jackson, 221, Pilot RAF Heaton Park was the nearest station to my home town of Southport that I was ever to serve on, being not far out of Manchester on the Bury commuter line. The camp HQ was in what I imagined must have been a stately home at some time or other, the domestic accommodation arrangements were unusual to say the least. Although all meals were taken on camp, virtually all sleeping was off base in civilian homes. I did not like this arrangement one little bit, with some householders saying that the front door would be locked at such and such a time, etc. It was obvious that compulsory billeting was anathema to many, apart from the odd merry widow by some accounts, and I could well understand that any intrusion of any kind would be so, I had only been with one family, who I hardly even saw, for about one week when salvation arrived.

One of my friends who had arrived late for a parade one morning was given what was known throughout the RAF as 'Jankers'. This was, basically, confined to camp for a few days which, amongst other things, meant sleeping on camp in a hut behind the NAAFI. Also in the hut were one or two cadets who had been given special tasks such as helping out in the cookhouse which, apart from ample food, meant a very early start in the mornings that precluded living off camp, I thought "That's for me" and immediately volunteered. After lugging sacks of potatoes around, and peeling same, plus washing crockery and floors, etc, I began to look around to see if anything else was on offer. Like all big organisations, there was a left and right hand order of things in that the twain never met. In this case I transferred into a 9 to 5 job, but still remained in the hut behind the NAAFI, although I should have again been in private digs. This second task was acting as a motor transport driver's' mate, so that I could assist in loading and unloading a three ton lorry as and when required.

My driver, on many occasions, was a very worldly wise WAAF Corporal who, luckily, I got on quite well with. One of our main jobs was taking beds and bedding to the civilian billets that were being brought into the scheme of providing accommodation for cadets or reclaiming same when, for one reason or another, households could no longer continue with this part of the war effort. On one particular drop a flighty, youngish lady made a point of informing us that her husband had just been posted overseas and she would welcome the company of a few cadets. Needless to say we had a chinwag as we drove away, but the WAAF Corporal had the final say when she said: "Ah well, I suppose a piece off a cut cake will never be missed," I fell silent for a time trying to follow the gist of her not too profound observation. Apart from that, I might well have forgotten about her, except that she was to confirm an event that was still being talked about at Heaton Park. It was to the effect that a son of Anthony Eden, Foreign Secretary and future Prime Minister at the time of Suez, having passed through there as a cadet, had been billeted out along with the rest. The story went on to say that after he left, this WAAF had been the driver when a complete house full of brand new furniture had been delivered to the house concerned. Later in the war it was confirmed that a son of Sir Anthony had been killed in action as a Sgt Navigator on Beaufighters in Burma. Not being commissioned was something of a surprise, no doubt he would certainly have had the educational qualifications, but perhaps that was the way he wanted it.

My time on the MT runs was suddenly ended when I went down with a throat glandular problem which put me in a makeshift RAF hospital for two weeks. This so called hospital was in what had been a massive private residence, probably a cotton baron's, or some such, the wards, for want of a better term, were very large bedrooms, fitted with about ten beds each. Each day, or so, a cadet seemed to be discharged without being replaced until I eventually found myself the sole occupant on my ward with two young WAAF nursing orderlies to look after me. I well remember one was from North Wales, not Anglesey I hasten to add, but if memory serves me well St Asop, I can still remember her first name because it was also mine, Ray. Still Ray at that time but Jacko for evermore shortly afterwards. One good thing about this spot of hospitalisation was that I instantly gave up smoking, which I had only started a month or so before, for life. On reporting back to my mates and regaling them with stories of poor little me being so well looked after by two little Waffies they showed marked signs of disbelief, to such an extent that I had no alternative but to ask both ladies to join us in a drink in our adopted pub, near the main gate. I was quite surprised that during the phone conversation they were more than pleased to accept. My friends were quite impressed, and it was a jolly evening all round but, sadly, the last due to our imminent departure to foreign parts. The girls both said they wished they could have been employed in the Park's sick quarters and not miles away in a so called hospital, they would have met more chaps like us was their final compliment.

The very next day we were issued with khaki drill, which the know alls said meant that we were definitely going to Canada and that the tropical outfit was to fox the enemy spies lurking around the country. Nonsense of course. One item of KD issued to us was a throwback to the days of the Raj and was never worn, it was the Pith helmet or Topee, the most useless article ever invented, an Australian bush hat would have been fine.

One group of cadets who seemed to keep themselves very much apart, possibly due to being somewhat older, to the rest of us, turned out to be all ex-police officers. The wartime term of "Reserved Occupation" meant that noone under that heading could be called up for military service, and policemen of all ages and ranks came within that definition. The one and only let out for those under that heading who wanted to join the military was to volunteer to join the RAF as aircrew. I did eventually get to know one or two of them, and I saw one of that particular group wearing police Sgt's stripes in Liverpool after the war was over but, unfortunately, it was from a train window as it pulled out of the now defunct Exchange Station. During the odd beer or two one night, two of these ex-coppers opined that after the war I would probably make a good one myself if all else failed, I have ever since wondered if that had been a compliment or otherwise!

CHAPTER 8
The long journey

When our special troop train pulled out of a sidings close to Heaton Park, no one had the faintest idea if it was bound for Liverpool or Greenock, near Glasgow, although the betting was heavily on the latter. Most convoys did, in fact, leave from the Clyde but with my local knowledge I was soon in a position to inform all in our carriage, at least, that it was to be Liverpool with so many local landmarks flashing past the windows, including the local funny farm at Rainhill. After passing through the eastern outskirts of Liverpool the train slowed considerably, before turning off the main line on to the dedicated dockland single track, usually only used for freight to and from cargo ships. Perhaps it was because the driver was not familiar with this stretch of rail, that by the time we got to within a mile of the Mersey landing stage we were down to walking pace. However, it gave time for literally hundreds of factory girls to down tools and wave like mad at us, which was duly returned with some vigour. At long last we trooped onto a ship called the "Orbeta" which was to be our home for 41 very long days.

The Orbita eventually cast her moorings and moved towards the Mersey estuary before dropping anchor, it seemed obvious, even to us greenhorns, that the ship was to leave home waters under cover of night fall and so it turned out. I don't suppose that from all the hundreds aboard her that many came from the Liverpool area, so it was particularly sad for myself and a few others, as we saw the very familiar sight of Formby Point, just two miles from my home village of Ainsdale, disappear into the darkening sky, our families not knowing of our departure, nor hearing from us for the next couple of months or more. Looking at the faces of many others around the rails, it was obvious that some were thinking, like myself, 'would we ever see dear old blighty again'. We need not have worried unduly because coming up on deck early the next morning, after the thumping of the engines had suddenly stopped, we found that we were surrounded by dear old blighty, albeit the Ulster bit, because Orbita was once again at anchor, but now in Belfast Loch! Later that day, December 14th, we really set sail, joining the main convoy of KMF27 which had exited from the Clyde. It was to be about two weeks later before the engines fell silent again. In the meantime we had ploughed due west for many a day before turning south, which meant that we were now out of range of European based long range aircraft, friendly or otherwise. It was on Christmas Eve, when heading east, that we spotted land for the first time since leaving home waters. It was the flatlands of North West Africa and later the unmistakable outline of the rock of Gibraltar that brought us to a high state of expectation. Whether the well known German agents in Spain ever caught sight of the convoy or not I will never know, but the entire fleet suddenly turned through 180° and retraced track until nightfall when, once again, there was another about turn and we headed for the straits of Gibraltar which were safely navigated during the dead of night. Being Christmas Eve, the padre had a brilliant idea which I'm not sure came off as expected. He rounded up the twenty or so Wrens on board and formed them into a choir to tour the mess decks, no doubt finishing in the officers' area- the cynics were convinced-, singing carols with one Wren having a lantern on a pole over her shoulder. On our particular mess deck the card school that had formed on day one went on playing without batting an eyelid, for the rest, they looked as if they wished they were a thousand miles away, a well intentioned event that did not quite come off.

History books now record that on that Christmas Eve of 1943, whilst the Wrens sang on, all hell had broken out in the Bay of Biscay, about 100 miles from our position, when 13 U Boats of the Borkum Group attempted not only to attack a slower convoy than ours, KMS360562, which we had overtaken in Mid Atlantic, but also to distract Allied forces trying to intercept the first of five blockade runners out of Japan. That ship, the Osorno, slipped the Allied net but finally ran aground in the Gironde estuary, but with its cargo intact. The U-boats, however, did manage to torpedo HMS Hurricane, a destroyer escort of the slow convoy but, luckily, with only two RN personnel losing their lives. This was due to the fact that the torpedo damage virtually allowed the entire crew to be taken onboard other ships before it was scuttled. The U-boats also scored hits on an American convoy out of Gibraltar for the States and one escort destroyer, USS Leary, was sunk.

A daily uplifting event on all of our 41 days on the Orbita was listening to the BBC's world news service and their signature tune of Lily Bolero, which is still played to this day. A mighty cheer went up throughout our ship when the programme announced that the German battleship Scharnhorst had been sunk during the night of boxing day in Arctic waters.

Although the ground war had finally finished in Africa in May of that year, the RAF was still well represented with many airfields spread along the entire northern coast giving us plenty of air cover, or so we thought at the time. It was two days after a very hectic stop over in Algiers Harbour for fuel and supplies that there was something of a surprise, to us lower deck mortals, when we discovered we had on board a barrage balloon which was duly inflated and launched. We thought it was to deter attacks by low flying German aircraft, however it was only in recent times that I read a book titled "Convoy Commodore" by Kenneth Creighton, published by Kimber, that another reason for barrage balloons on convoy ships came to light. One part of his book is that after being a convoy Commodore he was posted to a land appointment in Cairo and took passage in a ship which was part of KMF 26. It was on November 26th 1943 that the troopship Rohna in his convoy was hit by a glider bomb, HE293, dropped from an HE177 German aircraft. The damage was so severe that the ship eventually sank with over 1000 service personnel, including a number of ladies, losing their lives. Commodore Creighton was of the opinion that Rohna should have been beached on the nearby African coastline where many of the casualties could have been saved. The cost to the Luftwaffe? Eight HE177s shot down, so perhaps that was the start and finish of that type of attack. For the last day before reaching Port Said the balloon was not brought into use as we sailed close to the desolate coastline of Libya and Egypt, passing two very historic WWII sites- Tobruk and El Alamein- which, alongside Stalingrad, marked the beginning of the end for Nazi Germany. On our starboard side the vast desert area was also the place that my brother Harry had been charging up and down for two long years, first with the Army and then the RAF. His last address had been at an AMES (Air Ministry Experimental Station), which in effect was the pre-war code name for the then secret radar stations. My brother had last been heard of in hospital in Sicily, suffering from malaria.

Where now?, was one of my thoughts as we progressed towards Port Said for more fuel, etc. The Suez Canal southbound was the next stage of our journey when ships actually set off from both ends at about the same time with a convenient passing point being the Great Bitter lake which was more or less the half way point. A few miles down the canal saw the starboard side of the ship becoming more interesting as regards vegetation and population, to the extent that far more passengers gathered on that side compared with the port to the extent that the ship started to list rather badly, this brought forth a "This is your Captain speaking..." message over the tannoy system. The Captain did not sound to be best pleased and threatened to send us all below unless we evened out the numbers per side, the Wrens were the first to move en-mass, which ensured that many more followed. Lord Nelson would have been very proud of the twenty or so Wrens, now on the port side, a few miles later as a small work force of Arab labourers on sighting these lovely ladies looking at them over the ship's rail, all lifted their galabaers shoulder high, whilst shaking something! The girls did not avert their gaze, or even acknowledge that anything untoward was happening!

The next big event was the stop over in the Great Bitter Lake awaiting the north bound ships to arrive from Suez. Orbita dropped anchor next to two mighty battleships which turned out to be part of what had been left of the Italian fleet when they had opted out of the war three months earlier. I have often wondered what became of them, they had certainly departed by the time I started my Spitfire conversion from nearby RAF Fayid, just over a year later. On arrival at Suez, all convoy ships dropped anchor again and the sea around became a hive of activity with many of the ships embarking and disembarking personnel and stores. It was also a chance for the local Arab traders to come alongside in their boats and start business by way of whicker baskets attached to ropes with shouted orders and bids which was enjoyed by all, especially the traders themselves. A pity our ship, like all other troopers, was dry, or else we just might have managed a deal that would have broken our drinking fast.

Later, as we sailed on down the Red Sea the temperature increased day by day so it was not long before we all had to take to wearing our tropical uniform which included short trousers, a form of dress I never liked then or since. A view shared by many more in the British military and considered unthinkable by the American services. Our next port of call was Aden when most of the ship's that had been in the convoy since leaving the UK would depart direct to India. It was always interesting to watch the comings and goings by small tenders when not moored alongside. With only one gangway lowered on most occasions it was easy to spot the few leaving or joining the ship and it was a very pleasant surprise on this occasion when I instantly recognised a chap who had been on our team at Pershore, he was Jim Atkinson, who hailed from Tyneside, I espied him struggling up the gangway and now wearing Sgt's stripes. He had volunteered for aircrew service as an air gunner at the same time as I was accepted for pilot training and had left Pershore in just about as many days as it took me months to start my training. I must admit that we all thought he would be lucky to see this war out but fate had been kind to him. After his short training course, he had been posted onto Catalina aircraft and then found himself in the Seychelles in the Indian Ocean, to spend hours and hours patrolling that vast sea on anti-submarine duties. For some reason or another he was to sail with us as far as Mombasa and then fly to Egypt before going home to become an instructor.

What had been our fleet was, from now on, reduced to two ships plus two escort frigates. My friend Jim, with his local flying experience, told us that since the taking of Madagascar from the Vichy French the chance of an attack by submarine in this part of the Indian Ocean had been vastly reduced. It appeared that the French on that island had not been averse to re-fuelling both German and Japanese U boats. It proved to be the case for us, but a month later a ship was sunk near Mombasa with great loss of life, which included a number of ATS girls. On arrival in Mombasa we tied up against terra firma for the first time since leaving Liverpool. We noted that all securing hawsers had a spiked metal device around them which, in theory, kept land based rats from boarding. As one Wren noted, "a few more rats would not make any real difference as there were so many amongst the RAF aircrew already". Just what had they been up to?

Into the last furlong now with the Orbita heading south again towards our disembarkation point of Durban. Our entry into the harbour was quite something and particularly emotional. Standing at the sea end of a jutting quay was a lady dressed all in white, complete with a megaphone singing her heart out. Her songs included "Land of Hope and Glory", "Rule Britannia, and "There will always be an England". As ships of any real size are reduced to about walking pace prior to being secured, she kept walking alongside us for 10 to 15 minutes or so. This was a truly magnificent performance by the pre-war opera singer who had greeted every single convoy that had passed through Durban throughout the war in the same fashion. She even sang on the day that she had received news of the tragic loss in action of her eldest son serving with the Black Watch in Italy. She was Perla Gibson, and a dedicated book about her life called "The lady in white" was eventually published after the war.

After disembarkation we were taken to a transit camp called Clairwood which was about 6 miles out of town but luckily on a main railway line. There was only one shock during our first few days of living in Africa and that was when we were each issued with a palliasse and told to fill it with straw and that would then be our bedding for our stay, surely South Africa could do better than that was the unanimous opinion. As Clairwood was also the local equivalent of our Ascot we had to be very careful as to were we gathered our straw from! Otherwise, however, everything was absolutely marvellous after four years of wartime England. No blackout, plenty of superb food and alcohol, and a very pro-British attitude from the local whites, who, in the main, came from British stock. It was almost a nightly ritual to catch the train into Durban to savour the delights of a very civilised life. Being January, it was their summer, of course, with both high temperatures and humidity, but the sky was often cloudless which allowed sight of the Southern Hemisphere's night sky, which appeared to contain almost twice as many stars compared with northern latitudes. One famous cinema in the town had painted on the inside of their domed roof above the foyer, a remarkable imitation of a cloudless night's sky. It was not uncommon on some nights to hear people trying to decide if they were actually looking up into the open sky or an imitation, it was so realistic.

All good things come to an end, of course, but not in my particular case, until a very remarkable coincidence had occurred. I was standing in a queue at the food server in the mess hall one morning when I spotted a chap who caught my immediate attention. If I had not known that my brother was in Sicily, or even Italy by now, I would have thought that he was at least, a spitting image of Harry. As I moved up to get a better look he turned towards me as if he sensed my approach. Yes, it was my brother, last seen three years ago in the tranquil Buckinghamshire town of Wendover. He obviously wanted to catch up on all the news of family and friends whilst I was dying to know about the Eighth Army and the Western Desert. First of all, of course, we had to establish how this remarkable meeting had come about. It appeared that he, like myself, had volunteered for pilot training and was on his way to Southern Rhodesia, also like myself, for aircrew training. What a small world!

Just over a week after disembarking from Orbita, which survived the war by the way, we were on the move once again. This time it was to

71

be a two and a half day special troop train journey that was to take us through some rail stations with very famous names in the context of the British involvement in Southern Africa. The train set off from the local station at Clairwood with my brother aboard, but in a different coach to mine, which was a great pity because day two of the trip was also his birthday, and therefore we could not celebrate the occasion as well as we would have wished. It was not long after departure before we started the long climb onto the high plateau, spine of Africa passing through Pietermaritzburg, Johannesburg, Pretoria, Mafeking, before crossing into Bechuanaland and then onwards through part of the Kalahari desert to Francistown before entry into Southern Rhodesia near Plumtree for the final destination of Bulawayo. The reaction of bystanders as we passed through these various stations could not have been more contrasting with the two extremes being Jo'burg and Plumtree. Although our train did not actually stop in the capital of the Transvaal, you could sense the hostility towards us as our train passed slowly through the Central Station with virtually all the would be passengers on the platforms positively glowering at us. It was, and probably still is, a stronghold of the Afrikaaners of Dutch descent, many of whom did not support the Allies in the war, and in many cases were pro-Nazi Germany.

Some pilots trained in South Africa are of the opinion that some of the 350 plus British aircrew war graves in the Johannesburg War Cemetery were the outcome of aircraft sabotage by pro-German elements, who probably belonged to a group called the OBs, which stood for Oswag Brandwag. I suppose their attitude might well have been a legacy of the Boer War because in mainland Europe after the end of WWII it would have been impossible to find a race more pro-British and also anti-German than the Dutch people. One accolade awarded to the RAF in South Africa was "The blue plague", but people in the know insisted it had all started with the very first cadet pilots to arrive in those parts in 1940 at the commencement of the Commonwealth Air Training Plan. Those cadets had been very boisterous to say the least, for the rather staid local whites, but they all in fact wore the dark blue of the Royal Australian Air Force and not the lighter blue of the RAF. A typical case of give a dog a bad name and all that, I suppose. At the other end of the scale, a liberating army would not have been made more welcome than our train load of cadets were when , after crossing the Limpopo river into Rhodesia, we de-trained at the town of Plumtree for a meal and a truly fantastic welcome from the locals for such a short stay. At the end of this mostly pleasant journey from Durban to Bulawayo, the second town in Southern Rhodesia, we found our new base, Hillside camp, which had been a showground for the local area prior to the war.

CHAPTER 9
Aircrew Training and gaining Wings

At Hillside camp we slept in what had literally been cattle pens and were to stay there for a much longer period than we thought necessary. On reflection however, it was obvious that a pool of would be aircrew were necessary in a distant land, just in case a troopship with hundreds of potential flyers aboard was sent to it's doom. Two other factors that decided the length of the backlogs at various stages was that courses were often extended, or shortened, depending on the loss rates in front line squadrons at various times during the war. For instance, the bomber loss rate was particularly high in 1943 when the German night fighter force was at it's zenith. The second factor was that until about the same time, the RAF had not only to replace losses but had also to cater for the build up of extra squadrons which peaked in number at about the 480 mark in late 1943. From 1944 onwards it was all downhill as regards the training of new aircrew with many stations closing down. We at Hillside had been caught in the extended course period and joined part of another full ITW course being undertaken by cadets, such as my brother, who had come down from the Middle East and some from families who had settled in Rhodesia, and foreign countries such as Greece, Yugoslavia and even Argentina. Most of us, however, had already passed a full ITW course in the UK so we did not take this extra tuition too seriously, although two extra items proved to be of interest.

One was star recognition with the aid of slides, etc, although home study was possible on most nights during the dry season. The other extra item was an all day trek, in small groups, through the featureless Bundu (Bundu being the local name for the uncultivated wilderness of Elephant grass which covered vast areas). This was not along the all too familiar lines of 'escape and evasion' practiced at RAF stations in the UK. The aim on this trek was how best to reach civilisation in the event of a forced landing in the middle of nowhere. We were even briefed to aim for a main road, which, according to our map, was the only road in that particular area anyway. The briefing officer informed us that a lorry would drive down this road at a given time to pick up all groups, but if any failed to meet that deadline they would be on their own. Pigs ear, we thought. He went on to say that almost invariably any native (Kaffir in local parlance) we chanced upon would almost certainly be friendly but to keep well clear of any of their villages, a group of mud huts called Kraals, as one cadet who had actually forced landed for real and had ventured into one had been put to death because it was assumed that he must have noticed that they were in the process of dismembering a giraffe which they had recently slain for it's meat. A strictly forbidden act then and now, our group, now briefed, would most certainly not fall for that one, but another pit fall was to come. We set off at too fast a pace and later relaxed to the extent that we missed the deadline by about 10 minutes, yes, the camp transport had set off dead on time. Luckily, a local white farmer in his truck drew up and shouted "jump aboard". He seemed to fully realize what the problem was because he took us straight to the camp entrance which was almost twenty miles past his farm. We arrived at the same time as the official transport and could not hide our joy from the rest of our course who had made it on time. Soon their superior looking smirks faded somewhat. This lorry ride had been most interesting for the two of us in the front cab, not least because it was about the only civilian motor ride outside of towns that we would ever make, rail being the norm. The driver was a good talker and listener, which is a rare talent for most people, he had a laugh when one of us said we thought the road was supposed to be a main one out of Bulawayo. "Yes, it is", he replied, "these two strips of Tarmac that fit standard wheel tracks are all that you will ever see outside of towns in this country". We let it go at that until we met another car head on. We held our breath as neither vehicle showed any sign of slowing down until the last second when both took to the rough potted ground on what would normally be the kerb side in each case. I broke the silence by saying that "I thought this lorry had taken the rough ground rather well, hardly noticed any bumps at all". He said there was a certain speed in all vehicles that gave this effect over rough ground. I have kept this snippet in my memory bank ever since, particularly when passing over one notorious British Rail/Road crossing in Lincolnshire, it works rather well.

It was during my time at Hillside Camp that the very last intake of aircrew cadets to train in Southern Rhodesia during WWII arrived from the UK. One of those cadets that I recognised I had only known as Tony during our overlap back at RAF Heaton Park. However, it turned out that his full name was Anthony Wedgewood Benn, who now goes under the name Tony Benn, and could have been Viscount Stansgate if he had not declined that title on the death of his father. It was during Tony's pilot training at Gwelo that he received the very sad news of the death of his elder brother, Michael, in a flying accident in the UK. Michael had already completed a full tour of operations on Beaufighters in North Africa and gained a DFC. On return to the UK he had converted to Mosquito light bombers and the accident occured when trying to land with the airspeed pitot tube cover still in plave. Tony Benn's biography by Jad Adams (ISBN 3335588) makes remarkable reading and particularly so when recording Tony's father's career. He had joined the army at the age of 37 at the start of WWI in 1914, took part in the Dardanelles campaign, became a pilot in the RFC/RAF and Royal Navy, organised the first ever drop by parachute of a spy behind lines when in Italy. For his efforts during WWI he was awarded the DSO and DFC and also, by France, made a Chevalier of the Legion of Honour and awarded the Croix de Guerre and, by Italy, the War Cross and the Bronze Medal for Military Valour. He re-joined the RAF during WWII and was an Air Commodore serving in Italy when told of his son's death but managed to return to the UK the following day. He later gave lectures on air gunnery at various RAF stations and flew on some Bomber Command operations over Germany as a rear gunner at the ripe old age of 67. Surely the oldest crew member ever to do so. It was when he was nominated for another award that higher authority noted his age and ordered him to cease operational flights immediately. Much to Tony Benn's annoyance his father had, in December 1941, accepted a peerage under the title of Viscount Stansgate (Stansgate being a village in Essex in which the family owned a holiday cottage). His father also became Secretary of State for Air following the General Election held in 1945 between VE and VJ day. I have often wondered if any other father and son had both been awarded DFC medals?

My Brother and I spent a great deal of our leisure time at the municipal outdoor swimming pool and the nearby TOC "H" club each week end. Being from a Methodist family we were soon tipped off that the Sunday evening service at the Church of that faith was the place to be on Sunday evenings when after the service all military visitors were entertained to tea and sandwiches and also introduced to local families. The event soon became the highlight of our limited social life, but I got off to a familiar start, if only of a minor nature. One lady, who was obviously the person nominated to be on the look out for first timers to give them a special welcome, soon spotted my brother and myself and produced a visitors book to record our names and home towns. On noting two Jacksons and two Southports she gave us a quick look and asked, "cousins by any chance?" Where had I heard that question before? Ah yes, the WAAF driver at RAF Valley. The answer this time was, "No, brothers", which seemed to delight the dear lady no end because she went on to say, "well fancy that, we've never had two brothers here before". A good start.

It was policy in the Rhodesian Air Training Group (RATG) to allow leave at the end of each phase of the course, that in our case was ITW, EFTS and SFTS. The closeness of Victoria Falls was too good a chance to miss so 10 of us booked into the Victoria Falls Hotel which proved to be an excellent choice indeed. It had been built on the old colonial lines, that is to say for gracious living in all respects. It was managed by a Lancastrian from Preston who seemed to take a special interest in any of his guests in uniform. In the gardens one could see magnificent views of the falls which, even to this day, I consider to be one of the finest sights in the world. Whenever we decided to take afternoon tea, or even a beer or two, in these gardens we were often joined by a tribe of baboons, as if we hadn't seen enough of them on one barrack square or other during our time, but these provided a nice diversion. The journey to and from the falls from Bulawayo was by a steam train on one of the longest stretches of straight line in Africa. One predictable stop on the night journey was a town called Wankie to re-stock with coal because it was one of the very few places in Africa that mined this natural resource. Wankie was also the place that one or two of the chosen few were sometimes invited onto the footplate to complete the journey outbound. Alas, I never achieved that ambition, on a steam train that is, but later in life I did manage a Leeds-Kings Cross return on a 235 train up front.

After arriving back at Hillside Camp from one of the most relaxing holidays that one could ever imagine there was nothing to do except to sit around and await our destiny as regards allocations of who would be going to which EFTS. We had already established on the grapevine that depending on which elementary flying school (EFTS) one was posted to could be a deciding factor in whether we eventually flew fighters or bombers, so a great deal was at stake and tension mounted.

In the meantime, a short resume might be in order to pay tribute to

Southern Rhodesia's contribution to the war effort in general and the air war in particular. All flying stations in the country were located, for obvious reasons, near the main centres of population which were limited in Rhodesia's case to the capital, Salisbury (now Harare), Gwelo and Bulawayo, the equivalent distances in England being roughly London, Leeds and Edinburgh such is the size of the country. It might well be of interest to note that the white population at that time numbered of 95,000 which shot up to peak of approximately 300,000 post war, before declining after independence to about 120,000 or so today. It was therefore quite remarkable that they not only managed to support nine flying schools; 4 elementary (EFTS), 4 Advanced (SFTS) plus 1 instructor school, but they were also first off the mark in 1940 at the inauguration of the British Commonwealth Air Training Plan (BCATP). The four EFTSs, were all equipped with an American monoplane called the Fairchild Cornell or PT26A. It had started life with open cockpits, but later the Canadians had insisted on an enclosed canopy over student and instructor positions, to cater for their sub-zero winters. Now this type was here in the semi tropics where the sun beat down on most days, but that did not detract from a lovely to handle aircraft.

The four Advanced Schools had a 50/50 break down, two flying the well proven American Harvard, which had entered RAF service pre-war at Grantham, with the other two schools operating the Airspeed Oxford, a twin engined, British built aircraft, which had been uprated with American Junior Wasp engines replacing the British Cheetahs. The ninth flying school was an Instructor Training Establishment, operating a mixed fleet whose main task was converting recently graduated pilots to instructor status. To that end 5 out of every 50 passing out pilots were required to take this course and remain in Rhodesia so as to maintain the establishment of instructors at the eight Flying Training Schools. The total output of pilots in Rhodesia during 1940/46 was 7,600, a good part of the grand total of 58,000 fully trained pilots produced by Canada, USA, South Africa and Rhodesia. This was a magnificent effort on the part of all concerned, particularly from Southern Rhodesia with it's limited resources and manpower.

Another notable achievement was the raising of £70,000 by the native population to buy aircraft for the three Rhodesian Squadrons operating with the RAF. The average pay for those people was less than £1 per month at that time. A book covering the entire air training scheme in the four main participating countries is called "Flying by the seat of your pants", by Hugh Morgan. Hugh's father was one of the 58,000 pilots already referred to, and it makes excellent reading with many contributions from staff and students who took part in the scheme at various stages of the war and for a short period after it ended.

To return to Hillside Camp and the saga of who goes to which station for the real start of becoming a Pilot. The pros and cons, as we saw them at the time were as follows; The ultimate posting, if choice had had anything to do with it, for ambitious Spitfire pilots that is, would certainly have been a move to Belvedere for two very good reasons. Firstly it appeared that Belvedere was twinned with the advanced SFTS at Cranborne, which was equipped with single engined Harvard trainers and that would almost certainly lead on to single seat fighters in the long term. The second reason was that Belvedere was the only flying school within walking distance of a town centre, in this case Salisbury. The Advanced School at Cranborne was also near Salisbury, but out of distance for regular walking sorties.

The other side of the coin was that a posting to the only basic school near Bulawayo would nearly always lead to a move to one of the two Advanced Schools in that area equipped with twin engined Airspeed Oxford aircraft, which in turn meant employment on heavy aircraft only thereafter. A terrible thought for most, but a welcome release for the one or two who had not enjoyed aerobatics, which had been a discrete test during Grading School back in the UK. It appeared that due note had been made of this facet when our movement orders finally arrived a week later. For myself, and others, it was to be the dream posting to No 25 EFTS Belvedere. For the few who had admitted their dislike of aerobatics and also some approaching old age- over 25 that is- it was to be on the Oxfords that they finally achieved their wings.

The rail journey to Salisbury from Bulawayo was another longish affair, stretching well towards the 18 hour point, but this was mainly due to the fact that even on main lines, such as this one, they were almost invariably single track only for virtually the entire distance. When trains did pass, it was often in the middle of nowhere when one train would pull into a small loop and await the arrival of a train travelling in the opposite direction. There would then follow a small ceremony of handing over of the keys of that sector, the keys in fact were on a massive circular metal ring so there was little chance of misplacing them.

Our accommodation at Belvedere was almost regal after the cattle pens of Hillside, long wooden huts with a fair amount of bed space, they were also virtually on the airfield itself, which cut out travel time. Due to the climactic conditions of high afternoon temperatures, which in turn governed turbulence, early starts and early finishing of the flying programme was the routine throughout the year. On the admin side, about the only sign of discipline was by way of a retired Sergeant of the BSAP which stood for British South African Police. Although it was well known that he liked a snort or two virtually every night of his life, he never failed to do the Reveille rounds in person at 5 o'clock each morning on all flying days with flying commencing at six. We did have a bucket of coffee to help ourselves to, until a break for breakfast, followed after the first detail at 7.30, with flying finally finishing about 1 pm. I really took to the Cornell aircraft, with it's powerful Ranger engine, enclosed cockpit, flaps and even a braking system. The landing of this machine was infinitely easier than the Tiger Moth, which the Cornell had superceded six months previously, but not having flown at all for seven months and no experience on type, the time spent at grading school in the UK did not count for anything. Therefore we all started from scratch and no one soloed before 7 or 8 hours dual. One or two flights only stick in the mind's eye of individual trips, however I well remember my first solo on the Cornell.

I had the usual briefing of 'if you bounce on landing or are unhappy

Fairchild Cornell

about the approach be it too high or low, open up and go around again for another try, as often as you like until you're happy". Everything was going swimmingly until on finals when I noted two other aircraft also on finals, one either side at three or more wingspan distances. I had better explain that Tarmac runways just did not exist in Rhodesia at that time and only the general direction of the take off and landing was indicated for the big grass area. Well, I had not been briefed for this situation so I just ploughed on and landed dead ahead as did the other two aircraft. The check pilot who had launched me off said, after the usual congratulations, I don't suppose you noticed the other two aircraft just astern of you on finals did you? I replied that I had certainly noticed them after landing, which was perfectly true of course, and this seemed to satisfy him.

My nominated instructor at Belvedere, to start off with, was Pilot Officer Edwards, a born and bred Rhodesian who obviously wished that he was employed on anything other than instructing cadet Pilots. I think I coped as well as might have been expected and was not duly worried when I was reallocated to a newly arrived Flight Lieutenant Foley, just out from the UK. It was literally like chalk and cheese. He was a gent of the old school and nothing seemed to worry him unduly, he certainly gave the impression that he had seen it all before, probably been instructing for years. The only time that we met socially was at our passing out party before we moved up the road to 20 SFTS at Cranborne. It was during the party that I learnt that his wife had joined the WRENS at the outbreak of the war and was now stationed in the building in Liverpool that co-ordinated the RN RAF forces in the Atlantic and therefore took more than a passing interest in the convoy that she knew her husband was sailing on to South Africa. How I would have loved to have met that dear lady after the war to find out where, or where not, we had been during our meanderings in the Atlantic for the 11 days spanning the Christmas of 1943.

Our social life had once again settled into a routine, naturally, it centred on downtown Salisbury. With Flying finishing just after mid day, it was more often than not that we took a stroll past the racecourse and on into the town centre during the late afternoons. The rationale of an early start was that the licensing laws were very similar to those in Australia, at that time, which led to the well known phrase of 'the five o'clock swill'. It was only 7 o'clock in the evenings that the shutters came down as regards the drinking of alcohol in Salisbury. However, the cinema, called the Bioscope in Darkest Africa, was a little more liberal in that it did not finish until about 8.30pm, so on the few occasions that a film turned up that we really fancied we would pay the entrance fee twice over just to see it. On day one we would see the first half and leave in a hurry for a quick drink and on the next night, of course, have a quick drink before going to see the end of the epic or whatever. We never bothered with the Bioscope on Saturdays needless to say, those nights proved to be rather special with RAF types from the four other flying stations around Salisbury making their way into town one way or another. Although there were a few watering holes around the town, mostly in hotels and eating places, by far the most popular was the Meikels Hotel, the flagship of a hotel group going under that name. They even sported a dance band, and I am sure a bald headed drummer in that group must have been fed up to the back teeth at times by the barrage of flicked peanuts that was often aimed in his direction on Saturday nights.

On the flying side, the pace was hectic, although we did not appreciate it at the time due to our limited experience, we completed, on average, 110 flying hours each during the three month course. An annual rate of 440 hours in one year during training would probably be impossible in England due to the weather, if nothing else. Our basic training included the usual dual and solo night flying hours and it is flying during the dark hours that almost all pilots enjoy most of all. Without daytime turbulence, most aircraft fly without any real effort on the part of the pilot. Another factor is that on clear nights the visibility can be quite fantastic, town lights that appear to be about 20 miles away often turn out to be 50 or 60 miles distant.

During this period all course cadets were fully employed, either in the sky or on the ground helping the duty officer in charge of night flying as without a radio a lot depended on a squad of about 5 cadets, plus the officer of course. The landing direction had to be laid out with a line of Gooseneck flares, these flares looked just like flattened garden watering cans, but with longer spouts. When filled with paraffin and the wick, which protruded out of the spout, after lighting they would burn for a number of hours. Pre WWII these flares were standard at all RAF land based airfields because the one and only Tarmac runway in the service was at RAF Cranwell, and even that was only a few hundred yards in length, to support the vastly overloaded weight of a Vickers Wellesley, which was to attempt to break a long distance record by flying non-stop to Egypt. Tarmac and concrete became the norm for all airfields built in the UK during the war, but quite a few pre-war, grass only, survive to this day, for the use of light aircraft and gliders only.

Another, now historic, device that was under our care during our night flying duties at the end of the flarepath, was called the Chance light. This self contained electrical light, mounted on a four wheel chassis, was positioned so as to illuminate the ideal landing position, but for raw rookies like ourselves, we often found ourselves well beyond that point before touchdown. We also manned the Aldis lamps with a basic white light which could be changed in seconds to green or red, plus the ubiquitous Verey Pistol of course.

The only real aircraft accident on our course occurred whilst I was on these night ground duties when one wheel leg of a Cornell collapsed during a landing. The pilot concerned was a friend of mine called Paul Kent, who not only passed the course with flying colours, but later became the only other member of our entry to continue to serve in the RAF post war, reaching Wing Commander rank before his untimely death from natural causes. He told me after the accident that although the landing had been firm, it had not been much worse than many others. Many people on the station, including very experienced instructors, dismissed the event as 'the straw that broke the camel's back', that is, that metal fatigue after many, many unreported heavy landings was beginning to take it's toll.

Although I mentioned 'darkest Africa' at one stage, we could not have lived or worked in better surroundings, this was due, in part, to the average altitude of the country being close on 4,000' or so. With a normal drop of temperature of 2°c per thousand feet, what could have been 30°c at sea level was reduced to 22°c, similar to a pleasant English summer's day. Nothing for nothing of course, and purely from an aviators point of view, 4,000' of altitude was a big draw back for flying training type aircraft with their unsupercharged engines. The increasing temperatures during the day also reduced engine power, and therefore it was a real struggle to climb to an altitude that was safe for aerobatic and spin recovery training. I don't know if this long drag to altitude had anything to do with it, but a safe altitude seemed to be all things to all men amongst the 'gods' of the instructor world, which led to my only other well remembered detail. On this, my first solo spin and recovery flight, my instructor had rushed off to fly with another of his brood, but not before he had authorized my flight. Perhaps it was a throw back to his instructing days in the UK, but I noted for the first time that after Ex 14 (spinning) on the booking out sheet he had added 3000'. I remember thinking to myself, 'he must think I've got the hang of it now'. So off I went and carried out about 4 or 5 deliberate spins with full recovery, starting at 3,000'. Although the ground looked rather close during the pull outs I was quite happy as I returned to base and booked in. My instructor was now back on the ground and noting my flight time asked, 'you did climb up to altitude between each spin, didn't you?'. Like a flash I realised that he thought that with such a short airborne time I might just have taken a sightseeing tour around the area, but I managed to splutter, "must have got my take off time wrong sir", another quizzical look, but that was the end of the matter. Other cadets later put me right, 3000' on the authorization sheet meant 'must recover by, and that in turn meant a minimum entry height of 5,000', equivalent to 9,000' above sea level. How on earth had the Tiger Moth, the Cornell's immediate predecessor managed that, perhaps it never did, and operated to lower altitude parameters.

It was a little sad when we came to leave dear old Belvedere, not least because we were to be the second from last course to train there with the wind down of the entire training scheme now in progress. One small piece of history was made in our time when the first Hurricane fighter to be allocated to Belvedere for use by the instructors arrived, it did not fly a great deal: what a waste.

For some weeks prior to our departure we had been making plans as to what we should do during our leave period. Some on our course opted for one or other of the many offers of hospitality on tobacco farms, etc. Although we were still on very low pay, our little group of four thought that we could just about manage a week in Rhodesia's fourth largest town, which was in the Eastern Highlands, in those days it was called Umtali, right on the border with neutral Portuguese Mozambique, and a very wise decision it proved to be.

We had been recommended lodgings with a Mrs Quick, which was to be more than satisfactory, no house rules and we could come and go as we pleased. Umtali was not a garrison town and few uniforms were seen for most of the time, so it was quite something that the locals managed to run a coffee/tea shop for military visitors. As this facility was usually manned by two young ladies it was not often short of customers. I can still, in my mind's eye, picture it's location, it was situated on the Broadway, about a quarter of the way up the length of this main street from the railway station, nearly opposite was the residence of the Steel family, of Scottish descent, who often invited our group in for sundowners, or perhaps it should have been called midnighters, such was their hospitality. Still further up the inclined thoroughfare could be found the town's only two hotels, both were well patronized by the locals and ourselves alike. One local was a chemist, whose brother had gone missing whilst flying Spitfires in the Western Desert, or, in local parlance, 'UP NORTH'. He asked outright what we, as aviators, thought the chances were of his brother still being alive. As it was now eighteen months since he went missing it was difficult to say 'none'. No doubt his name will be on the

RAF's Memorial at Runnymede, or the El Alemain Memorial, along with the 10,000 plus members of the RAF with no known graves. In later days I have often wondered if his brother had been on the same squadron as Ian Smith, another Rhodesian, who was later to upset the British Government when he became the Prime Minister of his country and declared unilateral independence. He also had come to grief in a Spitfire in the Western Desert, but had survived with a slightly disfigured face which was the result of impacting with his gunsight after a crash landing. I have no doubt that his survival was to the benefit of his much loved country in the long term, but few in Britain saw it that way. Also, in the small town of Umtali was a girls boarding school which catered not only for the country as a whole, but also for the neighbouring state of Malawi. The inmates of that institution used to promenade up and down the main street from about mid afternoon onwards and were certainly not averse to engaging in conversation with our group, who just happened to be doing the same. Unlike today, young girls of, say, 15 to 17 in this country looked very much their age, whereas those who had lived in the tropics since birth, often looked and acted well beyond their years. Our time in Umtali was rapidly running out, but we all resolved to return on our next leave, having enjoyed our first real taste of colonial life so much.

The next challenge was to master the Harvard trainer which had a certain reputation, particularly the difficult art of landing the beast. On arrival at No 20 Service Flying Training School (SFTS) at RAF Cranborne, I was allocated to Sergeant Austin, known to all, except students that is, as Bunny. The fact that he was still a Sergeant indicated quite clearly that he had been selected for these duties immediately after gaining his wings. We soon found these instructors were absolutely dedicated to teaching others, whereas some of the senior staff who had completed a full tour of operations had quite understandably developed a 'live for today' attitude to life, however both types had a great deal to offer in their differing ways. Quite by chance, I was to come under the wing of two instructors from the extremes of both groups, but they came in the correct sequence as far as I was concerned.

The first phase of our six months SFTS course, not only included conversion to type but also the all important under the hood flying. That was flying by reference to instruments only and universally known as I.F. when precision was all important and certainly insisted upon by Ulster born Sgt 'Bunny' Austin. Later on, in the second, and last, part of the course, which included live .303 firing at ground targets and both dive and low level bombing, I was lucky enough to have as my instructor on many flights Flt Lt Huggins who, incidentally, was the son of the then Prime Minister of Southern Rhodesia. He had completed a full tour of Ops in the UK which might explain his real 'gung ho' attitude. Low flying really meant just that and, at times, I was fearful of applying too much bank on the aircraft in case a wing tip touched the ground. In this very egalitarian part of the British Empire being a son of the PM counted for nought, he was regarded by all as a bit of a character, which was a fair description in my opinion.

Once again, there is always an event or incident which will be put in

RAF Harvard

the memory bank for all time from one's early training days. Early days at Cranborne converting onto the Harvard started on day one, and before we had even left the ground, Bunny had given me a good walk around the aircraft during the pre-flight inspection during which I had thought how large the aircraft now looked after the Cornell, although I had seen many before in the UK. It was just after start up that we saw a formation starting their take off run from the far side of the grass airfield. If everything had gone according to plan they would have been to the left of our position and about 50' high by the time they passed our parked aircraft. However, the no 3 aircraft of the formation, that is the one due to pass closest to us, seemed to be lagging somewhat and also starting to move towards the rear of his leader, whereupon he was caught in the leader's slipstream, flipped on it's back and slithered along the ground past our port wing tip upside down. After a second or so of silence, Bunny said over the intercom from the back cockpit: "Funny, I've never seen that happen before", before I had time to button my lip I blurted out: "And I hope it's the last bloody time too". Such intemperate language from a student was just not on but Bunny chose to ignore it and shook me rigid by saying: "Now for the pre-taxy checks". Yes, we did carry on and complete the first dual exercise on the Harvard, but I'm not sure that I learnt much on that first occasion.

The usual routine progressed at a fair pace; stalling and spinning with both being far more hectic than the Cornell, followed by the now familiar circuits and bumps until deemed ready for first solo on type, which in my case came after 5 hours. Apart from the normal basic controls we now had two new devices to contend with. The first was a variable pitch propeller (RPM) which meant we now had control of the revolutions of the propeller as well as the boost control via the normal throttle lever. The second device was a lever that selected wheels up or down and was only fitted to the front cockpit which, in effect, meant that the student pilot was in sole charge for most flights. This strange arrangement on the Harvard led to an incident before our time, but which was still much talked about.

Instructors would often merge two lessons together which in many cases was one hour of IF, carried out with the student in the back cockpit, under the hood, and the instructor in the front, keeping a good visual lookout in addition to imparting the odd word of advice. After the hour was up, the Instructor would gladly seize the golden opportunity of actually flying the aircraft himself for a change, and as often as not landing at our satellite airfield about ten miles to the east so that he and his student could exchange seats with the engine still running. On this notorious occasion, the Instructor, after landing, actually taxied the aircraft back to the take off point and, after unstrapping, clambered out only to find that his Greek student was still under the hood, with his part of the cockpit canopy still firmly shut. Not particularly pleased, he re-connected his speaking plug and whilst still standing on the wing shouted "Open up" into his microphone, meaning the two hoods of course. There was a mighty roar as the engine was given full throttle by the Greek student, blowing the instructor, still strapped in his parachute, clean off the wing. After the aircraft was airborne the student gave the usual request of "Undercarriage up please, sir", getting no reply he repeated the request until nearing 7,000' (11,000' above sea level) before he released his IF hood and got the shock of his life when he found the front cockpit empty. However, he managed to descend and land the aircraft safely back at Cranborne after managing to pin point his position. During the inevitable grilling by his flight commander the student stated that having found the front cockpit empty with the hood open he assumed that his instructor had become so fed up with his flying he had bailed out on him. It was never recorded what the instructor and student said to each other after the instructor finally managed to return from the satellite field, perhaps it's just as well! I have often tried to put myself in the Greek student's shoes. The concept of a cadet learning to fly using a foreign language and in an aircraft type fitted with a particularly poor intercom system beggars belief, perhaps this was an incident just waiting to happen.

It was not only the intercom system that lacked sophistication, the radio- as fitted to the Harvard- could have been one of Marconi's earliest models. It was known to one and all as the coffee grinder because to try and tune in to a required frequency it was necessary to wind a handle and read a metred gauge at the same time. During one night flying session, not only did a student manage to wind on to the local radio station, but also to jam the press to talk switch on to permanent transmit. It was most unfortunate that the instructor flying with him was not only born and bred in Salisbury, and with a very recognisable voice and a pillar of his local church. According to many God fearing civilians it was language most foul that assailed their ears as the instructor castigated his student for not being capable of making radio contact with Cranborne at the end of a night cross country flight.

Our social life was more or less a continuation of that at Belvedere, although slightly curtailed due to the distance from town, although Saturday nights in the Meikels Hotel was always a racing certainty. One addition to our civilian contacts was a local family by the easy to remember surname of Leopard. The popularity of that family was partly due to the fact that they had seven daughters. I can only re-call one of them now, going by the name of Rosie, and that was because she had taken a shine to our unofficial team leader, Ray Jones from Wrexham. A nice touch from Ray was that well after the war, and remembering our joint interests in football, he waited for the Saturday that my home town, Southport, was due to play away at Wrexham and positioned himself on the road between the town rail station and the football ground, just in case I turned up. What a reunion! I had arrived by train, however it was from the south and not Lancashire as Ray had guessed. He had not reckoned on the fact that as an ex-brat I was still on contract to the RAF at that time. It was not all good news that he had about our original gang of four who had served together throughout our time in Rhodesia and fighter conversion in Egypt. Ray himself and George Duffy had elected to train on P47 Thunderbolt fighters whilst Alf Harding and myself chose Spitfires. The bad news was that George, a superb athlete during his schooldays and beyond, whose coach had predicted a brilliant career over the 100 yard sprint, had been involved in a very nasty accident after their joint posting to No 5 Squadron in India. George had survived a crash landing after engine failure in his P47, but had suffered a broken back which put paid to his dreams in the athletic world, to say nothing of other implications.

Back to Rhodesia and our association with some of the civilian families that entertained us so well. Two topics of conversation that occured sooner or later were "the rains" and a rather unusual one called the "suicide month". Despite the chat I never did discover if the suicide month of October was the result of day after day of unending clear skies or the thought of losing them when the rains arrived. It might even have been an accumulation of many years of predictable weather combined with the fact that all tropical countries have twelve hours of daylight, and twelve hours of night at all times of the year, very boring indeed, but surely not a suicide issue? However, from a flying point of view, the predictable end of the dry season in late October or early November was our own particular concern. We had been lucky so far, all our Elementary and half of the Advanced flying had now been carried out in almost perfect weather, with only a phenomena called 'Gutti' to worry about, this local name referred to short lived low cloud forming over hills just after day break, which normally dispersed as the day wore on. Would the rains curtail our flying, was the main question? In the event, it was the late morning and early afternoon rise in temperature that normally caused the build up of very active thunderstorms, with ensuing rain during the slow progress south of the inter-tropical disturbance line that was the real problem. I was one of the few on our course who was caught out when, after a solo bombing detail, I concluded that discretion was the better part of valour and diverted to Mount Hampden airfield after seeing a vast thunderstorm covering all of Salisbury, Belvedere and Cranborne. I collected a few brownie points from my flight commander for using my 'loaf', after eventually returning to base.

The start of the last stage of the course to the award of wings was the final hurdle, however, we had all taken a full flying test towards the end of training and in my own case, there was a bit of a wink, wink, nudge, nudge during the de-brief after that test. I concluded that it had been the big one, and it was most unlikely that anyone would be scrubbed (suspended) during the last stage, so why not relax and enjoy it was the testing officer's final advice, it certainly was enjoyable, with both types of bombing. On low level bombing I soon found out that if you really got low and waited until the engine oil air cooler duct on the port cowling came in line with the target tripod, a bullseye would ensure if you pressed the release button at that instant. As for dive bombing, I think all pilots who have tried it will confirm that a 40° dive looks more like a vertical one, and the recommended 60° dive appears from the cockpit to be well past the vertical, with the harness straps taking some strain. For both types of bombing we carried 7 lb practice bombs with four under each wing, they had all been produced locally as part of the Country's war effort and the locals were, quite rightly, very proud of this. The firing of live rounds from our one and only .303 machine gun at ground targets was also highly popular, but it turned out to be most unfortunate that we had not been warned about 'target fixation'. This comes in two forms, the first is when a pilot gets his target firmly in his sights he becomes so obsessed with keeping it there before firing that he momentarily shuts out of his mind the danger of diving too low and either flies into the target or else starts his pull out so late that his aircraft mushes into the ground, both invariably end in complete disaster for machine and man. The second type of target fixation mainly takes place in war situations when a pilot on a ground strafing run sometimes, at the last thousandth of a second, suddenly realises that it is not a military target that he is attacking but cannot bring himself to stop pressing the firing button anyway. Just after the war I served with a fellow pilot who had a recurring nightmare about having shot up an aged couple driving a horse and cart in Italy in just those circumstances.

The Christmas of 1944 fell about six weeks before the end of our course time and although it proved to be infinitely better than the previous one aboard a troopship, it was a low key event for most of the time, except on Christmas day itself when a rather drunken party around the camp swimming pool got completely out of control, with one or two young ladies from downtown being thrown in fully clothed. It was just as well that they joined in the fun, otherwise the disciplinary consequences would have been unthinkable.

As for our course, we had only ten days left before our Wings parade when one of our cadets flew straight into the target on air to ground firing. He was one of the most popular and likeable chaps you could ever wish to meet and it was a very sad day indeed when we laid 'Stoney' Mason to rest in a cemetery in the middle of Salisbury, the local populace paid due tribute as we slow marched the few hundred yards of Stoney's last journey.

Other well remembered strokes of ingenuity during training included a practice standard beam approach system (SBA) that was not actually tied in with any airfield, it was based well out into the Bundu, on an imaginary airfield. The student would try to stay on a steady beam towards the phantom site, whilst flying on instruments in the usual manner, while the instructor looked out at a thin line across the ground that the locally enlisted natives had cleared for several miles along the direction of the transmitted beam. The instructor could of course have also listened to the dots and dashes, plus the steady beam, but by visual reference he got a far better idea of how far off the beam a student was at any particular time, and how he chose to regain it. Another plus factor was that a beam approach onto an airfield that operated up to 50 training aircraft would have been dangerous in the extreme. On another occasion we were issued with maps with graticules overprinted as per AA maps, and told that a stream of Avro Ansons from an Air Navigation school would be passing through a sector, given to us in advance, at a certain level and time, and it was up to us to intercept as many as possible. Great fun was had by all. It was also on this part of the course that we were allowed to carry out solo dummy head on and quarter attacks on fellow pupils after a thorough briefing, of course.

At the end of our training to 'Wings', we all had approximately 320 flying hours under our belts, which was more than double that which many of the Battle of Britain pilots had acquired when they joined their first squadrons. At long last it was all over and our award of Wings was set for February 2nd. It was a very formal affair and took the format that we had seen twice before when our two senior courses had passed out, however, it must have been tedious for the rest of the station turning out every other month to witness such occasions. The week prior to the parade we had all been interviewed to test our reaction to a possible posting to the Instructors School at Norton and thereafter retained in Rhodesia on those duties. For most of our 50 or so cadets it was unthinkable, but one or two went so far as to say if that was what the RAF needed they would go along with it, not surprisingly, it was from this last group that the five needed were selected. With promotion to Sergeant for most of us, or Pilot Officer for a very few, came a vast increase in pay so for our final leave in Umtali we decided to live it up a bit and booked into their top hotel for a week.

Needless to say, we were in particularly good spirits on this last leave in Rhodesia after having just gained our wings at long last. Many of the locals paid us the compliment of mentioning that they well remembered our last visit, in the nicest possible way I'm glad to report. The tea/coffee canteen was still a morning must and the Steel family opposite to it laid on yet another sundowners session. Our thoughts, obviously, did at times stray ahead as to our immediate future. We had already been informed that most of us would be going to a Fighter Operational Training Unit (OTU) in the Middle East shortly. In the past some cadets had even travelled north by train from Bulawayo to Victoria falls, over into Northern Rhodesia, and then the Belgian Congo before catching a ferry across Lake Tanganyeka before completing the epic journey by air to Egypt. Yet others had been given cash to buy civilian clothes so as to pass through supposedly neutral Portuguese Mozambique as passengers in a Short 'C' Class flying boat on the Durban-Cairo sector of the pre-war Imperial Airways 'horseshoe' route. Whichever, it was very sad indeed to bid farewell to all our well wishers in the Eastern Highlands.

The return to Cranborne was, yet again, by the night train and a little nostalgia crept in as shortly after dawn we could see from the train windows the first detail of Harvards taking to the sky from our Cranborne airfield. Two days later it was farewell Salisbury before setting off on another night train to Gwelo to catch a northbound flight to Egypt. A nice touch crept in at this point, when it turned out that one of our instructors, Rhodesian born Flt Lt Meredith, organised some of his friends to take us around the town with final drinks at Meikels before waving us goodbye from the platform, what a lovely note to finish on. After a days rest at Thornhill airfield, Gwelo, it was to be very early morning calls for the next three days of flying forever northwards. The aircaft we flew in was a Lockheed Lodestar, looking remarkably like the type Dick Merrill had flown across the Atlantic from Southport Sands. It was fitted with sideways facing bench seats which accommodated about 10 or 12 of our course. In those days, unlike today, it was a requirement to record in RAF log books all passenger flights in a special column, it might be of interest to modern aircrew and passengers to tabulate our progress. First of all the aircraft was registered as 6-AGBU and the pilot throughout, a Captain Hodgson.

Day 1	Gwelo- Kasama	3:30
Day 1	Kasama-Nairobi	4:05
Day 2	Nairobi-Kisuma	1:00
Day 2	Kisuma-Juba	2:05
Day 2	Juba-Malakal	2:00
Day 2	Malakal-Khartoum	2:20
Day 3	Khartoum-Wadi Halfa	2:30
Day 3	Wadi Halfa-Cairo	3:10

After our first landing at Kasama for fuel, in what was then Northern Rhodesia, we set off for Nairobi on the longest leg of the entire journey to Egypt. With the inter-tropical conversion zone (ITCZ) way down in Southern Africa it was to be almost ideal flying weather throughout the journey, and this combined with perfect visibility meant that we could relax and enjoy the scenery for a change. On arrival at Nairobi we landed at the pre war RAF base of Eastleigh, with it's well impacted runway of red earth, which I was to become familiar with some fifteen years later when I first joined Transport Command. Accommodation was on camp, but as we thought it might well be our one and only chance to see the town, only a few miles away, we resolved to take a taxi from the main gate where we were assured one would turn up sooner or later. While talking to one or two locally based NCOs, also awaiting transport, we were a little surprised, to say the least, when about 5 girls in WAAF's uniform appeared and started to chat us up, all with a pronounced foreign accent. One of our new found friends told us that the girls were all from Poland and had arrived via Russia and the Middle East. A rumour had got around that if they later wished to enter the UK it would only be possible if they were engaged or married to someone British. They soon established that our group would only be in Kenya for 24 hours, at which point their interest soon faded, and even an offer of a night on the town was politely, but firmly refused. You cannot win them all.

Many years later after joining Transport Command and being introduced to a Flight Engineer's wife, I realised that she was of Polish stock. When asked how they had first met she replied, 'overseas, during the war'. 'Nairobi, by any chance?', was my next question. 'No, it was Karachi in fact, but some of the friends I made in Russia ended up there', was her reply.

The next day's flying was a little strenuous to say the least. Although the airborne time was again only between 7 and 8 hours, an extra fuelling stop was required. Two of the landing sites, at Juba and Malakal, both in the Sudan, were about the most desolate places one could ever imagine, how on earth they managed to transport aviation fuel to stock remote places beggared belief. However, the accommodation at the end of day two was a real surprise, not on the RAF base as we had expected, but in the best hotel in Khartoum with the very British name of the Britannia.

The last day was very straightforward indeed. The River Nile was within sight for virtually the entire day and, like day one, only one re-fuelling stop was involved which was at Wadi Halfa now, as is well known, under several hundred feet of water as a result of the building of the Aswan Dam. After our final landing at Helliopolis, near Cairo, we were quickly whisked off to a transit camp at Almaza for the night, before leaving the next evening on the Cairo to Alexandria train, bound for an Aircrew holding centre at a semi disused airfield called Gianaclis, just into the Western Desert, from the Nile delta. After six long days of constantly being on the move, with all our earthly belongings this last journey was beginning to take it's toll, so some sleep was called for. Being in one long railway carriage, our group piled all our kit bags together in the centre aisle, near the toilet door, and then proceeded to unscrew all lamp bulbs as a sleep inducing measure. Thank God we had decided to leave the toilet lamp on with the door closed, because during one brief stop an Arab, a race well known in those parts for thieving from the British military, must have managed to climb onto the train roof and then later, at an appropriate moment, lowered himself down to gain entry into the train through the bars of our toilet window. It was the opening of the toilet door that gave his game away with the sudden illumination at that end of the carriage. I was first on the scene after vaulting the stack of kitbags but only just in time to see him disappearing between the toilet window bars which was followed almost immediately, by a very loud shriek. He must have lost his hold on the train roof, poor chap. Although the incident was duly reported, no one seemed to be particularly interested.

CHAPTER 10
Spitfire conversion

We were to spend only two weeks at Gianaclis awaiting our next flying posting, but it was long enough to get a feeling on this ex- South African light bomber airfield of what life must have been like during the hectic days of desert fighting. One startling feature was the very low temperatures during the night hours in the early Spring, one member of staff told us to place old newspapers on the ground under the camp beds and also under the last blanket which did, indeed, ensure some regress.

Our OTU postings were duly announced with half our number assigned to RAF Ismalia and the second to RAF Fayid, we did not realise the implications of this divide at the time, except that Ismalia was near a town and Fayid was in the middle of nowhere. We soon learnt however that those trained at Ismalia eventually went to Italian based squadrons whilst those from Fayid were mainly sent to the Far East, with just a few to Italy. One of the strangest questions ever asked of budding fighter pilots was put to us on arrival at RAF Fayid, but only after a briefing explaining a few pros and cons regarding what answer we might wish to give. The question was straightforward enough. Which of the following five aircraft did we hope to train on: Spitfire, P47 Thunderbolt, Mustang, Kittyhawk or Tomahawk. The pros and cons were mainly about our own estimation of our ability at landing aircraft during our training to Wings standard. If in any doubt ask for Thunderbolts, which with their very wide wheel base were very easy to land. For others who had found no particular problems in that art, Spitfires, with their narrow undercarriage, was a good option. The three remaining types were mainly used for ground attack and all were based in Italy but, in any event, the numbers required had dropped dramatically with the end of the war in Europe now in sight. Even before the war ended it was assumed that RAF squadrons flying American built aircraft would be the first to disband come the end of hostilities because of the lend/lease agreement which, briefly, called for a return or scrap of these aircraft. The Thunderbolt, however, was used by only the RAF in the Far East and the end of the war in those parts still seemed a long way off, with the Japanese likely to fight to the last man. Our gang of four all got their first choice and, as already mentioned, Ray Jones and George Duffy went on to Thunderbolts and Alf Harding and myself on to Spitfires, all in the Far East.

The conversion course got off to a cracking start with not only more Harvard flying, but also some of the most thorough briefing sessions on aircraft type one could ever imagine. Our first solo on the Spitfire would, apart from taking off in an aircraft without the benefit of dual instruction on type for the first time, involve operating an aircraft fitted with the standard British aircraft braking system. During our training in Rhodesia, both the Cornall and Harvard American built aircraft had toe operated hydraulic foot brakes which could be activated without moving the rudder bar. On virtually all British aircraft, including the Spitfire,

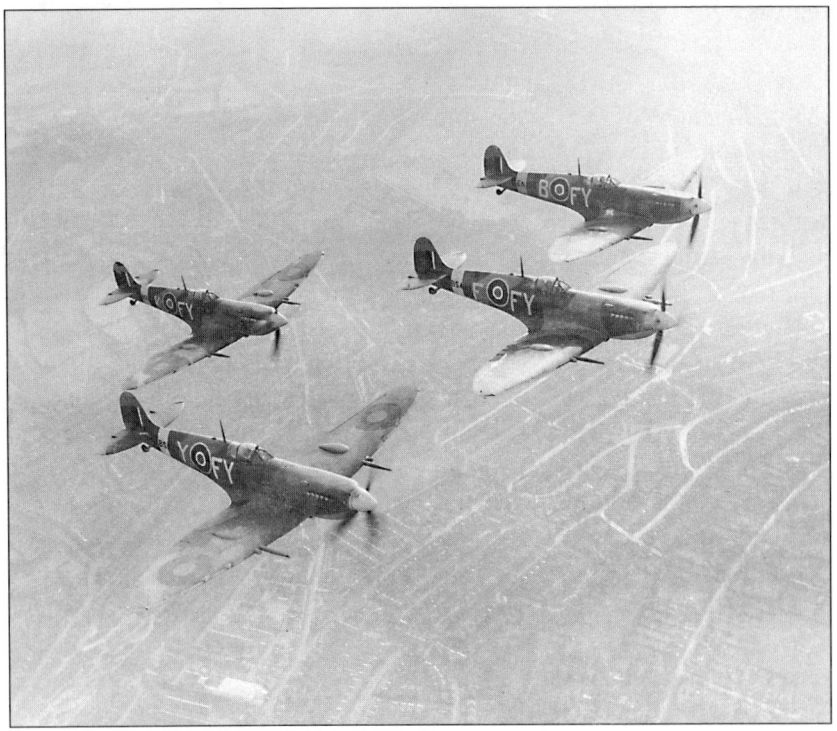

Supermarine Spitfire

of that era, the brakes were on the hand operated differential type. This meant that a pilot had to use one hand to apply the pneumatic tyre brake lever, and also apply full rudder if braking on one side only was required. I never suffered brake failure on hydraulically operated systems, although it was a way of life on air operated ones, and particularly so in hot climates, and/or during landing runs on marginally short runways. It was a requirement at 73 OTU to pass an oral test on the following type systems before first solo; fuel, oil and hydraulic systems, engines and airframes, blindfold cockpit drill, action in the event of fire, the system and use of Oxygen. The signed certificate inserted into our log books also recorded that we were proficient in the use of the VHF radios which we had not had the benefit of before that time. In those days only four pre set VHF frequencies were available in all RAF operational aircraft, each operated by A,B, C, and D buttons. These letters stood for the following: "A" for airfield now called 'Tower' or 'Local', "B" for bearings and now called approach control, "C" for common to all RAF airfields, and finally "D" for distress, now an international frequency. The 10 week course, during which I recorded the following flying hours of Harvard 13 and Spitfire 59, which included six at night, was full of incidents.

With the entire flying staff having completed at least one operational flying tour before arriving at Fayid, for what was described as a rest tour, for them, it was not entirely surprising that high jinks crept in at times, for those survivors, this way of life was not exclusively confined to the lower echelons of the officer corps and NCO instructors. Even the Station Commander, ex-Brat, Group Captain Frank Carey of Battle of Britain fame, with 28 confirmed kills, was not averse to taking to the skies in his own P47 Thunderbolt with the 'ace of spades' emblazoned on the engine cowlings and making dummy attacks on any aircraft or formation that he chanced upon. His excuse, not that he needed one in his exalted position was that he was testing reactions to sudden attack from behind and out of the sun. But why a P47 and not a Spitfire with his background, was the general feeling amongst student pilots. It was before I had even soloed on the Spitfire that I thought my number was up, and that was to be only the first of three such incidents before the end of my fifty two years of continuous flying. This first occasion was during a dual formation check out on the Harvard. It was a two ship affair and when each of two students had satisfied their instructors, they each took control and a vicious dog fight ensued, quite frankly, I was not sure what was going on. Up to Wings standard we had only indulged in basic aerobatic manoeuvres, and at a reasonable sedate pace compared with this melee. It was soon abruptly cut short a few minutes later when we came within a whisker of a mid air collision. In the bat of an eyelid it was all over but not before I caught sight of the other Harvard in a vertical dive, passing dead ahead in our line of flight. Such a close up view of the student and his instructor in their cockpits, less than 50 yards away or about a second at our speed of 130 mph, was a real shaker. "How close do you reckon that was?" came the question from the back cockpit. "About 50 yards", I managed to say after trying to compose myself. "Better be going back I suppose", was his riposte, he flew the aircraft back to Fayid and also carried out the landing, which was probably a wise move.

After a final check on the Harvard it was to be the big day and the realisation of one of my dearest dreams; first flight in a Spitfire, and one that I will always remember, like all other pilots before me and since. After being strapped into the tropical version of the Mk 5 Spitfire by my instructor, who then carried out all the pre- take off checks that could be achieved before actual start up, he then walked out along the port wing and sat down facing forward and gave the thumbs up. This was it, pressing the Booster coil and start buttons together the engine fired up, and after the removal of the starter trolley and chocks we were away. The instructor stayed perched on the port wing tip until reaching the holding point of the runway in use when he gave a final check of the coolant temperature, which was always likely to rise out of limits in hot climates in a matter of minutes, then he jumped off the wing and gave a final thumbs up. The take off run was not as bad as I had feared, probably due to my gingerly use of throttle on this first effort, which resulted in the swing being no worse than that of the Harvard. After take off all went as briefed, brakes on/off, undercarriage up and climbing power set, next followed a procedure not required during training to wings. On the Spitfire, take off with the cockpit hood open was the norm, so that a pilot could be extracted more easily by fire crews in the event of a mishap. However, to ensure it remained open it was locked in the backward position by latching the left entry door slightly open. This, of course, required the pilot to pull the door to the fully closed position and then close his hood soon after take off. Other features new to me included using oxygen, flaps only having two positions, full up or fully down with no intermediate positions. And finally having to open and close radiator shutters to keep the Glycol liquid, which cooled the Merlin engine, within limits. Glycol, by the way, had two virtues which varied with it's strength, of having both a high boiling point and a low freezing point. When I had time to settle down after take off, at a steady altitude, I became amazed at the effectiveness of the controls, it was a pure delight to fling around the sky with pure abandonment, with thoughts ringing in my ears of "I've made it, I've made it!" However, there remained the little difficulty of bringing it back to earth all in one piece. The landing proved to be one of my best of those days, so I was on cloud nine as I taxied back into dispersal. I was a little taken aback recently when going through my log books and noting that my flight time on that Spitfire first solo was 1hour 35 minutes. I doubt if my instructor intended me to stay aloft so long, but time does tend to fly by when one is enjoying oneself.

On the ground, life was pleasant enough and particularly so in the Sergeants' Mess where we were treated as equals by all and sundry, even by our own instructors. Another unexpected feature was that it was not Arabs who waited on us at meal times but Italian POWs, who all seemed quite pleased to be seeing the war out in that capacity. One NCO instructor we became pally with during evening sessions in the bar asked if we would like to borrow the Station Flight's Fairchild Argus aircraft for a weekend jaunt to Cairo, we did not take up the offer just in case it was the beer talking, although he seemed serious enough. However, I did take to the skies in a Fairchild over 40 years later when the then Wing Commander, now Air Chief Marshal Allison allowed me to use his personally owned model, it proved to be a very good aircraft to fly, as it turned out, after all those years of wondering.

I had found the stall and recovery in the Spitfire very similar to the Harvard, but what if we got into an inadvertent spin in such a powerful aircraft, was very much on our minds, I think some of us might have chickened out if we had been told to go up and have a go. The powers that be had obviously foreseen this problem, so part of the course called for an instructor to lead a formation of five aircraft and, after circling around in long line astern at about 15,000', he would call on each one of the four students to pull way in turn and carry out a three turn spin and, after recovery, re-join the formation. Once again the fear of the unknown had been allayed, the spinning and recovery of the Spitfire was innocuous enough, however, it was just as well that we had that one under our belts because a week later a Spitfire actually got into a flat spin and impacted with the ground within the airfield boundary. At the end of flying that day a group of us took a hike across the airfield and marvelled at how intact the Spitfire looked, just as if it had landed wheels up. Looking into the cockpit, nothing seemed amiss there until one of our group noticed that the medics who had removed the pilot's body had failed to take away one of his shoes which was on the cockpit floor, under one side of the rudder bars. Could this have been an indication of why the pilot had failed to recover from a straightforward spin, which would, as night follows day, lead to a flat spin eventually, if the recovery technique of full opposite rudder is not taken? Perhaps the Pilot's shoe, having come loose, jammed the rudder bars in only a half on position. Should all pilots have been forced to wear standard RAF flying boots, regardless of climactic conditions, in fighter type aircraft?

During ground training sessions a mental groan went up when it was announced that we would all have to undertake another five hours in the LINK trainer, had we not suffered enough in Rhodesia in this synthetic instrument flying monster? However, this was to be so different and really good fun. This time it was not with the hood of the device firmly down, in fact it had been completely removed. The idea was to look through a standard gun sight whilst "flying" the link trainer and laying off the correct deflection on target images projected onto the walls around a domed structure. When we thought we had the correct deflection set, the pressing of a button would activate a beam of light towards the dome wall and an instructor would be on hand to analyze the results, excellent training we all concurred, because most of us had got it horribly wrong on our first few attempts.

Another unique device for those days was a decompression chamber, which certainly brought home the fact that loss of oxygen at altitude would not be noticeable to a pilot and, in fact, brought on a sense of euphoria in many. I was never to see another decompression chamber again until close on 25 years later, when the then Transport Command decreed that all aircrew converting to transport aircraft that were pressurised had to take a course at the Medical Aviation School at RAF North Luffenham. During the pre-chamber briefing the Medical Officer in charge asked for a show of hands of those who had been in one before, about 5 of us on the 20 strong course put our hands up and he then asked each in turn where and when. He seemed quite happy when the others said Farnborough, but not so when I said Egypt. "Egypt?", he queried, "What were you doing taking one in that country?". "Converting to Spitfires during the war". "Spitfires during the war?", he repeated, "never knew that those pilots needed to go in one". Neither did I for that matter until I had arrived at RAF Fayid.

It seemed a little strange at RAF Fayid that in ten short weeks we should serve on three different Flights and therefore under three different Flight Commanders, whereas at our Advanced School in Rhodesia it had been only two stages, basic and advanced, in two different squadrons over a six month course. There was a certain rationale to it in that the first stage at Fayid was training in general handling only, the second stage was advanced flying and unarmed dummy attacks on both air and ground targets using cine cameras to assess results, and the final stage was devoted to live air to air firing against towed drogues and ground targets such as captured tanks, etc using both .303 machine guns and 20mm cannons.

I have already covered the first stage of learning all about the Spitfire in some detail and all that remains is to say that the Flight Commanders surname was very famous at the time, and therefore easy to remember, as he was the brother of Ivy Benson who led an all ladies band of that name, which was all the rage both during and after WWII.

It was during the second stage at Fayid that I used up the second of my nine lives, this time death looked a racing certainty. The flight itself should have been straightforward enough, it was to be a height climb to whatever the service ceiling of the allocated Spitfire turned out to be. Service ceiling was deemed to be the altitude at which the rate of climb falls to only 100' per minute, in the event it came at 35,000'. It was whilst testing out the controls, as briefed, and keeping a watch on my position that I spotted a very large aircraft carrier heading southbound through the Suez Canal. I thought I could get a better view of it if I throttled back and put the Spitfire into a steep dive, so that the carrier would be visible over the top of the engine cowling, which turned out to be a very steep dive indeed. The airspeed shot up and the altimeter unwound at a fantastic rate. Then the aircraft started to shudder and I wondered if the engine had over revved and given up on me, a quick glance at all the engine instruments indicated that everything was normal in that department. At approximately 20,000' I thought 'enough is enough', and I had better ease out of the very uncomfortable dive. The elevator was eased back, but the nose did not respond and panic began to set in. Repeated attempts to get the nose up, so as to reduce speed met with no response whatsoever, except to produce more airframe vibrations and I concluded that some type of structural failure had occurred. At about 12,000' I thought that the aircraft would eventually dive into the desert so it was time to try and bail out. I reached up and pulled the hood Emergency Release handle, and although the wire was easily pulled out, the hood remained in position. My next move was to go for a crowbar that was normally fitted to the left entry door, to try and prize the hood open, however it was missing and reason enough for very verbose complaints later. Now down to about 7,000', one more effort on the elevators brought, much to my surprise and, needless to say, thanksgiving, a response in that the nose rose and the airspeed started to drop. I applied throttle but the airspeed still dropped off and quickly neared the normal landing speed so I quickly lowered the nose again so as not to reach the stall. I assumed, wrongly, that the engine must have now failed during the dive and a belly landing in the desert was the only remaining option. The vibrations were still violent, however I put that down to the thermal currents that are part and parcel of low altitude flying over the desert after mid morning from Spring through to Autumn. I was still confused as to why the speed wanted to bleed off so quickly, even without engine power, so now down to less than 2,000', and a crash landing looking me in the face, I gave one last go at the engine controls of boost and revs and noted that they both responded as normal. So, from less than 1,000', and more in desperation than anything else, I pulled back on the stick and immediately found myself in a violent climb that only tailed off at 7,000' or more. The airspeed indicator had obviously been around the clock, and although some Spitfire pilots have poured scorn on this ever happening it is recorded in one book that a Hurricane pilot had lived through an almost identical experience. After pulling myself together, I made my way back to RAF Fayid and breathed a sigh of relief as I finally put the Spitfire down on mother earth in one piece. No, my previous life, such as it was at that time, did not flash before my eyes during the dive, but I did think for a split second, what would my parents think when the news broke.

I trooped slowly back to our crew room, with my parachute over my shoulder wondering how to put into words what had actually happened. After knocking on the Flight Commander's door and being admitted, I found his deputy was also present on other business. They both listened in silence and then gave me a grilling on oxygen. "Was I sure I had more than half full on the gauge before take off? Had I taken my mask off during flight by any chance? Did it fit properly? Was the rate of puffs from the mask normal?" I mentally gave up and, as I left his office, he shouted "don't forget to let the engineers know about pulling the hood release wire, it might come off on the next flight if you don't". Fat chance, I thought. However, if it had come off when I pulled the wire I would be dead by now, trying to bail out at that speed, which was a very sobering thought. I was assured that that particular Spitfire would be the subject of a rigorous technical inspection taking days, but noted that it was flying again the very next morning. Needless to say, I took a close interest in it from then on, wondering if I would ever have to fly in it again. Although I did not, I was not unduly surprised that twice later it dropped a wing, port side both times, during holding off to land, resulting in minor damage on each occasion.

It was in the mess that evening, during a few recovery beers, that a P47 Thunderbolt Pilot Instructor mentioned the possibility of "Compressibility", a word I had not come across before in the context of aviation. He explained that no aircraft would ever fly faster than the speed of sound because a wall of air built up near the front of aircraft wings which limited the top speed and control of any aircraft. He then came out with a story about a P47 Thunderbolt formation disaster which he said had occurred even before his time at 73 OTU. This story was to the effect that an instructor leading a formation of four students had put them into long line astern at altitude for a tail chase. During one steep dive all lost control, despite the leader, and probably the students as well, throttling right back. The leader claimed later that it was only after he reversed the throttle position to fully open that he regained control and landed safely, whereas the four students dived into the desert. The storyteller claimed that he had actually seen four black marks in the desert where they had flown in and gave a final twist to the story by saying that the Americans had offered to fit air brakes to P47s built for the RAF, but the offer had been declined as they had never thought them necessary before.

With hindsight, I find it quite remarkable that we never had a lecture on high speed flight at that time because there is now ample evidence that adverse control effects had been experienced by a fair number of pilots, when one reads their recollections of war time flying in single seat fighters. A big debate ensued after the end of the war as to whether any aircraft had, in fact, flown supersonic before the jet age in uncontrollable dives. The argument came down heavily on the side of 'not possible', but some years later it was reported that a Victor "V" bomber had broken the sound barrier, although it had certainly not been designed to do so.

Other incidents came thick and fast, although we were still only half way through our second stage of dummy attacks, when some briefings called for low flying plus attacks on targets of opportunity. This meant all things to all men of course. This ranged from Arab Dhows on the Gret Bitter Lake to patrolling the long straight Tarmac road between Port Tewfick at Suez to Cairo. The road, of course, stuck out like a sore thumb and was well used by British Army lorries. After sighting a lorry, pulling up from low level followed by a wing over brought an aircraft into an excellent position for simulated firing. Pilots would then mutter to themselves 'dagger, dagger, dagger'. Some pilots, and I am certainly not admitting to being one of them, would often fly off for a few miles after their dummy attack and then re-appear at almost deck level flying along the road head on to their victim to see who would chicken out first. Some army drivers, who had seen it all before, held their nerve but many did not, probably new boys to the area, who swerved off the road and got stuck in the soft sand. In the evenings some of the pilots would say knowingly, 'got three confirmed today'. These stupid antics came to a sudden end after one pilot pulled up and banked his aircraft the wrong way from the road taking the only telephone wires in the area with him. The British Army were not best pleased to say the least. Pity the wires between Army GHQ in Cairo and Fayid which ran along the Sweet Water canal connecting the Nile delta to Ismalia and then Fayid did not suffer the same fate on that particular day, they remained red hot for some time. All Spitfire paint work was duly inspected by a bevvy of instructors but our own, far more discrete, inspection much later established that most Spitfires had scratch marks of one sort or another. In any event, the snapping of a very thin phone wire might not have left any tell tale marks to look for anyway. Dummy attacks on Dhows were now also strictly forbidden as a result of a P47 Thunderbolt pulling up after a dummy attack and went into a zoom climb just at the wrong moment. With the aircraft mushing as it did so, the Dhow's sail caught the full blast of it's slipstream and promptly capsized, luckily with no loss of life.

It was at about our mid course point that we lost the second pilot from our original start point in Rhodesia. The late Ted Dovey had been one of our course who had asked to train on the Thunderbolt and got his wish. It had been during a two student air to air cine only dummy firing attack that Ted had been in an air collision with the second student. It has never been established at what stage the collision took place during the detail. What is known, however, is that these sessions always started with each of the two student pilots taking it in turn to fly dead astern of the other aircraft at, hopefully, exactly 200 yards distance and take a sighter burst. That involves manoeuvring the aircraft so that the dot in the middle of the gunsight is positioned about two thirds of the way up the rudder of the target aircraft and then press the firing button which activated the cine camera, but not the unloaded guns. The later developed cine film was then used by assessors, using the first few seconds of the sighter burst as a datum point, and award marks. The mock attacks which followed these formalities came from many different positions and heights. Before pressing the firing button students had to assess the deflection required on his sight, depending on the angle off between the lines of flight of the two aircraft and also the range. Although the harmonisation of the guns was set at 400 yards in those days, Ginger Lacey once told me firing at more than 200 yards was a waste of time. It seems highly likely that the pilot of the attacking aircraft got carried away and flew into Ted's tail section.

Those of us on the Spitfire segment of our course were due to complete our 6 hours of night flying that evening with a 1.30 cross country, and had been stood down for the daylight hours, so it was whilst lounging around in the ante-room of the Sergeants' Mess that we first heard the sad news. It prompted one of the old timers of the NCO instructor world to recall that some time ago another disaster had struck two Spitfires on the same exercise. It revolved around the fact that a student pilot had booked out a Spitfire, which was obviously unarmed for the exercise, but proceeded to climb into a plane parked next to his. Came the sighting shot and the rest was history as they say, his fellow student was shot out of the sky and killed. I must say that during our time at Fayid it would have been virtually impossible to mistake an armed Spitfire for an unarmed one, such was the number of warning placards, perhaps they were a result of that incident. The Spitfires in our day were still parked in one long line, regardless of which of the three different flights they belonged to, something of a surprise even to us new boys.

Needless to say, the mood was, quite naturally, somewhat subdued that evening as we prepared for our last night flight of the course which was to take in Cairo, Alexandria and Port Said. I had certainly not lost any of my love of night flying, although I had suffered a shock to the system on my very first night take off in a Spitfire a couple of weeks before. On opening the throttle I had thought for one brief second that the engine had caught fire, such was the stream of flames on each side of the cockpit. Our briefing officer had failed to mention that the Merlin engine exhaust was alongside the cockpit, day or night, when the engine was running, but only visible as flame during the hours of darkness. Looking back on those days, it seems quite remarkable that although I was to fly Spitfires later with three different Squadrons and two other units that had them on strength, this was to be my very last night flight on type. The most exciting part of the course, live firing from the world famous Spitfire, was yet to come and eagerly awaited.

In the meantime our social life was virtually non existent, we had ventured into Ismalia one weekend, but concluded that it did not warrant a second visit, no matter how desperate we got. The tedium was broken for one day at least, when a New Zealand Armoured Division, recently withdrawn from the fighting in Italy for a rest break, invited a visit from RAF Fayid. Our course was chosen to represent the Station and we were very much looking forward to it, particularly myself, because I had always fancied a ride in a tank, which was part of the offer attached to the visit, I did have a ride, but not quite as I had visualised. It was on top of a tank, not in it, and with about four others clinging on like grim death as we careered up and down a practice range, which included several fairly steep sand made obstacles. All good fun I suppose but I would still have preferred to have been inside.

A minor diplomatic incident occurred one day when a Group Captain stationed in Italy arrived for a visit and found student pilots being trained on Mk 4 Mustangs, which sported bubble canopies, whereas the front line Squadrons were still flying the much older Mk 3s, to say he went into orbit would be an understatement.

The final part of our course was now upon us and a steep learning curve it proved to be, both in the air and on the ground. For instance, I never knew before then that Spitfires could not carry much more than 12 seconds of .303 ammunition, and that 4 seconds of continuous firing was about the limit per burst. The much more effective 20mm cannon was prone to mis-firing, which really put you off your aim if the gun in one wing stopped firing and the one in the other wing carried on. This of course, gave quite a swing towards the dead gun side, as I was to find out on at least two practice sessions.

We had three different types of targets to practice on. I have already mentioned air to air and air to ground on fixed targets, but a third was particularly unique and only possible because of our remote location and the climactic conditions pertaining in that part of the world. I have never heard of it taking place in any other location and certainly not in the UK. It was called "shadow firing" and the idea was for two Spitfires to go off in formation at 500' to the eastern side of the Suez Canal which, in theory, was deserted and then fire at the shadow of the other aircraft. The results were very obvious as the tufts of sand being thrown up from the desert were easily seen, I had assumed that the lead aircraft would always be flown by an Instructor. Wrong! It was two students who took to the air each time with both having a crack, I think it was pure bad luck, rather than judgement, but my co-student managed to put his shadow over a herd of wild camels one day, just as I pressed the firing button. Being an avid animal lover, the incident has lived to haunt me ever since. I doubt if I ever mentioned that disgraceful episode to more than five or six people during my flying career, but one of them must have been a young teenage girl manning the Ops Desk at Sherburn Aero Club when I went there as CFI, after leaving the Royal Air Force in 1983. It was at least six years later when Joanne Richardson, now a mature, fully qualified school teacher, but still helping the cause at weekends behind the Ops desk, was on duty with myself on what was a poor day for flying. With both of us looking through the club house windows for any sign of improvement in the weather, we saw one member of the engineering staff returning to his hangar with a shotgun and a brace of wood pigeons. "Barbaric sport", I said idly. In rather measured, school ma'am type speech she said coldly, "and what about those poor camels in Egypt then". Game, set and match to Jo.

I found the air to air firing quite exhilarating. Here at last I was firing guns at an air target, even if it was only a red drogue towed up and down one straight line by a slow moving Hurricane. Obviously, one aircraft of this type could not be launched each time one student was due to fire, so the answer was to use about five different colours on the tips of bullets fitted to five different Spitfires for each detail. Every time a bullet struck the drouge it left it's tell tale colour mark to be counted later when the Hurricane slipped it's towing wire at low level over Fayid airfield, before returning to it's base near Port Said of Balba. I was pleasantly surprised to achieve a very respectable score on my first attempt, I hope I had flown in the right aircraft, as regards bullet colours.

The air to ground firing, particularly with 20mm cannons, was great fun, not only was this against targets of substance, we could actually see bits of old lorries being flung into the air after hits. In our mind's eye, we could imagine them to be German or Japanese army convoys on the move. It had been a fantastic course and apart from the lack of a briefing on high speed flight, already mentioned, the only other disappointment was that we were never given a presentation on aerial combat from one of the many distinguished fighter pilots on staff.

Our time in Egypt was nearing it's end and so it was back to the transit camp at Almaza to await further instructions. It appeared that there would be a delay of about two weeks before transport to India by air was available, and an offer of ten days leave in Alexandria or Tel-Aviv was thankfully accepted. Our gang elected for Alexandria, the French influence from days of long ago was still evident in some quarters and we soon found lodgings in a pension run by a lady of obvious French descent. As always, a routine soon set in and most mornings, after a continental breakfast, which in itself was a nice change from the eternal fry ups of camp life, it was a trot around the town in a horse drawn garrey. After that, it was a few Stella beers in some dive or other before the inevitable call in at the famous, or infamous, depending on your outlook on life, Fleet Club.

This club will forever remain in my memory because of one spectacular incident during our stay in Alexandria, I can still pinpoint the day that it occurred because it was VE day 1945. Most British servicemen, including our little gang, really went on a bender but still managed to make the Fleet Club for a few final drinks before calling it a day, or night I should say. The big surprise when we entered was that Housey Housey was still on, although we should have known better, the game being something of a religion in the Royal Navy. For non players, such as ourselves, a special area behind screens was always available so we could drink and talk without distracting the rabid punters. I suppose it must have been the drink, but one of our group suddenly shouted "House" as a joke. It came at a point in time during the game when there must have been quite a few players just awaiting one more number to win. A lot of grunting and groaning could be heard from the losers, followed by the noise of bingo cards being torn up. A deadly silence then followed for the next few seconds, before it was realized that no winner had stood up, then all hell broke loose. Some convinced would be winners had set about the occupants of the table just on the other side of the screens on the assumption that the shout of "house" must have come from their table. I will never know if it became one ship's company against another, but as we tried to beat a successful retreat we were regarded as neutrals, being in khaki drill and not whites. Progress to the exit became so dangerous with bottles, chairs and any other movable object flying through the air that we took cover in an alcove until the RN shore patrol eventually arrived to restore order. By that time the scene was one of complete devastation, even Hollywood could never have hoped to emulate the bar room battle that had just taken place. To return to Tony Benn for a moment, last seen in Bulawayo, he records in his memoirs that on 'his' VE day he had spent a lovely day sailing on Lake Galilee, the Sea of Peace. Lucky chap! Unbeknown to us at the time our group would also be on the Sea of Peace within the next week.

During our last few days in Egypt, now living in tents again at Almaza, another, but unusual event for that area occurred when a thunderstorm broke during the night hours causing a flash flood. Living in a tent on one of the lower points of the camp site we caught the worst of it with water edging up to about the half way mark of our camp bed supports. Why on earth should I remember a thunderstorm over fifty years later? Well, although our kit dried out fairly quickly my very precious first flying log book had suffered damage to it's binding after some water had just reached it's storage in my kit bag. Being a trained fabric worker I repaired it as best I could later in Poona, India with red dope and aircraft fabric, no big deal, but the red marks of the dope often raised questions and I was glad when I started on my second log book. However, some years later the Station Commander at RAF Leeming, Group Captain Lowe, had, for reasons unknown, decided to inspect all aircrew log books on his Station. When they arrived back it was with some apprehension that we all went through our individual books, in mine I had got as far as page 1 when I noted a large pencil circle mark, complete with an exclamation mark around the rank of LAC. Although I had reached the dizzy heights of Flight Sergeant, I was, like all others after the war, reduced by one rank. I had a real shock a few minutes later when someone came rushing in and said the Station Adjutant is on the phone and he wants to speak to you personally. 'Good God', I thought, 'must be something to do with my blasted log book and rank of LAC'. Not quite, the adjutant said the CO had found the entries about my flying in Japan very interesting indeed, but what on earth had disfigured my log book so much, with red marks front and back? When I tried to explain to the first non-aircrew adjutant I had ever met, he gave a running commentary to my explanations, starting with "Didn't know they had thunderstorms in Egypt". Neither had I until the night in question, and as regards my repair job in India he said, "so you'll be able to say 'when I was in Poona' in future years Sergeant". The saying of "When I was in Poona" was something of a music hall joke at that time because so many retired Colonels were supposed to have started conversations with this phrase from their favourite seat at the end of pub bars over the years. The adjutants final fling was, "let's get this straight for the Station Commander. You were sent out to Egypt where your log book was damaged, then you repaired it yourself in India and finished up in Japan, Right?". "Not quite, Sir", I replied, "I first went to South Africa for pilot training". "Good lord, you did get around a bit, didn't you?" I suppose I had, come to think about it, but the phone had gone dead before I could put anything else into words.

It is always difficult to look into the future, particularly when you are still young, but even in our wildest dreams it would have been difficult to imagine that our leave in Alexandria was to be our last for another 18 months, and after we had eventually returned to England. Our immediate concern was which type of aircraft we would be passengers on for the outbound passage to India. It appeared that three types were in regular use at that time; a transport version of the Liberator bomber with just one fin and rudder, the pre-war Armstrong Whitworth "Ensign" which was a four engined high winged monoplane and the world famous Short 'C' class Empire Flying boat. Flying from Rhodesia to Egypt had been straight forward enough, all passengers were aircrew and of the same rank of Sergeant. Now, however, we were stationed at one of the main centres of the trunk route from the UK to India. Surely there would be many more important people, such as diplomats and high ranking officers of all three services, who would be given higher priority as regards passenger seats than mere Sgt Pilots. So, a longer wait than first stated might be our fate, not so, as it turned out, aircrew still had priority one status despite an ever growing surplus back in the UK.

CHAPTER 11
Forever Eastwards

At roll call one morning I was one of ten aircrew told to be ready to move out at 2 o'clock the next morning, without any additional information. However, when the five ton lorry pulled up at a jetty that connected with a one time Nile houseboat, with a Short "C" class Flying Boat at her moorings in the distance I was euphoric. The formalities were minimal, name asked and given, ticked off against the passenger manifest and that was that. Just as dawn was breaking we were ferried out in a small tender for the trip of a lifetime. As already recorded, it was at this point that I caught sight of Sqdn Ldr Tyroll-Martin, how I would have loved to have told him that some of his boys had made it to Spitfires. My log book records the following details of the two day voyage East.

Short "C" class Empire Flying Boat
6-AFBJ
Capt: Whittaker

Day One	Cairo- Kallia	2:15
	Kallia- Habbaniyah	3:20
	Habaniyeh- Basra	2:00
Day two	Basra- Bahrein	2:15
	Bahrein- Dubai	2:00
	Dubai- Karachi	5:00

The take off seemed to take a fair stretch of water but as it turned out was much the same during the next five over the two day flight. Our group had seats nearest the cockpit, and whenever time permitted Capt. Whittaker seemed to enjoy coming down and having a chat. He treated us like fellow pilots, rather than passengers, which was a real boost to our morale. Particularly so, as virtually all other passengers were of Officer rank or privileged civilians of some importance, no doubt. The aircraft, like all others of it's era, was unpressurised so cruising altitude was limited to about 10,000'. A spin off was that manufacturers could afford to build in much larger windows than is technically possible in todays aircraft. That feature, along with the fact high wings were necessary on flying boats to keep propellers well clear of water runways meant that we had magnificent views of mother earth throughout the flight. As we passed sedately across the Suez Canal towards our first water landing on the "Sea of Peace", we kept our fingers crossed that Group Captain Frank Carey was not up and about on one of his dawn patrols! The unloading and loading of human cargo was a slick operation after alighting, as it was throughout, even the taking on of fuel seemed to be a well practiced art that kept down time to about one hour or so.

The next stage was to Lake Habbaniyeh, near Baghdad and it came as something of a surprise to RAF passengers, at least, that in addition to the well known RAF land base of that name there was also a nearby lake which could cater for flying boats. The name of Habbaniyah was part of RAF folklore, even before WWII as it had served as the RAF's linchpin for keeping dissident rebel tribesmen under control by way of pre-warned air strikes against villages that aided or abetted them in the area then known as Mesopotamia. From 1939 onwards it had also been used by the RAF to house No 4 Flying Training School, which had been based in Egypt until the start of WWII. This FTS came into great prominence in 1941 when the Iraqi's, thinking that the German and Italian armies were about to capture the Nile Delta, and then the rest of the Middle East, revolted and surrounded the base in strength. All the flying training aircraft were modified to carry bombs and went into action, and so helped to quell the insurrection.

The night stop came next when we alighted on the Shatt-Al-Arab river near Basra although it was very close to another very famous pre-war RAF Station called Shaibah, which even had a song named after it called "These Shaibah blues". We were all billeted, aircraft crew and all passengers, in a delightful small hotel overlooking the river, very close to a bridge which crossed into neighbouring Persia, as it was then known. Captain Whittaker was certainly looking after us extremely well and went out of his way to let us know that we should avoid buying the bottled beer that would undoubtedly be offered to us, as it would cost five shillings per bottle, that was just under half a day's pay. When translated into today's money it would be approximately £15. During this small briefing we took the opportunity to ask about the next day's flying. He said it would certainly be Bahrein, Dubai and then, hopefully, direct to Karachi, although it was possible that he might have to alight at a place called Gwadar for more fuel, although he had no particular wish to ever land there again. His wish was granted, but there must have been a nice story behind that Remark.

The second day went just as smoothly as the first with the highlight, without doubt, being the landing on Dubai creek, an idyllic spot in aviation terms, if ever there was one. Even a landing on the Thames near the Houses of Parliament could not have matched this setting, with the comings and goings of Arab Dhows plying their trade as they had done over the centuries adding spice to the scene. We had already flown for more than four hours that day when we left Dubai for Karachi, with the possibility of a fuelling stop at Gwadar which, in the event, did not materialise and so it was another 5 straight hours to Karachi. However, with an immaculately clad pre-war steward on hand to cater for all our needs as regards food and drink, the time passed quickly enough, it was only after our final landing, in what is now Pakistan, that life took an unusual twist. We had heard plenty of stories about life in the sub continent from the old hands and it had been made very plain that everybody, but everybody, would go down, probably sooner rather than later, with Delhi Belly, such was the hygiene standards out there. Before we had set foot ashore at Korangi Creek, near Karachi, an incident occurred. After the Short "C" Class had been made secure to a buoy, we noted a small boat pulling alongside our entrance door with some very important looking gentlemen aboard. They were the local Customs and Immigration officials who, after boarding the aircraft did not hang around for any length of time before they departed, only to return about ten minutes later. Whilst aboard, they had deposited what appeared to be fumigating devices, which implied that we might be carrying something nasty that might be detrimental to the health of the Country, a little rich we thought, after all that we had heard previously about these parts. I came across this procedure once more during my flying life, and that was fifteen years later in Northern Australia, after landing at Darwin, a close run thing as to which was the more ironical.

After finally stepping ashore we found ourselves in another tented transit camp at Mauripur, our stay was to be for about 10 days before it was decided who was to go where and when. For the fighter boys it was to be Poona in the Bombay area for Spitfire pilots and Yellowhammer, near Bangalore, for our Thunderbolt pilots, so it was that the parting of the ways for our gang had finally arrived.

During the ten day wait, we gradually came to terms with a new way of life, being shaved in bed by our bearers was certainly a novelty, as was the serving of tea, or char as it was always called in India. We also had a "Dobie Wallah" who would collect, launder, press and return our clothing before nightfall. Although the cost of both services was ludicrously low they both catered for enough transients to make it well worthwhile by local standards, in fact I must have overpaid my bearer because he threatened to follow me to my next camp. When I asked him how he intended to travel, he replied with a big smile, "on top of your train sahib", I didn't realise until later that was the normal way of travelling for the many who couldn't afford the fare. We also had a chap who approached all newcomers and asked if we had any foot corns that needed attention, I did have one on a toe and much against my better judgment submitted to his proffered tinkering around with his miniature scalpel then it took an unexpected turn when he produced a substance akin to clay and made what can best be described as a miniature animal's horn. This he placed over whatever was left of my corn and then proceeded to warm the substance with a naked flame from a small device which was probably fuelled by Methylated spirits. After some light tapping on the horn he whipped it off and out came the residue. It was not until recent times that I had any further need of the services of a chiropodist and when I asked the dear lady in the midst of her work if she had ever heard of the type of treatment I had received in the Sub-Continent, all I received by way of a reply was a look that was a cross between shock, horror and disbelief.

It was only a question of time before the eternal question of "Like to see mongoose fight snake Sahib?" was asked, it was one of the biggest non-events of all time, if only for financial reasons, the so called fight was never allowed to get out of control. It was now time to be moving on again, this time by train and for one reason or another I was put in charge of a complete railway coach which was to be for the exclusive use of our squad of about 15 Sgt Pilots. It seemed strange at first when I was called before a movements officer to be briefed on what I thought would be a straightforward journey, however, very little was particularly easy in India, as I was to learn then, and once or twice later in life.

First of all, the journey would take about six days because the hot season had started and therefore the quicker route across the Sind Desert was not an option for passenger traffic until much later in the year. A great pity because I would have liked to see Jodhpur on that line, and it would also have cut travel time down by a couple of days. The route we set out on was to Lahore, well to the north, and then New Delhi, Agra, Jhansi and Bombay. There a rail traffic officer (RTO) would make arrangements for us to change to another line and coach for our destination of Poona. Other points included the information that "K" rations would be issued for the entire journey, which turned out to be a number of small cardboard boxes for individual use, containing tinned Spam, cheese, etc, the ingredients for making tea and coffee were also added. When I was stupid enough to ask where we would get the hot water from for a brew up I was told some cans would be provided and I was to try and scrounge hot water at any station we happened to stop at. The cans turned out to be old petrol ones with the lids cut off, and on at least two occasions the hot water came straight out of the steam trains engine boiler, thank goodness our issue purifying tablets worked. One other item on the briefing list was that as obviously one train would not be going all the way from Karachi to Bombay, via New Delhi, our special coach would be disconnected at certain points and then re-connected to other appropriate trains. Although the system had worked fairly well in the past, with Indian rail officials knowing the RAF's requirements, it would be just as well to keep an eye on things at these points because we didn't want to arrive back at Karachi did we? I certainly concurred with that. The carriage itself was even more primitive than those in Egypt and that was saying something, the seats were all wooden and ran the full length of the central area of the coach, back to back, facing towards the open windows. The toilets were of the usual hole in the floor type, with two straining bars, all right for the constipated, I suppose.

Day One of the journey north went off reasonably well, it started with a full breakfast at the transit camp and then off to our coach on the train. Although the temperature remained pretty high throughout, after leaving the coastal area the humidity dropped steadily to a rather pleasant level. The inside of our coach was strictly off limits to other travellers but outside on top of the roof there were crouched many freeloaders, accompanied by their worldly possessions. All went well with our coach change to another train at Lahore, which led to a false sense of security. The first hiccup occurred at a station in the middle of New Delhi, when our coach was left high and dry for several hours at the end of one of the main platforms awaiting a southbound train to hook up to. The overhead swivel, with it's water supply pipe for replenishing steam trains proved too much of a temptation for many of our group who could not resist the chance of a shower after three days on the move. Stripping down to their underpants before partaking of this unexpected luxury did not meet with universal approval from the rather staid Hindu passengers on the opposite platform, in fact, it did not win any approval whatsoever, rather the reverse in fact.

It was in the Agra or Jhansi area that a real disaster struck. We had heard a great deal of clanking plus pushing and pulling during the night but thought no more about it, other than just another train change. That was until the next morning, when just after day break, one of our gang said shouldn't the sun be coming up through the other window? Right, we were heading back north again. It was three hours later before the train made an enforced stop for water replenishments. The driver thought it was very funny when we explained our predicament and seemed quite delighted to have a bit of shunting practice, manoeuvring our coach into a siding, not so the driver of the first to arrive southbound train, who also stopped for water a few hours later. He was one of the 'rules is rules' brigade, which was not uncommon amongst the English trained Indians of those days. It was only after piling kit bags on the line in front of his train, during the refuelling of water process that we extracted a promise of co-operation from him and I must say that when an Indian gives you his word it is invariably met. Another English trait perhaps? I'm still talking of 50 years ago, of course. It was when we reached Jhansi, perhaps for the second time within 24 hours for all we knew, that a member of our group called Scanlon was seen to become rather emotional. Apparently he had been born and bred in that town and his father was well up in the railway world until 1937 when they had returned to the UK. He was one of the very few from those days that I met back in England when, after I had landed in a Harvard after giving an aerobatic display at Wellsbourne Mountford in 1950, he appeared from the crowd to have a chat, a very nostalgic reunion indeed.

By a strange coincidence a fellow pupil at my last school in Southport before joining the RAF, had also returned to the UK from Jhansi at about the same time, and his father was also ex-Indian Railways. I can only recall his surname of Henderson, and that he was something of a teacher's pet, possibly because they, mistakenly, thought he might have missed out as regards education in far off India. Perhaps it was about 1937 or so that locals throughout the Empire began to realise that many of the "Englishmen only" tasks could be carried out just as well by locally trained people. I well remember that as late as 1956, during the Suez conflict, it was suggested in some newspapers that Egyptian ships' pilots might make a real mess of things if they were ever allowed to navigate the canal. Pure tosh of course.

Eventually our saga came to an end after more than six days and the RAF Station at Poona, high up in the Western Ghats, proved to be a very pleasant location indeed. It provided brick built accommodation and was within walking distance of the town with it's own AFI Club (Auxiliary Forces India), equipped with a swimming pool which we made full use of most afternoons at the end of the flying day. AFI Clubs throughout India provided an oasis for all military personnel lucky enough to be stationed within reach of one. They were graded in the usual way of officers/other ranks. The officer only clubs tried very hard to uphold the traditions and standards of the pre-war Raj, and there was usually someone on hand to keep a look out for any transgressors of the perceived standards. One RAF officer who visited such a club in mufti was none other than the Earl of Bandon, often referred to behind his back as 'Paddy the abandoned Earl', and not particularly well known for his immaculate dress. On trying to gain access to one club he was accosted by a rather pompous Army officer, also in mufti, who stated "I am the Club Secretary, Captain the Honourable (whatever his name was), I don't think your dress measures up to our standards". To which Paddy replied, "And I am Group Captain the Earl of Bandon, now that's got you F***** on two counts, get out of my way man". Just over ten years later Paddy had mellowed somewhat, having risen to Air Marshal rank and in charge of all RAF forces in the Far East, he was then always immaculate in uniform or mufti. The day came when the new swimming pool at the Officers' club at Changi, Singapore was ready to be officially opened, and he was invited to do the honours. When he arrived with the pomp and ceremony that befits all C in Cs, he was duly shown to a dais to address the large gathering of officers and their ladies, however, he declined to mount it and instead stepped onto one of the diving boards, and after shouting "I now declare this swimming pool officially open", he dived in head first in full ceremonial dress, and still with his monocle in position, which he had taken to wearing in later life. One of the last great characters, along with the Attcherley twins, of the RAF.

No 3 Refresher Flying Unit at RAF Poona was somewhat misnamed in that for Spitfire pilots, at least, it was more of a conversion to a later mark of Spitfire, plus dive bombing practice, which we had not covered in Egypt, rather than actual refresher flying that took place there. In fact I only flew two dual details in the dear old Harvard during our time there. The first was a cross country, covering the local flying area and then I was let loose in the four bladed Mk VIII Spitfire, a tropicalized version of the Mk IX, which had proved so successful in Europe, with it's much more powerful Merlin engine. It had also been highly successful in Burma against Japanese fighters, although we had been told at one briefing that the Japs could no longer mount more than twenty or so aircraft at any one time in that area due to losses and petrol shortages. The course was almost entirely given over to formation dive bombing, plus strafing runs, but I must admit that every time I put one into a dive my mind went back to the unpleasant experience in Egypt when I was convinced my number was up. If only we had been told about high speed flight, and the fact that control problems would only occur at high altitudes when the indicated airspeed is so far removed from true airspeed, whereas at sea level they are identical in the ideal atmosphere of 15° C and a pressure of 1013 millibars.

After about fifteen hours of ground attack flying, which took me past the 400 hours total mark, and still not on a squadron, we were off on another train journey, this time it was of 2 days duration to a place called Bhopal, in central India, for a jungle survival course. This was of two weeks duration and very demanding physically, with some long treks through semi jungle lands and fording rivers as best we could on make shift rafts. The school was run by a Canadian F/Lt who, apparently, had spent some years out there, he was now well into his forties but seemed to enjoy his task immensely. I don't know if he was pulling our legs or not, but during a briefing prior to one trek he said it was unlikely that we would meet any Tigers there had not been any sightings in recent times. We didn't really want to know about a possibility. Many of his staff proved to be interesting characters. They were certainly from Burma, and possibly from the Karan tribe who were reputed to have been head hunters until recent times and living off the land was their stock in trade, blow pipes with darts and that sort of thing. One incident I have never forgotten was that when one of these tribesmen was proudly showing me his own hand made crossbow, he suddenly loaded it with a bolt and in a flash shot a Chipmunk out of a tree at quite some distance, it was just as well they were on our side.

Returning to Poona was yet another two days of primitive life on an Indian train, but we would now be moving on to a squadron in Burma, having had our log books all signed up as being fully qualified in ground attack work on Spitfire VIII aircraft before departure to Bhopal. In the previous two weeks whilst we had been away, Poona had not only received a brand new type of Spitfire, for the Far East theatre, the Griffon powered Mk XIV, but had also been tasked with not only converting about 10 of us onto type, but also to give us training in the art of taking off from aircraft carriers. This mark of Spitfire was so different from the Merlin engined type, that no lesser a person than Air Vice Marshal Jonnie Johnson, the allied top scoring fighter ace of WWII, with 38 victories, stated that it should have been given a completely new name. The Griffon engine produced a power increase of more than 100% over the Merlins of Battle of Britain days, and also drove a propeller that rotated in the opposite direction to that of the Merlin, which we had to become accustomed to. I never found out a satisfactory explanation for the change because up to that point American and British engines differed in that they had opposite traction rotations as standard. From a practical point of view the pilot had now to have full right rudder trim 'on' in the Griffon, as opposed to full left in the Merlin, for take off to counter swing. Under the concept of "Old habits die hard" some departures from the runway on take off were not unknown when pilots first converted to the later model, much to the consternation of the old hands in the fighter world.

These brand new aircraft were all fitted with gyro gunsights and this device was certainly a bit of magic. Etched on the base of these gunsights were the designations of various enemy aircraft types, such as the ME109, FW190, Zero (Japanese fighter), etc. All that achieved was to either enlarge the round circle, or reduce it, th٠t was reflected onto the glass of the gunsight, this related to the known wing span of the selected aircraft. This meant that if firing did not take place until the sight of the enemy aircraft's wings just touched this circle at two points it would take care of one of the two major variables in air fighting. This was the harmonisation range of the guns, set up by armourers, which would produce an ideal spread of bullets and cannon shells in the area of the target. The other major factor was to ensure that the fired ammunition arrived at a point in space that the enemy aircraft was likely to be in when the bullets and shells arrived. This was known as deflection shooting which did not apply, of course, if the attacks were carried out from head on or directly astern. Both these types of attack, however, relied upon the victim not altering his line of flight which was most unlikely unless, of course, he had failed to realise that he was about to be fired upon. The angle of bank was also fed into the gyro system to cater for the allowance of deflection required. It appeared that during the war anything new, in the aircraft world, such as the gyro gunsights, was mainly fitted on the production lines and not retrospectively, particularly so in far off foreign places. During the reading of Group Captain Gray's book "Spitfire Patrol", I noted that although he had been a fighter pilot for most of WWII he had not flown an aircraft sporting such a gunsight, it may well have been because his last two years or so were spent in North Africa and Italy. I have never come across any literature on the background, as regards the invention of the Gyro sight but have often pondered on the effect it might have had if it had been produced earlier than it was, a great deal, I suspect.

Another novelty, as regards the Griffon Spitfire at least, was the fitting of a cartridge starter to the engine to replace the dear old trolley ACC electrical ones. The only other RAF aircraft that I ever flew with this fitted was the DH Chipmunk and I noted with interest that whenever one was sold off to the civil market that the Civil Aviation Authority insisted that it be replaced with an electrical starter before they would grant a civil licence, perhaps they knew something that the RAF never found out.

Before flying in the Mk XIV we were given one last fling in the Mk VIII, the very last trip we thought at the time. The conversion to type consisted of one general handling detail only before starting on dummy deck take offs. As mentioned previously the Spitfire, whatever the mark, had only two flap positions, fully up or fully down. To cater for the ideal position of 15° of flap for a really short take off it was decided to use two blocks of wood to jam the flaps in that position. This was achieved by selecting flaps down and, after the ground crew had inserted the blocks between the wings and flaps to select flap up again, the take off proved to be very short indeed. The technique was to get full power on as quickly as possible, whilst holding against the breaks for as long as they held, which gave rise to a massive torque reaction resulting in an alarming left wing down situation that even full right aileron did not quite bring the left wing up to the normal level position until about 50 mph. The lift off was carried out at a lower speed than normal and it was the first time that a saying of the day meant anything at all to me. It was called 'hanging on the props' and quite apt for a few seconds until the speed rapidly climbed to the norm for initial climb. Obviously, we could not leave the wooden wedges in position as we would need full flap for landing, so we had been briefed to the effect that as these pieces of wood were expendable, we should fly over wasteland behind our dispersal area at about 300' and then select 'flaps down' which would allow the wooden wedges to drop away to the ground, then we could select flaps up and climb away to normal flight conditions.

The call of nature had to be catered for in our dispersal hut and an open air urinal, of the dry sump type with ashes, was fairly close at hand, but for the more serious business, a sit down latrine had been constructed in the wasteland referred to above. Although no casualties were ever reported from flying pieces of wood, it was not for want of trying from our low flying, flaps down, woods away pilots. A far more serious threat was posed to the customers of the sit down open air loo by the fact that they were built on the continuous running water system, as per troopships, but the seating arrangements were very different in that they were only a few inches above the water level, which led to some rascal making miniature boats out of paper and, after setting them on fire, launching them from an upstream position when some of their mates were doing you know what. Talk about being caught with your pants down!

As an ex-airframe fitter I was amazed to note that the port rubber tyres of the Spitfires needed changing after about 10 dummy take offs due to so much pressure being put on them by the port wing being almost half way down to the ground for most of the short take off run. In England and elsewhere it was after reaching 208 landings that a mandatory change was called for and even then, on grass airfields in particular we often thought it was a very conservative figure.

It was during this conversion course that we lost another member of our original group a most likeable chap called Paddy Alexander, the son of a family butcher who hailed from Belfast, he had a fantastic sense of humour, and it was always a pleasure to be in his company. He met his end when engaged on an aerobatics practice detail during which his Spitfire, a new Mk XIV, broke up in mid air. The reason was still unsolved by the time we moved on to Ceylon, and I never heard of a final resolution. I trust Paddy's sense of humour was still with him when we laid him to rest in the military cemetery at Poona, we sincerely hoped so because to say it didn't go according to plan would be a massive understatement. The South West monsoon was now well established and it was a rainy afternoon when we set off on Paddy's last journey and I was one of the pall bearers on this very sad occasion. We had been briefed on the location in the cemetery of the prepared grave but as the padre was leading the procession we knew all would be well. As I was holding up the front left of the coffin it was probably at the same time as the Padre that I saw that a prepared grave had already been used in the very recent past and was now covered in soil. The proceedings, needless to say, came to an abrupt halt, while the parson consulted his notes, we soon set off again for quite a walk before reaching another recently used grave. This was certainly too much for the padre, and for us carrying the coffin for that matter, but for two very different reasons. He allowed us to gently lower Paddy to the ground whilst he made off to make urgent inquiries. I don't suppose I should use the phrase third time lucky, but a third grave was available and the ceremony duly completed. Not a day that one wanted to remember, but it proved otherwise over the years.

Back at RAF Poona, a fair amount of alcohol was put away that night, but one feature of all evening drinking sessions was that a chap, who we all thought needed medical attention, was invariably present and sooner or later would start singing "Lloyd George knows my father, My father knows Lloyd George", time after time and hour after hour. Apparently he was a member of the permanent staff and had been doing this for several months.

Another ongoing event which had been taking place for years, rather than months, was that at a precise time every evening a wailing noise, of very high intensity, would start up from Poona's prison, which was well within earshot of our camp. Our Indian bearers told us that the custom had started well before the war when Mahatma Gandhi had been held there by the British for acts of civil disobedience, it was a show of solidarity by the other inmates, which had continued even after he was long gone.

We still managed a few more afternoons by the pool at the AFI Club, and it was during our leisurely strolls into town that we always gave a quick glance towards the veranda of a certain colonial style bungalow. Almost invariably there would be an aged white couple, certainly British, who would both be sitting there in their dressing gowns, regardless of the time of day. It seemed particularly poignant, even at our young age, that sooner or later one or other of this obviously devoted couple would depart this world and then what would happen to the one left behind? It was well known that many ex-military types and civil servants of the Raj decided to spend their retirement years in India, such was the spell that it cast over so many people. The other side of the coin was that some servants became so interwoven with the lives of their employers that they were well prepared to continue serving them come what may, so that was some comfort to us as regards the couple in Poona.

We did not stay in the sub-continent long enough to fully appreciate all of it's attractions, but one outstanding feature plain to all was the friendliness of the local population. Most traditions of that area are well documented such as the sacred cow having right of way at all times, the caste system, young girls being forced to marry men they had never met before and, of course, widows throwing themselves onto the burning funeral pyre of their late husband. One other way of disposing of the dearly departed by the Parsee's was sometimes talked about, but I have never seen the gruesome details in print so I will leave it at that.

A hot item of gossip doing the rounds at that time included a snippet that the activation of "Exercise Zipper" was imminent, which was the invasion of Malaya. Some people, including the Japanese agents no doubt, even knew that the ports of departure would be Bombay, Madras, and the Royal Navy base of Trincomale in Ceylon. Was that why the Japanese had suddenly left Rangoon, leaving behind their ex-pows to inform the 14th Army and RAF of their departure or perhaps they had gone to defend their probable landing beaches around Penang. One reminder of dear old blighty was the large number of British troops sporting the 'Crossed Keys' badge in down town Poona, I well remembered last seeing it in the Forces Canteen in Worcester.

It was finally decided what our fate was to be, in the immediate future at least. The carrier take off training had been given, almost needless to say, so that we could take part in Operation Zipper, but not actually on a Squadron. The general plan for Operation Zipper was that Royal Navy fighter aircraft would cover the initial landings of the army from their aircraft carriers and only when the ground forces had made bridgeheads, which included captured Japanese airfields large enough to operate RAF fighter aircraft from, would the carriers return to Ceylon, to disembark their own aircraft, and then make another two round trips with RAF aircraft on one only take off missions. The first of these trips would take twenty Spitfires from No XI and 17 Squadrons and launch them in the Malacca Straights for a landing on one of the fields. The second voyage would be to take another 20 Spitfires which would be a 50/50 split of squadron aircraft and replacements for an estimated loss rate of 25%. So it was that we at Poona would provide 10 pilots and aircraft, to be in position at RAF China Bay for the second wave of the RAF involvement, which might well be as late as mid-October, even if everything went according to plan. As Poona did not even have ten Spitfire Mk XIVs on charge at that time, our ten carrier trained take off pilots were despatched by train, yet again, on another two days of very basic living, to a maintenance unit at RAF Nagpur, not all that far from our jungle training at Bhopal, to collect as many Spitfire Mk XIVs as they had managed to uncrate and re-assemble from a recent delivery from the UK. This train journey was to prove far more significant than it was possible to imagine at that time. News was given to us at one rail stop that a device called the Atom Bomb had been dropped on the Japanese city of Hiroshima and had caused unbelievable devastation and loss of life to such an extent that the Japanese must surely now surrender. A state of euphoria soon developed amongst us during what was left of our train journey, with speculation rife as to what would happen to us now. A quick return to England after the formalities of retaking the British, Dutch and French territories still in Japanese hands? Life is never like that, of course, and decisions in very high places would take some time to make. After arrival at Nagpur, it was to be a wait and see situation, luckily we now had an officer with us who had joined our group at Poona, he was Flight Lieutenant Johnnie Taylor, whose Spitfire flying went as far back as the siege of Malta. He had actually flown off a carrier to help reinforce the island at the height of the battle, but for his prodding and probing for the next few days, I fear we would not have had much in the way of news. However, he came rushing into the Nagpur Sgts Mess one morning to tell us to pack our bags as soon as possible as we would be flying to Bombay in about two hours time. This was to be my first trip in the world famous DC3 Dakota, a type I flew 52 years later, thanks to Eamonn Williams, and Air Atlantique of Coventry Airport.

During the three hour flight into Bombay from Nagpur, Johnnie Taylor briefed us all on the latest situation. The C in C, Lord Mountbatten, had decided to let Operation Zipper go ahead as the most sensible way of re-occupying South East Asia, but in a modified form, which called for a change of name to Exercise Zipper now that the Japanese had surrendered, this was after the dropping of a second atomic bomb, this time on Nagasaki. This had led the Japanese to think that there must be an unlimited supply of them, which actually was not the case. He also informed us that the ten replacement aircraft to cover a probable loss rate would no longer be required, but they still needed 10 pilots between the two squadrons because many of their own pilots were nearing the end of overseas tour dates and would therefore be leaving for the UK very shortly. Another factor in rushing back to Poona, and then on to Ceylon, was that although the Army would land on the Malayan beaches as planned, it would be a waste of time for the Royal Navy fighters to provide air cover against a non-existent enemy fighter force. So the first return voyage of HMS Trumpeter, one of the escort carriers, with only 420' of flight deck, would set sail with 20 Spitfires on board, and not Navy fighters as in the original plan. The planners had, presumably, taken note of the fact that this first RAF wave would be way ahead of it's original timing by about a week and they must have assumed that with the army landings being unopposed all would be all right on the night. It never is, of course, and when Squadron Leader Ginger Lacey, being first off HMS Trumpeter, leading from the front, having six other Spitfires behind him on deck, reducing his own take off distance to 350', he could not have known what he would faec upon landing. This was at a place called Morib, near Port Sweneham where he was met not by a British Army officer, but a Japanese Major, who surrendered not only his sword but the entire airfield as well. Lacey was bewildered and it was to be another couple of days before the army finally arrived, having been delayed as the beaches had proved unsuitable for a seaborne landing and it had turned into a shambles.

After the DC3 aircraft landed at Bombay, we were taken to the main railway station to catch a commuter train back to Poona. This was a luxury train compared to what we had seen hitherto and the fact that we would only be aboard for an hour or two was an extra bonus. Being able to occupy any vacant seat enabled most of us to strike up conversations with some of the obviously prosperous business men. This was the first and almost certainly, the last time that we would be in verbal contact with the higher levels of Indian society. It was an eye opener in that they thought that the British Army was second to none in the world and would be a benchmark for when they took over, now that the war was ended, music to the ears indeed.

We had one more day at dear old Poona after our final arrival, and then it was to be another epic train journey to Madras and then on to Ceylon. This was at eight days the longest yet, but with two nights in a transit camp at Madras and another night in Colombo, after a ferry boat ride across the narrows that separate India from Ceylon, it had some pleasant moments. Train journeys in India had another problem in addition to those already mentioned, in that it was not until 1997 that a standard rail gauge was finally achieved, from the three different ones in place during the time I was there. That meant of course that travelling from A to B often entailed diversions of some length and history books tell us that it even happened in England, the birthplace of steam travel, so perhaps we should not be too critical of the Raj.

The two full days off in Madras re-charged our batteries and although we had pleaded to be away sooner it fell on deaf ears. It seemed everyone needed to be some where else very quickly now that the floodgates of re-occupying Malaya and Singapore were well and truly open. We could not even produce a piece of paper to say which Squadron or unit we were on, which did not help our cause one little bit. The journey south from Madras to catch the ferry was probably the best part of our many days on the move during the previous two months. It had mostly been during daylight hours with frequent stops which invariably meant a char wallah would be on hand to cater for our liquid needs at least. At one stop we noted with interest that it was a change point for the line into the French enclave of Pondicherry. Had they thrown their lot in with the British in 1940, or just been left to their own devices for the rest of the war, we never did find out. The ferry ride to Ceylon was short and sweet, but very relaxing nonetheless. The verbal travel instructions for the last part of our journey to RAF China Bay were the vaguest yet. After disembarking from the ferry a train for Colombo was ready and waiting as predicted, and so it was a case of all aboard and off we went to spend a night there and then on to the RN base of China Bay the next morning.

On arrival at China Bay we were taken to the Royal Navy's Chief Petty Officers quarters, rather than the expected RAF Sgts Mess. Although our stay was for two short days before embarking on HMS Trumpeter at the adjacent naval base, it was just long enough to get a feel for some of the traditions of the Royal Navy, including drinking the daily rum ration, which reminds me of a story that if true was tragic in the extreme. One of the CPOs told us that two identical twin brothers in the RN had both died of alcoholic poisoning on their 21st birthday. Apparently it was a result of their mess mates managing to hoard portions of their rum rations and then plying the twins with it to celebrate what should have been a very happy day.

I had been aboard a warship once before, and that was as a schoolboy when HMS Liverpool, a cruiser, visited the city of that name, even then I thought that it was claustrophobic below decks, but it was a palace compared with an Escort Carrier. At the end of the day these ships were nothing more than cargo vessels which had their superstructure replaced with a flight deck. Having said that, they had performed magnificently on convoy protection duties during the war, particularly so before the Allies gained the use of airfields in Iceland, and later the Azores, to close the mid-Atlantic gap as far as land based long range anti submarine aircraft coverage was concerned. Our sleeping accommodation for the next five days was in the recreation area of the CPOs mess, which was on bench seating, and little different to the train journeys in India, the food, however, was superb and almost unlimited, what would people back in semi-starved England have given for this type of fare?

We were to sail South Eastwards to pass North of Sumatra before entering the Straights of Malacca, the first sight of land on this voyage however was the southern most tip of Car Nicobar Island, well remembered because we saw a merchant ship beached and on fire. As HMS Trumpeter steamed serenely on news seemed to be rather thin on the ground at lower deck level and on one occasion, when our group were taking the air on the flight deck, we were asked by two ratings if we had any idea where the ship would be going to after this second RAF transportation exercise. They thought it strange that we were as much in the dark as themselves, having noticed the more relaxed relationship that existed between aircrew officers and NCOs than was the case in the Royal Navy. One big surprise to all RAF members aboard came after entering the Straights when Paravanes were deployed, surely we were not going to be mined a month after the Japanese surrender, especially as this was Trumpeter's second venture into these waters. Many other allied ships must have passed this way by now, better safe than sorry must have been the theory.

The final day arrived, and with a steady 10 k South Westerly blowing, combined with an all out effort from the engine room, which gave Trumpeter it's maximum of about 18 knots, we had no problems with the short take off run, this led to something of an anti-climax. The real shock came after landing in Malaya when we were told that although our aircraft were required, the ex-Poona pilots were not. Flt Lt Johnnie Taylor our mentor was not best pleased, along with the rest of us, however he kept our best interests at heart, which produced rich dividends a few months later. The rail journey south to Air Headquarters in Singapore, from Kuala Lumpur, was particularly interesting in one respect in that at each and every rail stop there were always very smartly dressed soldiers armed with rifles and red stars in their hat badges standing guard, they were of Chinese descent, with not one Malayan amongst them. Who had equipped and trained them other than the Japanese, and that being so why? The Japanese had obviously left some potential trouble behind, which surfaced in a big way with the onset of the Malayan insurgency in

1948.

On arrival in Singapore we were directed to Air HQ, which at that time had recently arrived and taken over one of the best known hotels in the English speaking world- Raffles and we were told that we would be staying the night there and interviewed the next morning. Once more it was a case of sleeping on a bare floor, as left by the departing Japanese, as they did not go in for such refinements as beds, and the RAF had not yet managed to have some Charpoys made locally. An interview on the morrow sounded very strange indeed and gave us something to chew over that evening. Probably some Flt Lt on staff had nothing better to do we thought, but we all became shell shocked when paraded before the Air Officer Commanding, AVM Breakey, who had just taken over from the abandoned Earl. Pity we missed him. The message was loud and clear, don't go and kill yourself with any reckless flying, the war was over and we all wanted to return to England didn't we? He did mention that a Sunday church service in the Cathedral had been disturbed when two Spitfires buzzed the city the week before, and if that ever happened again someone would be for the chop. The staff officer conducting our entry and exit from the Holy of Holies then read out our postings, for five of us it was to be RAF Tengah in the North West of the island to join No 152 (Hyderabad) Squadron, flying Spitfire Mk VIIIs.

CHAPTER 12
On a squadron at last!

No 152 Squadron along with at least one other had been financed by the Nazam of Hyderabad as part of his contribution to the war effort. Above and beyond that I was to find out later he also provided ample funds for members of his Squadrons to celebrate the Christian Festival of Christmas each year, which was more than commendable for a Moslim. At that time who could have foreseen that within two short years India would not only have gained independence, but also partition from Pakistan, and most of the state rulers would have lost much of their power and influence. In the case of the Nazam, it was extreme indeed and a decade later his state did not exist, having been broken up into three parts and absorbed into neighbouring States, a sad business all round.

It was great to be on a squadron at long last, even if it was not the one I had hoped for. No 152 Squadron had been heavily involved ever since re-forming at RAF Acklington in Northumberland, almost immediately after the start of World War II. For almost the entire Battle of Britain period it had operated from RAF Warmwell in Dorset, my last ground station before taking to the skies, tasked with the prime objective of defending the Royal Navy base at Portland. In 1942 it took part in Operation Torch, the invasion of North Africa, and later supported the British Army in Tunisia, Malta, Sicily and Italy before moving on to India and Burma late in 1943. After the Japanese surrender, No 152 Squadron flew direct from Burma to Penang and then Singapore in early September of 1945, using 170 gallon drop tanks to increase their Spitfires' range by about 150%.

On first seeing the Squadron aircraft I was very impressed by the Squadron logo. It was a black Panther painted on each side of the fuselage, as if jumping through the standard RAF roundel.

The amount of flying per month did not amount to much, but it always seemed to have a purpose. In addition to dummy formation bombing attacks, we had a fair number of full squadron formation flights to overfly parades being held to mark the laying down of arms and disbandment of certain irregular forces. These consisted not only of the Japanese trained and equipped members of the Malay Communist party, but also local saboteurs trained by the British 136 force, who had operated against the Japanese for some considerable time. Perhaps some of the railway station guards we had seen on our journey south from Kuala Lumpur were standing to attention below us as we swept overhead on each occasion.

One flight which was to prove a good omen to us was a sortie to escort an RAF York inbound to the Kalang RAF Station in down town Singapore, with the C in C of all forces in South East Asia Command (SEAC) aboard. It was of course Lord Mountbatten who was relocating his HQ to Singapore from Kandy in Ceylon. His entire staff eventually arrived and they contained a fair number of WAAFs who seemed quite delighted to visit both our Sgt's Mess and to meet us at one of the NAAFI Clubs in Singapore, this Club was located alongside the RAF base at Kalang, which had been Singapore's civil airfield before the war. As befitted it's pre-war name of the Singapore Swimming Club, it boasted one of the best pools on the entire island and had been one of the focal points, along with the Singapore Cricket Club on the Padang, for European society until the Japanese came along. One of the WAAFs we felt particularly sorry for was, at just over 20 years of age, a Bomber Command war widow who hailed from Leicester. Another had spent a couple of years at RAF Pershore starting at about the time I was leaving there so it was nice to hear about the station again. The only girl I can recall was Jennie Barr from Guildford, and it was her name that came up in a casual conversation in the 1970s when Penny Thomas, our RAF neighbour at RAF Brize Norton, mentioned that she had served with the WAAFs in Singapore immediately after the war and knew Jennie very well. It transpired that Jennie too was now a widow after a very happy marriage.

Also based at RAF Tengah was No 155 Squadron and together we formed 902 Wing. No 155 Squadron, which did not re-form until 1942, on the North West frontier of India, had the misfortune to be issued with American Mohawk aircraft for the first eighteen months after their re-birth, and were now more than happy with their Spitfire Mk VIII. With each squadron having a large percentage of NCO pilots, as was the norm in those days, it was not possible to house all in the Sgts Mess, so we NCO aircrew were allocated quite a few of the pre-war airmens' married quarters. This worked out very well indeed with the extra distance from work being such that transport was required. It was a motley crew that sat on the road kerbside each morning outside these quarters, awaiting the crew coach, with most of us dressed in lightweight jungle green battledress, with just a few having reverted to khaki drill, and with head dress, or lack of it, varying from official issue slouch hats as per the Australian style, to blue Glengarrys, and in one particular case no headgear at all as the offending NCO's kit, except what he stood up in, had been lost in transit from Burma.

On the flying side our superiors always tried to lay on a low level flypast of any departing troopship known to be carrying a tour ex pilot from the wing, no matter what his rank was. With Air HQ still being on the Singapore waterfront, these beat ups no longer took place in the harbour area, but only after the ship was clear and off the west coast of the island. One particular flypast of this type was very nostalgic in that it was for the departing Commanding Officer of No 152 Squadron. In addition to the two Flight Commanders making a first fly by, all other pilots on the programme that morning flew to catch up with the ship before it got out of range to give further salutes. Sqdn Leader Kerr had obviously been held in very high esteem by all ranks, and had become something of a legend even before his time with the Squadron, having been involved in operations against the German Luftwaffe from early in the war, and had taken part in the operations against the two capital ships of their fleet when they made a dash up the English Channel.

I was beginning to think that the Spitfire and I just did not get on together, being involved in three incidents during my six months on the Squadron. My flying had been on the "Better be safe than sorry" side since my high speed dive in Egypt, but that did not keep me immune as it turned out, I had been on the Squadron for less than a month when the first incident occurred. My Flight Commander was still only a Flying Officer, although his flying went back to early Mohawk days which made him a very experienced fighter pilot indeed for that time. The other Flight Commander, however, was a Flight Lieutenant and, therefore, higher up in the pecking order, although he had spent most of the war in the instructional world. Even at our NCO level we thought a certain something had developed between the two of them. On the day in question both A and B flights were airborne, with formations of four aircraft in both cases, and also with the respective Flight Commanders leading. I was flying No 2 to my boss, Flying Officer "X", on ground controlled interceptions, after which we were put into line astern for a tail chase. It was when we were in a steep dive that I spotted the four aircraft of "A" flight flying in a bit of a gaggle well below and to say it was like a red flag at a bull would be the understatement of all time. We changed direction like a flash with my leader heading for an attack on the senior Flight Commander from the rear, hell bent on teaching him a lesson in aerial dogfighting, no doubt. As we pulled out of the dive to deliver the attack from his six o'clock position, I, No 2, could only see my leader and his intended victim. 'What had happened to the other three aircraft of A flight?', went quickly through my mind. Not for long though, as I was shattered to hear the roar of a Merlin engine and see the under belly of a Spitfire less than 20' above my cockpit, which then carried straight on into the tail area of my flight commander, about 50' ahead. For a few split seconds I was completely mesmerised by the sight of the propeller of the aircraft in front, having become detached from it's engine, going up and to the right in a gigantic arc. Having taken avoiding action I found myself, as so often recorded in many reports of dog fights, in what appeared to be a completely empty sky. As No 2, I made a radio report back to base in what must have been absolute gibberish so often was I asked to "repeat my message and speak more slowly, please". I made my way back to Tengah in a bit of a state, trying to stay cool but all for nought because on finals, although I checked for three greens, it was not until the last moment that I noticed that although the undercarriage lever was down it was actually in it's safety slot, and a heavy landing might well have resulted in it going to the 'select up' position. It was a case of full throttle and round again for another go. However, I thought "to hell with this, I'm off on a tour of the island to cool down a bit". When I eventually landed about thirty minutes later I was met with disbelief by some of the pilots in the crewroom. Some remarks were along the lines of "That was pretty cool wasn't it? Completing your detail and not knowing if the other two pilots were alive or dead". They had a point of course, and I was just as chuffed as everyone else to learn that both had landed wheels up without injury, one on Sembawang airfield and the other in some wide open place on the island. Although I do not believe in premonitions, I did have a dream about seeing a mid air collision and making a radio call about it some nights before it occurred. The strange thing about that dream was that I could still recall the details the next morning which, I understand, is sometimes unusual, it has certainly been so in my case over the years.

One problem of overseas postings during the war, and particularly so when moving locations in rapid succession, was that large gaps occurred in receiving mail from family and friends in the UK. It must have been well into the autumn of 1945 when I received my first letter in Singapore from my dear mother, a very religious lady, to say she thought the dropping of atomic bombs, even on the Japanese, after all their atrocities, was against her Christian beliefs. Not a view shared by anyone who had taken part in Exercise Zipper, instead of Operation Zipper.

Although the repatriation of ex-prisoners of war released by the Japanese on the mainland of South East Asia had been achieved in a remarkable short time scale, it was proving very difficult indeed to recover some of those unfortunate enough to have been incarcerated on Java and other islands in the Dutch East Indies group. The role played by the ground and Air Forces in this task is graphically described in a book called "Forever Eastwards" by Air Chief Marshal Sir David Lee, who himself took part as Officer in Command of a P47 Thunderbolt Wing. He records that the force employed was not welcomed by the local population who thought the British were hand in glove with the Dutch government and hell bent on restoring a colonial regime to the area. No doubt the Japanese, just as they had in Malaya, had fanned the flames of discontent against European rule in the Far East, during their own occupation. However, the Japanese co-operated fully with the British on a number of occasions when asked to help in trying to restore some semblance of law and order. The price paid by the liberating force was heavy, with the British 23rd Division suffering over 1000 casualties, which included 250 killed, during the first few months of the re-occupation task, this was more than that division had lost in the previous twelve months of fighting in Burma. The RAF lost 21 killed in the same period, plus many aircraft damaged by ground fire. The most tragic incident occurred after an RAF Dakota had force landed in a paddy field, after which the entire crew and passengers were executed by the local insurgents.

We, in Singapore, were only called upon to fly "show of strength" flights over some of the nearest islands on occasions, but that was about all we could do as one piece of jungle looked very much like any other and, in any event, the chances of seeing rebels who might have been below was nil. It was to be many months after the Japanese surrender before the last of the Dutch civilian internees were finally rescued from their prison camps, and we sometimes saw groups of the newly released in the Raffles area of downtown Singapore, during our odd forays into the city, and had a chat with them whenever possible. On one such occasion we noted that all but one of the party were suffering from malnutrition. As usual the odd one out was a female who stood out from the rest in that she obviously had not gone short of anything. The disdain in which this particular lady was held by the rest was all too obvious, being completely ostracised, however, she was lumbered with having to stay with the group until transport back to the Netherlands became available.

The much maligned NAAFI services were absolutely marvelous during this post war period in the Far East, they took over the "Cathy Cinema" in Singapore city centre, on behalf of the military, to show morale boosting films. It's one and only drawback being that it was located directly opposite the pre-war YMCA, which had been used by the Japanese as the Headquarters of their Kempetai, an extreme version of the German Gestapo. Near the waterfront, at Collyer's Quay, the famous Robinson's store had also been taken over, more or less as an off duty drinking den. No danger of getting drunk, however, with only one bottle of beer per person, per trip to the counter, and with a queue a mile long most of the time. The beer itself was nothing to write home about, having been brewed in Australia with some sort of chemical in place of hops. In the wine world it would probably have been described as "Does not travel well"! For those who did not mind the occasional punch up, there was also a NAAFI establishment called the "Pegasus Club", which was mainly for the use of Army other ranks, but they did not seem to mind the RAF making use of their facilities.

The second of my three incidents whilst flying the Spitfire from Tengah duly occurred and it was the only one that I had to hold my hand up to. It was during a hectic aerobatic solo detail that after throttling back, coming out of a dive, that the engine failed to respond when I opened up again. I tried all the usual things to restore power, but to no avail and no matter how slowly I opened the throttle lever, the engine just would not respond. I was getting near the 'bale out', or 'pick your crash landing site' height, and still without any response from the engine, so I elected for a crash landing and set course for the nearby coastline on the west of the island, with the intention of belly flopping into the shallows, beam on to the waterline, but not too far out, although our survival pack actually carried shark repellent. After tightening the safety harness as never before, and opening the cockpit hood, it was a case of one last go at the throttle lever. Eureka!, or umpteenth time lucky, she actually fired up, so it was back to base. My Flight Commander, now a Flight Lieutenant Plumb, listened to me in complete silence and then said, with some emphasis, "I take it that you had pressed the de-airating button", There was no answer to that. I had never heard of a de-airing button before, but soon found out that it was something that had been first fitted to the Spitfire Mk VIII. As far as I was concerned it had never been mentioned at RAF Poona during our conversion course, such was the training in those days.

Our squadron took some pride in organising away from it all day trips, and some of them proved to be particularly interesting indeed and two of them have lived on in my memory ever since. The most evocative was to the war cemetery of Krangi, near the bridge over the Jahore Straights. Many of the names listed from all three services of the Allied cause were, of course, as a result of the Japanese attack on the island in early 1942. Many others indicated that they had died as POWs after capture and, in some cases, for some weeks after the liberation of the area in 1945. Our guide told us that one or two recent deaths were the result of some members of the liberating force taking drinks which had been spiked with wood alcohol by the Japanese at the time of their surrender. This tied in with the fact that we had been warned about this possibility after first landing in Malaya. The second part of that day trip that I well recall was that after leaving Krangi Cemetery we crossed the Jahore Bridge on the way to see an abandoned Japanese built jungle air strip. This proved to be a big surprise in that the number of Japanese aircraft left around the airfield far outnumbered the total that the intelligence reports suggested would be available to the Japanese for the defence of the entire Malay peninsular. So much for their homework, could have done better, was the general mood as we made our way back to Tengah.

One day one of our pilots reported seeing two mighty warships making their way down the Malacca Straights and assumed them to be Royal Navy. Wrong, as it turned out, because Tengah was asked to provide 26 RAF personnel as guests of the French Navy, aboard one of the two Battleships anchored in Singapore harbour. It was 152 Squadron's lucky day because from an admin point of view the easy option was to send aircrew from either 152 or 155 Squadron and 152 must have won the toss. So it was that we had a super day out on the Battleship Richelieu which was, with another one whose name I can no longer recall, on passage to Saigon to help repossess the French colony of Vietnam. Already trouble was brewing in Indo-China, but nothing compared with what was to happen 20 years later. The French had obviously gone to a great deal of trouble to ensure that the visit was a success, with conducted tours of the entire ship from engine room upwards. One big difference to the British system of having three grades for messing, i.e. Officers, SNCOs, and other ranks, was that they seemed to have six, or it could have been more, because we lost count. The reason for losing count was that each mess deck insisted on their visitors partaking of French wine in larger than normal sized glasses, red wine always did give me a thick head, however this was something different. The Royal Navy, cunning as ever, had sent along as their representatives a group of immaculately dressed WRENS, they stole the show, of course, and impressed the French no end. We did not know how long these ladies intended to stay aboard, but they saw fit to stand looking over the ship's rails as we boarded our liberty boat to return to the quayside, and gave us a few waves and cheers. Looking up at them from about 30' below they were a pretty sight to behold and a mighty cheer went up from our half drunken gang when one Wren lifted a foot onto the first rail of the decking and, the rest of the girls did likewise, result, a chorus line. I remain convinced to this day that they never thought about what they might be showing in such strong sunlight.

The last of the three incidents during my short time on No 152 Squadron took place when flying No two to Warrant Officer Eddie Eden, a man very popular with all on the Squadron. His rank indicated that he had been around a bit and that was very true, having already completed tours in the UK and Italy on Spitfires amassing over 1,000 hours on type which was almost certainly higher than any other RAF pilot. On February 28th 1946 when taking off, with our wings over-lapping, with my port wing behind his starboard one, just before lift off I got the distinct impression from the feel of the throttle lever that he must be slowing down, and as we were well past the half way mark of the runway length, I gave it full blast and pulled back on the stick at the same time. This did lift me off the ground for a split second, but I would still have hit Eddy's wing but for the fact that he had lifted his undercarriage and was sinking on to the runway, to save over running the strip. For myself, I had just enough runway left to accelerate and lift off in the last few yards of Tarmac. I was told by air traffic to hold off a bit while they arranged for the runway to be cleared. I think that they must have forgotten about me because I had eventually to ask for a diversion to RAF Seletar, when the fuel indictor was getting decidedly low. It was not long before night fall when I made the 10 minute dash back to Tengah from Seletar and the initial inquest was well and truly over by that time.

I never found out what caused the power failure on that occasion but what is well known to all Spitfire pilots is that you can start a Merlin engine with the fuel selector "off" and it will still run on petrol already in the lines for a good few minutes until fading away. After some pilots had found this out the hard way, mostly whilst taxying for take off, and blocking all following aircraft, it was decided to wire all fuel selectors in the "Fully on" position, with the wire locking only to be broken by ground engineers as and when required and by pilots to deal with engine fires. One weakness with the Merlin engine in the tropics, when fitted to a Spitfire, was that if you did not get airborne pretty damn quick after start up you weren't going anywhere because the engine Glycol coolant would soon reach it's boiling point of about 115° C, demanding an immediate engine shut down. This made for faster taxying speeds for pilots when making sure that they beat the deadline, and if the fuel cock was not "on", the failure was more likely to occur just after take off, rather than when still taxying. In temperate climates engine coolant temperatures rose more slowly and, therefore, taxi time was not of the essence, except on scrambles of course. As is the case with many so called practical solutions, it had it's drawback in that some pilots began to assume that the petrol cock was bound to be on and that was one less check to carry out. The Chipmunk aircraft had a related problem in that it was decided to wire the hot/cold air selector in hot, which would get rid of any ice, but also reduce power slightly. The loss of power suffered when in the hot position was deemed, by higher authority, to be acceptable. Not so by some mad keen aerobatic pilots who often broke the wire to obtain the cold position and so have maximum power for their antics. Once again, it was assumed by some pilots to be wired hot, when it wasn't. This "always in hot" theory was a typical case of taking the cure before catching the cold.

The cleaning up of RAF Tengah went on apace, with almost unlimited labour in the form of Japanese POWs working 12 hours a day. The only time I saw any of them relaxing during their working day was when I went into a hangar that was in the process of being turned into a camp Theatre and found them all leaning on their shovels, gawking at the already built stage. They looked completely stunned, and for once I could fully understand their feelings. Up there was a young airman, who I later found out was from the theatrical world and in charge of the project. He was prancing around like a ballet dancer. "A penny for their thoughts" did not quite fit the bill. Although all military establishments took advantage of the labour force available there was still a surplus, with 125,000 POWs to find work for, so the residue were packed off to an island just off Singapore called Rempang. I never did find out if they were supervised, or just left to their own devices, with food being delivered as and when. Whenever I was on the first detail, and flying by myself, I loved to give that island a buzz because they always carried out a full parade with a flag hoisting ceremony every morning at a precise time, which made it quite a spectacle from the air: Particularly so from low level, of course!

We thought all our transport problems of getting into Singapore and back when off duty had been solved with the arrival of an RAF Airfield Construction Squadron, with plenty of motor transport on hand. This proved to be the case in the short term, because they had regular runs into the city centre with their five ton lorrys, and you only had to be in RAF uniform to cadge a lift. No sooner had they arrived than they went to work with a vengeance on the secondary runway, which we had never used, to both reinforce it and also to extend it to the RAF norm in those days of 2000'. This was fine as it was more into wind than the one we had used so far, and also longer. In Singapore, by the way, the wind normally blew from the North East for six months of the year, and the South West for the other six months. Such was the devastation that the constructors made to the landscape around the airfield that they soon earned the nickname of "Moonmen".

There was mounting tension amongst the civilian population of Singapore Island towards Christmas time, with a shortage of food being one factor, plus a demand for higher wages for all. This unrest reached such a peak that we were only allowed into the city centre in groups of three or more, and each armed with a revolver. This situation did not last all that long and was all over by the time of the first post WWII Christmas. This turned out to be a somewhat subdued affair with most minds focused on distant places. My log book indicates that I was aloft during the daylight hours of Christmas Eve and again just after Boxing Day. Only one clear recollection of that particular Christmas Day remains and it occurred as a result of the re-introduction of the pre-war custom of Officers' and NCOs' waiting on at table to serve airmen their Christmas dinner. As luck would have it, at one stage I was behind a very young officer, recently arrived from England, and behind me was the Station Commander. The main dish was roast beef and the young officer had the grave misfortune to place it on the table in front of the one and only Hindu Indian based at Tengah. It is difficult to describe the look on the Indian's face, his eyes were popping and with twisted lips he began snarling. The

CO was onto it like a flash and after dumping the plate he was carrying in the middle of the table, he raced forward and removed the Indian's dish in a trice, and with a look that could have killed in the direction of the mystified young Officer. In England the equivalent would have been serving your best friend their pet dog.

In January of 1946 the unthinkable occurred as far as the RAF was concerned; strikes, and for the first time in the RAF's short history. They had already broken out in India, Ceylon and Burma, but why on earth in Singapore at RAF Seletar? Accommodation for all ranks was in pre-war purpose built buildings, the food was adequate, and certainly more plentiful than in England. The leisure activities, as one might expect on a tropical island, included water sports and sailing. The only gripe seemed to be that they all thought they should be back in the UK now that the war was over. Life is never like that, of course, and priority had after the repatriation of all ex-pows and civilian internees, been given on the basis of first in, first out, and certainly not to last in first out. My first thoughts that the Communist party must have had something to do with the situation has never changed over the years. One tiny irritation for all ranks who had been east of Suez for some time was that an election had been called in England shortly after VE day and not held over until both the main enemies had been defeated. This had lent weight to the saying of the "14th (Forgotten) Army". It would have been good if Winston Churchill had still been in power on VJ day.

The Station Commander at RAF Tengah called for all ranks not on essential duty to assemble on the station parade ground one morning when he would address them. The Group Captain's message was very much to the point. He had no doubt that sooner or later RAF strikers from Seletar would try and gain access to his station with the intention of attempting to spread strike action. If that came to pass anyone under his command had his express permission to detain and imprison intruders in the guardroom using whatever physical force was necessary. Very strong stuff, but fully supported by all ranks. The strike at Seletar was short lived and put down before we had any need to flex our muscles. Air Chief Marshal Lee, in his book "Eastward", concurs with the decision of the Air Ministry to call these disturbances "strikes" and not "mutiny". He also refers to the time that Air Chief Marshal Sir Keith Park, C in C of the RAF in the Far East, was shouted down when trying to address airmen at RAF Seletar, if that was not mutiny it is difficult to understand what is.

The only genuine grievance I came across was from airmen who were well past their overseas tour time of 3 1/2 years, with no sign of an early return to the UK. A shortage of shipping was the only reason given for their retention 7,000 miles from home on RAF Stations that were grossly over manned; 3,000 at Seletar, for instance, which coped quite well with half that number later. Morale was dented in that context when it was reported that the Queen Mary was carrying 20,000 GI brides across the Atlantic per round trip. Good riddance, was the opinion of many, thinking that at least some of the brides were probably the instigators of "Dear John" letters which were often received in the Far East, as elsewhere. Those of a deeper thinking nature took the view that if the larger liners could not negotiate the Suez Canal, they could at least ply the Alexandria- Marseilles sector, which was the Southern terminus of the already in place land route across France to the Channel ports. This would have doubled the number of troopship departures from the East if they had confined their sailings to Suez and back, instead of going all the way to the UK, before returning. Happily, the problem ceased to exist by mid 1946 when mid-tour leave in the UK had been established, even for the Japanese occupation force, but if you had already passed the mid-tour point it was a case of tough luck!

Squadron Leader Harding, later Air Vice Marshal, who had taken over from the revered Sqdn Ldr Kerr, followed his predecessor's bent for innovation and, unbeknown to all other 152 Squadron pilots, until the actual briefing that is, had arranged for a mock dog fight between Royal Navy, American built, Corsair fighter aircraft, operating off a carrier in the Malacca Straights, and our own entire squadron. For one reason or another, the Squadron Commander was to lead our section and made it obvious that he was looking forward to the contest with high expectations of his Squadron. On signing my form 700, a log book recording all work and inspections on a particular aircraft, I was, as an ex-fitter airframes, more than interested in the last entry which read; "Rudder removed and replaced, alignment and locking checked satis.", or words to that effect. No reason as to why it had been removed in the first place was given and my mind returned to the days when I was ground crew. Damage had occasionally occurred to aircraft when moved in and out of hangars, and the most likely area of damage was to the moving parts such as flaps, ailerons, elevators and rudders. This type of damage was universally referred to as "Hangar rash" and sometimes Flight Sergeants in charge would give the nod to a new part being fitted whilst discrete repair work was carried out. The nod would certainly be given if any lack of supervision by the Flight Sergeant himself could be construed. I did not take a rudder replacement as seriously as I would have if it had been an aileron or elevator, the rudder being mainly used for ground use, such as taxying, take off and landing and only used in normal flight for keeping the turn and bank ball central, which was imperative during air firing. The climb away after take off, which is carried out at a relatively low speed, seemed to go as usual, but after levelling off at altitude, with a decided increase in speed, I found that I had some difficulty in arresting a developing crab like motion with opposite rudder. Even after winding on full rudder trim a lot of pushing on the right rudder bar was still required and I began to wonder how long I could keep this up before getting leg cramp. Then it all happened, the radar vectors that we had all been listening to on our radios from the ground station suddenly announced contact with out opposing force and after giving a few heading alterations our CO called visual and put us into a steepish dive, with this increase in speed the holding on of the amount of rudder required became impossible so I reduced speed and pulled away. During the de-brief the CO told me not to place the aircraft unserviceable until he had flown it to see how bad the defect was. In the event, the flight never took place, the technical NCO's had heard on the grapevine about the problem after the de-brief and carried out a quick inspection which revealed a lack of tension in one rudder control cable. I did manage a few free beers that night in the Sgts Mess from the technical NCO who had countersigned the original work. I knew from personal experience that countersigning was sometimes regarded as a formality depending on both the type of work carried out and the experience of the tradesman employed.

One accident that occurred over Singapore island during our time was both tragic and sad, it had actually been seen by an NCO pilot of our sister Squadron, No. 155. When airbourne he had spotted a Mosquito aircraft spinning into the ground with one wing missing. Two aircrew being killed through no fault of their own in peacetime is tragic enough, but for it to happen so soon after the end of the war, and before they had a chance of returning to England and family, made it a double tragedy. It was also sad because it left a slight stain on the reputation of probably the second finest military aircraft ever built in the UK, coming a close second to the Spitfire. However, need it have happened? Could not the fact that hot and damp climates might not suit wooden fuselages held together with glue been foreseen? A false dawn may have been caused by the fact that structural failures only began after individual aircraft had been out there for a year or so. Although most people have laid the blame at the door of failed glue joints, a friend of mine, who was also trained as a Fitter Airframes, told me that red ants getting at the wooden main spars was another factor to contend with.

About my only moment of flying madness during my time in Singapore came when I was on a solo detail and I thought a few minutes of really low flying over the sea up the Malacca Straights might be in order. The sea was dead calm, as is so often the case in the tropics, which makes the judgement of height above water just a little more difficult. I soon realised that I was far too low and even noticed out of the corner of my eye that the sea surface was being disturbed by my prop wash. As all pilots can confirm, an aircraft will always mush down a little as you ease back on the stick to break the descent for landing. Although I was in level flight this would still happen with the prospect of the propeller striking the water unless I was ultra gentle on the controls. I managed to do just that in the event, and heaved a mighty sigh of relief at the same time. I never flew as low as that ever again, except for landing with wheels down of course.

I have already mentioned that the "Moonmen" provided transportation for us in the short term, but it was to be very short indeed. They had completed the donkey work of moving thousands of tons of earth for the re-construction of the short runway and now needed to dig up part of our only usable strip at it's intersection with the one that they were working on. Although we all thought that we might move over to Seletar for a few months and return after the reconstruction work was completed, it was not to be. We did have two weeks notice that No 155 Sqdn would be moving to Medan in Sumatra in early February and our own No 152 Squadron would be returning to India at the end of that month to fly Tempests. I don't know if it was a case of the left hand not knowing what the right hand was doing but no sooner had these arrangements been announced than Spitfire Mk XIVs started to arrive. Our little gang of new boys thought it ironic that although we had flown this type before those who had come down with No 152 Squadron from Burma had not even seen one close up until they arrived. Nor had they seen a gyro gunsight for that matter. The old hands took it in good part when we pointed out where they had gone wrong when occasionally they failed to start up the Griffon engine on their first few attempts at using the Coffman cartridge system. The CO of No 152 Squadron decided that these new aircraft would be flown first of all by those with no previous experience on type so that they could gain experience and those who had flown them before, could wait until last. The last never came, not until I took off for K.L. and No XI squadron.

Flight Lieutenant Johnnie Taylor had moved on to become a Flight Commander with No XI Squadron, now based at Kuala Lumpur, along with No 17 Squadron, and when it had become known that those two squadrons would form the RAF Fighter Wing in the British Commonwealth Occupation Force, bound for Japan, with an increased establishment, he remembered our little ex-Poona/HMS Trumpeter group and managed to arrange a transfer for three of us, plus the Mk XIV aircraft to his Squadron.

CHAPTER 13
Commonwealth Occupation Force: Japan

It was sad to be leaving our first squadron and Singapore, but the prospect of being part of an occupying force, particularly of Japan, was quite exciting and something to look forward to. For many other pilots on the squadron, who had been overseas for some years and had no intention of remaining in the RAF now that the war was over, the temporary closure of RAF Tengah at the end of February also marked the end of their flying career. For Alf Harding, who I had served with throughout my training days in Rhodesia, it was not to be Japan but Java instead. However, it was the second best posting available in that he would not only still be flying but off water as well as land. He was to join an air sea rescue flight flying the Sea Otter Amphibian aircraft a very similar type to the one I almost had a flight in during my first time at RAF Sealand. After we had gone our separate ways I never saw him again but I had a very pleasant surprise over thirty years later during dinner in the Officers' Mess at RAF Coningsby, one of the cooks shot out of the kitchen to tell me he had an Alf Harding on the phone who said he knew me from his Singapore days, did I wish to take the call? You bet I did. It turned out that my name had been mentioned on TV as the pilot of the Lancaster, which had flown over London that afternoon in connection with the Royal Tournament. My dinner was quite cold by the time we had finished our conflab, but another one was soon rustled up.

It is very rare, if not unique, for a fighter pilot, or any other pilot for that matter, to take an aircraft with him on posting to another squadron. However three of us took Spitfire Mk XIVs off from Tengah for Kuala Lumpur, 1 hour and 20 minutes later we had become No XI Squadron pilots. We also had with us all our worldly possessions stacked away in the empty ammunition bays. Although that was my last Spitfire take off from Tengah, I was to return again 25 years later as Captain of a mighty

Short Belfast freighter of No 53 Squadron, airlifting RED TOP air to air missiles back to the UK as part of the RAF's final withdrawal from Singapore.

With Kuala Lumpur not being a permanent pre-war RAF base we thought we may have to live under canvas, or at best in locally built Basher huts, so it was great to find that all NCO aircrew of both XI and 17 Squadrons shared the requisitioned down town mansion of some former tycoon. The officers also had similar accommodation and the RAF police managed to acquire one next to ours, which they both worked and lived in. Too close for comfort, but it provided a target one night after we had decided that we could reproduce the V2 rocket by using the Griffon engine starting cartridges, attached to sticks, just like a bonfire night rocket, and get ignition by way of a very primitive fuse. They proved to be quite good, actually, and after slight tilting of empty beer bottles we placed the sticks in and could just about predict the area that they would land on, i.e. the police accommodation. They soon put a stop to that, of course, misuse of Government assets and all that.

Our new squadron often referred to as Legs Eleven, after the bingo cry, and some unofficial logos often depicted one leg of a girl, which, rumour had it, was from a photograph of Betty Grabel in a glamorous pose, but this was never seen painted on the fuselage of any of the squadron's aircraft. In fact, the Spitfire Mk XIVs that had arrived so late at Madura in India for Operation Zipper, were still without any Squadron markings of any kind, official or otherwise, and remained so even in Japan, which seemed very strange indeed.

In the context of aircraft markings, No XI Squadron almost made a name for itself when it was decided to strip off all paint down to the bare metal on our aircraft before departing for Japan. As no ground crew could be spared for the task, it was decided to use NCO aircrew, but after we had taken two full weeks to complete just one aircraft the scheme was abandoned. However, one very important job was completed successfully and that was the repainting of the RAF roundels on the sides of each fuselage to the full red, white and blue standard. The white had been omitted throughout the war with Japan because it could have been misidentified as the Japanese markings of the rising sun. I might add that we had precious little else to do other than paint stripping and repainting of RAF roundels as my log book records that during the five weeks that I was at Kuala Lumpur I made one flight. This was due to the fact that no sooner had we landed our Spitfire Mk XIVs at Kuala Lumpur from

Tengah they were all grounded because of a magneto fault which required all mags to be sent to a maintenance unit in Singapore for rectification and returned just in time for one air test per aircraft before our departure, along with No 17 Squadron, to RAF Seletar, and embarkation on HMS Vengeance for Japan.

One benefit of living off base in Kuala Lumpur was that we had easy access to the town centre, such as it was, but it did have a cinema showing British films of uncertain vintage. One night I was the only one from our mess who was interested in the latest film on offer so I took a lonesome stroll into town and picked up a local paper, printed in English on the way. My seat was in the front row of the gallery and whilst awaiting the start of the show I had a glance through the recently bought paper and came across a list of recent awards to the British services for their part in the recent war. This was not unusual as these lists had been a regular feature over the months. For some reason or other I assumed that before names appeared in print the persons concerned would have been informed one way or another and as no one on our wing had mentioned a recent award I only gave a casual glance to the RAF section. Under the DFCs however, a name leapt out at me. It was for a Flying Officer George Dak and as an officer of that name was now on our squadron- having completed a full operational tour with either No 20 or 28 Squadron, surely that must be one and the same. Now a remarkable coincidence occurred in that five officers from our squadron arrived and also took up seats on the front row, but on the opposite wing to myself. Yes, George Dak was among them and as I still assumed that if he was on the list he would have been informed about it by now, I thought I would just add my congratulations by way of pointing at him from a distance and giving a thumbs up. All five officers looked mystified and started pointing at each other to try and establish which one I had in mind. When I made a horizontal movement across my left chest, in the area that a medal ribbon would be worn, one of them went back up to the exit and then down again on my side of the cinema to ask me what it was all about. I just gave him my paper, pointing at George's name. This officer took the same route back at a fair rate of knots. I watched his return with anticipation and was very pleased indeed to see handshakes and backslapping all round before they got up and left, but not before George had pointed back at me and gone through the motions of drinking a glass of beer. I don't suppose many officers have received the news of an award in such unusual surroundings. Drinking a few beers was now a better bet than sitting through a film. George Dak was a well liked and respected officer, so when I broke the good news back at the Sgt's Mess a unanimous decision was taken to invite George and his friends over for drinks, an invitation they gladly accepted, which led to quite a riotous ending to a memorable day.

About the only other entertainment in the mess, other than drinks in the evenings, was the dart board, some people managed both of course. One pilot was particularly skilled at the game, treble tops coming thick and fast when he was on song. One night he shook all others present, and even himself, I should think. His first dart was a treble twenty, which was not at all unusual, but the second was a dead centre hit on a mouse he had spotted out of the corner of his eye, running along a skirting board, all of 10' away: deflection shooting par excellance. He quickly looked back to the board and scored a bull's eye with his last shot. No one could quite believe what they had just witnessed. A one in a million chance indeed.

Our monastic lives suffered a slight technical hitch, as the saying goes, when one night a WAAF from our Singapore days managed to track us down, and phoned to speak to Frank Cull in person. Frank was on hand and reported later that the WAAF would be coming up for a few days over the next weekend and would love to see us all again. Perhaps we could even show her around the town. She had foreseen the problem of accommodation and said a friend of hers at Air HQ in Kuala Lumpur had arranged everything in that department. Frank Cull, a fellow NCO pilot, was a bit of a ladies man and must have left a deep impression, but how on earth could we keep a lone WAAF entertained for a long weekend? Day one was a disaster in that we had already arranged to go into town to see a civilian boxing match, and took the dear lady along with us, she hated every minute of it! The next evening, however, was a complete change when we decided to go en-mass to a dance hall called the BB. We had often seen it on our prowls around the town but had kept clear, as we thought that British servicemen without partners might not be to the liking of the locals, but now we did have one, so in we went. Frank and his partner, who I can still recall came from Beverley in Yorkshire, became a real show stopper with their jiving and jitterbugging. At times they had the floor to themselves with all other dancers keen to be spectators for a change. We left Frank to sort things out for himself for the remainder of the visit, which passed off quite well apparently.

The last few days of our stay in Kuala Lumpur soon slipped away and then it was a two squadron formation take off for RAF Seletar. After arrival, we only had five days before embarkation, but it was long enough for a mass gathering of all those going to Japan to be addressed by an Air Vice Marshal who would be our Air Officer Commanding when we arrived there. Some cynics thought that five days had only just been long enough to hear him out. He was called "Boy" Bouchier by all, having been known by that nickname at the height of the Battle of Britain, during which he had served with great distinction. The AVM had started his present tour in the Far East in Burma, and was to continue in his new post of AOC until the end of the RAF involvement in the occupation of Japan in 1948. His briefing did go on a bit, with his main message being repeated in many forms, this was that the British would show the Japs a thing or two. The Union Jack would be flown from many buildings and on every conceivable occasion, dress to be immaculate at all times, no fratting, justice would be seen to be fair and dispassionate and our heads were to be held high at all times. Yes, the Japanese would be shown a thing or two about how the British conducted themselves. Any novel writer taking up his theme might have added that AVM Bouchier, after a year or so in Japan, fell under the spell of his former enemies and their country to the extent that he decided to spend the rest of his days out there and his doting widow carried on that tradition after his death. That is exactly what happened.

The big day arrived with the arrival of HMS Vengeance, a purpose built fleet aircraft carrier which appeared to be at least twice the size of our previous one, HMS Trumpeter. After she had dropped anchor, just off RAF Seleter, all our Spitfires were ferried out on barges to join No.4 Royal Indian Air Force Squadron, which had already embarked in Bombay. This squadron was also equipped with the Griffon engined Spitfire Mk XIV. After weighing anchor, serene progress was made down the Jahore Straights towards the South China Sea, with all hands manning ship. Although the RAF had been told to stay below decks, a kindly Chief Petty Officer had pointed out a position which would give us a good vantage point without being seen from the bridge. A fair number of military spectators on the verandahs of military buildings in the Changi area gave the sailors the odd wave which could not be returned. Perhaps the proposed move of the HQ Air Command South East Asia from the Collyer Quay area of Singapore to RAF Changi had now taken place, as predicted by our WAAF visitor to Kuala Lumpur. She might even have been one of those wishing HMS Vengeance, and Frank Cull, bon voyage.

With the war now passing into the history books, food and drink, or vitals as the Royal Navy preferred to call them, were plentiful and the seven days spent aboard was more like a pleasure cruise for the RAF contingent, than a military operation, except for the sleeping arrangements which were on bench type seating as usual.

The first sight of many countries is at it's best from the deck of a ship and Japan must rank alongside Norway in that respect. I did not know what to expect as regards scenic beauty when we first spotted mainland Japan from the flight deck, but as we entered the Inland Sea from the south, my mind certainly went back to my school days when I entered a Norwegian fjord for the first time on the troopship Navasa. It was an experience never to be forgotten. I had already seen two Italian battleships in the Great Bitter lake in Egypt, and two French in Singapore, and now we came upon two Japanese ships of that type, but with a huge difference. They were both upside down with their propellers sticking out. Was this due to aerial attack or the Japanese Navy committing a scuttling, we never did find out. It was not until we were actually in the Inland Sea that we were informed we would not be taking off from the carrier after all. The reason given was that the Captain was not prepared to allow any take offs because there was an Admiralty requirement that an escort (rescue) ship had to be in attendance on all such occasions and none was available. Bad planning? It would have been nice to be involved in a full three Squadron Spitfire formation flypast over Hiroshima, but it was not to be. We came ashore at the Iwakuni Naval Air Base on mini floating flat tops which would later ferry all our Spitfires ashore, an undignified form of arrival for the RAF we thought.

The base itself was a shambles as a result of repeated American bombing raids and many accommodation buildings were still without a roof and combined with a late, cold spring after our two years in the tropics did nothing for our morale at all. We still had yet to see a Union Jack, let alone an RAF ensign. We were to spend only one full week at Iwakuni before flying up to our permanent base of RAF Miho, which was located on the northern coast of the same main island of Honshu, more or less facing Korea. No XI Squadron, was commanded by Sqdn Ldr McGregor, known to the officer ranks at least as "Wee" McGregor, due to his diminutive figure. The legendary Sqdn Ldr James (Ginger) Lacey was still at the helm of No 17 Squadron, although he was due to return to the UK within weeks after over three years in the Far East.

It soon became common knowledge that both COs had set their sights on becoming the first pilot to fly a Spitfire in Japan, which led to heightened tension as ground crew made frantic efforts to check out their mounts on day two of our arrival. There was only one runway available for use at Iwakuni, and it was assumed that whoever started to taxi out first would certainly be the winner of the unofficial contest. As the boss of "Legs Eleven" Squadron fired up first and moved off, it seemed certain that he would be first past the post, however, another Spitfire also started to taxi shortly afterwards, but did not follow the one already underway. It was seen to be moving rather rapidly to the opposite end of the strip, surely one of the two pilots had made a mistake as to the runway direction in use and would have to return sheepishly to dispersal? The unthinkable then happened, both Spitfires lined up for departure, facing each other, and started rolling. Everyone stood transfixed, even the Japanese labourers, awaiting what was surely going to be a head on crash with fatal results for both pilots. Suddenly, one Spitfire leapt into the air and passed over the other, still on the runway with just feet to spare, so James Lacey became the very first Spitfire pilot to take one off from Japanese soil. The Japanese had their Kamikaze pilots and now the RAF had pilots who played Russian roulette. I very much doubt if that was what our AOC, AVM "Boy" Bouchier, had in mind when he harangued us in Singapore. The thought of repercussions that would have ensued if the very first two RAF Squadron Commanders ever to be based in Japan had both been killed in such an accident is mind boggling.

However, the sight of what was, for all intents and purposes, a Spitfire, was already a familiar sight over the land of the rising sun long before our arrival I refer to the Royal Navy's Seafires, operating off aircraft carriers. It was the pilot of one of those aircraft who virtually became the last British casualty of WWII when, after surviving a crash landing in Japan, he was put to death between the time of the two atomic bombs and the signing of the Japanese surrender in Tokyo Bay three weeks later. A close run thing with an unhappy ending.

We all had to air test our own particular aircraft before our formation departure to RAF Miho in the North. Needless to say, all headed for Hiroshima, a few miles up the road, to gain an aerial view of what was left of that city, seeing the devastation from the cockpit of a Spitfire was no doubt a unique experience, but also a very sobering one. Surely we had seen the end of world wars for the foreseeable future if one aircraft carrying one bomb could inflict such damage? Basically, that has remained the position over the past 60 years, no matter what anyone else may have thought in that time. Minor wars continue as ever, but the great powers have had a good reason for a pause for thought in their disagreements. The increasing number of states possessing atomic weapons might well change the situation dramatically in the future, but the possession of such weapons will continue to act as some deterrent. A ground tour of Hiroshima only underlined our thoughts, although none was really necessary. The only puzzle was that one or two of the buildings, of modern reinforced construction, had survived the blast. These included the local brewery, but present day atomic weapons are far more powerful than that first bomb, no building, not even a brewery, would now survive if near the epicentre of the blast.

Later, whilst returning to Iwakuni as passengers in the back of a standard British 5 ton lorry we all felt a terrific vibration and a rumbling noise. I thought for a moment that perhaps the engine had given up on us but looking out of the back of the lorry I could see some buildings shaking slightly. My first and, hopefully, last earthquake experience, perhaps the Japanese war gods were not best pleased with the white devils that day.

The only disappointment on our formation flight from Iwakuni to Miho was that our CO, as leader, was the only pilot who had a good view of the Japanese countryside, so intent were the rest of us on keeping station, but we would certainly make up for that later on during solo details.

The airfield at Miho was in a reasonable state, not having suffered as much bomb damage as Iwakuni, for the obvious reason that it's location was further away from the Pacific and, therefore, the American and British Aircraft Carriers. The first week at Miho was largely given over to settling in, but at the end of it No 17 Squadron were to say a sad farewell to their boss, the top scoring Battle of Britain pilot, Squadron Leader James "Ginger" Lacey. The first leg of his journey home to dear old blighty, and his beloved wife Sheila, was due to begin from outside the Officers' Mess, when he would drive his own jeep to the local railway station at Matsue to catch a train to Kure, and then board a troopship. The actual time of departure from the Officers' Mess soon became an open secret on the Station, so a large turn out was a possibility. The Officers' Mess, by the way, was part and parcel of a very large wooden building, which also contained the Sgts' Mess and Station Headquarters. The possibility of a large turn out soon became a reality as it was not only members of No 17 Squadron who wished to bid him farewell, but also most of the rest of the Station, judging by the size of the crowd that gathered. Many of the Japanese civilian workers must have sensed that the event was of high importance as they were also well represented. When the jeep eventually got underway I caught a glimpse of the great man surreptitiously wiping away a tear. Obviously, command of No 17 Squadron, which had an iron gauntlet as it's badge, must have meant a lot to him.

The British Commonwealth area of occupation covered about one third of Honshu and relied heavily on air power as a see and be seen force. This consisted of seven single seat fighter squadrons, plus one transport flight. The Royal Australian Air Force produced nearly half the fighters, with three Mustang squadrons based at Bofu (No 76, 77, 82 Squadrons) an airfield to our south west, forming 81 Wing. As at Miho we had three Spitfire squadrons in No 4 of the Royal Indian Air Force and Nos XI and 17 of the Royal Air Force. The seventh squadron being No 14 of the Royal New Zealand Air Force, flying Corsairs, who shared the Iwakuni base with 1315 flight equipped, mainly, with Dakota transports, plus a few Harvards and Austers for local communication work. The Dakotas were, literally, our lifeline to the outside world as regards mail, running frequent services to and from Hong Kong and Miho.

Being a mere F/Sgt pilot at Miho, who could certainly be spared from flying duties for a couple of days, I was told one morning to pack overnight kit and be ready to board a Dakota that afternoon that would be returning to it's base at Iwakuni. The briefing was short and sweet. No XI Squadron had been informed that it's silver, which had been put into storage on the North West Frontier of India at the outbreak of war, had now arrived at Kure docks but would need an escort before release. That was me. On arrival at Iwakuni, transport would take me to the docks, then by train back to Miho with the crates. A straightforward task, one would have thought, and all went well until I was supervising loading into an old fashioned type guards van. I did not realise that the train was under the command of the American military until a US Army Sergeant, after doing a double take at my RAF uniform, said "Say, what'ya got in them there crates, bud?" I replied that they contained an RAF Squadron's silver, which had been in storage for the duration of the war on the North-West Frontier. His response to that was, "Squadron silver, North west Frontier, that silver rates an armed guard in my book". So it was that I had four rifle toting GIs for company during the journey back. The officers of 'Legs Eleven' were so pleased with the silver that they invited me into their mess that evening for a quick look see. I could well understand their pleasure, as some silver models of bi-planes that No XI had been equipped with in pre-war days looked absolutely magnificent.

I might have forgotten about that trip, except for a remarkable coincidence some 15 years later after leaving Japan. I was then flying

Hastings transport aircraft and although flying hours were plentiful they tended to come in short sharp bursts, which left quite a few days of doing absolutely nothing. It was on one such day that I must have been driven to distraction, because I started to read Air Ministry Orders (AMOs) for the first time in many a day. Imagine my astonishment when I came across one that, freely translated, indicated that No XI Squadron were trying to trace their missing silver which was last known to have been in storage in India at the start of WWII. It so happened that my next transport trip was a day return flight to the very base in Germany that No XI then operated from. On landing, it being lunch time, I made straight for the Officers' Mess and soon tracked down the bachelor Wing Commander now in charge of the Squadron. However, he seemed far more interested in a female school teacher than the ramblings of an obviously deranged trucky pilot. Perhaps it was the Squadron custodian who had framed the AMO without informing his CO?

Before setting sail for Japan, we had managed to obtain a book written by an Englishman who had spent many years in that country at the turn of the century. In it there was one very telling comment which stated that in Japan there were two very distinct races- male and female. This we found to be quite true, the men very much as we had expected them to be, with the females very caring, dedicated workers and, on one occasion, particularly sentimental and emotive. The occasion I have in mind occurred when No 17 Squadron suffered a fatal accident with the death of W/O Grey in an off base Spitfire crash. During breakfast the next morning a No 7 Squadron pilot told us that a party who had arrived to remove the personal effects of W/O Grey could hardly get into his room because it was overflowing with bunches of flowers. It turned out that every single female member of the Sgts' Mess staff had spontaneously brought along a floral tribute. These ladies ranged in age from just out of school to late middle age, and their genuine sorrow was evident.

The younger ones seemed to recover first, and we began to notice that one word would quite often be used depending on who they were serving. In my own case it was always "Butcher San" as a plate was placed in front of me, and other NCOs also collected names. Due to the fact that I had been appointed as a kind of go between for our squadron in dealing with the Japanese labour force allocated to us, I became quite friendly with their English speaking leader. He had been a Professor of English at Tokyo University in his time, so I had no trouble in passing on our requirements and at the same time getting some insight into all things Japanese, including their attitude to the war. This was simply, "If the Emperor says jump, you jump". When I asked him what "Butcher San" meant in Japanese he paused just long enough to arouse suspicion, but that did not last long after he told me that it was a little difficult to give an exact English translation but "son of a prince" was about right. As the chattering and giggling continued whenever "Butcher San" was mentioned, I went back to the well and told the Professor that he had better come clean about it's true meaning. After some thought he came out with it- "Baby Face" was my nickname, not "Son of a prince". Probably better than some of the others were being called was my only consolation. Perhaps I should have left well alone.

Most of our routine flights were patrols of individual prefectures, such as our own Tottori and adjoining Hiroshima, Okeyama and Shimane as well. Most of these patrols were flown in pairs or fours, but very occasionally as singletons. On one such patrol, an American Army Air Force P51 Mustang came alongside my aircraft at a distance of about half a mile and called on the common frequency used by all the occupying air forces to say, "Spitfire over Matsue, this is USAAF P51 (followed by his number), can I formate on you to get a better view. I've never seen a Spitfire before". As soon as I had agreed I wished I hadn't. He got so close I thought he wanted to get into my cockpit. Shortly after, he pulled away a little and called, "How about seeing who is fastest?" Although our Spitfires' top speed was when flying above 20,000', I again agreed, although we were only at a couple of thousand feet or so. He then said, "You say when", meaning when to give full power to the engine. Out of courtesy, I replied "You give the word". "Now", was the split second reply, so he had some initial advantage, but I soon pulled ahead. His last transmission was "Gee, that was really something", and off he went. I would love to have known what tale he had to tell back at his base. He would assume, no doubt, that our Spitfires were still using Merlin engines, like those fitted to his own Mustang, and not the much more powerful Griffon ones used by the British in their latest Mk of the Spitfire.

Our social life was fairly limited but an excellent beach and a small village were well within walking distance, as was a large lake inland, with a long hot summer setting in we made full use of the beach for late afternoon swimming sessions, and longer periods at weekends. We soon got used to the antics of an elderly lady who often appeared, and provided

On patrol over Totorri Prefecture, Japan, April 1946 in No XI Squadron Spitfire TAC/R Mk XIV

she could find a spot that was not within 50' of anyone else, take a dip in the altogether. It was after I had been back in England for a number of years that I bought a book in the "World in Colour" series called "Japan" and read with astonishment that our Miho shoreline got a mention. In that book it states that according to Japanese mythology the beach at Miho was so tempting in the sunshine that one day an angel flew down from heaven to bathe there leaving her feather dress hanging on a pine tree, a fisherman seized it, and the daughter of heaven was unable to fly away. The fisherman, consented to return her dress if she danced for him, it goes on to say that the legend of the feather dress is often enacted at high class weddings to this day. Perhaps the old lady had been enacting it every summers' day for years.

Our local village looked as if nothing had changed much over the years and after making contact with a local shop keeper, who seemed to be open all hours and spoke excellent English, our visit became more frequent and took on a new dimension. He seemed happy to talk about virtually anything with the one exception of his past, so after we got the message the subject was never mentioned thereafter. One offer he made on more than one occasion, however, was that all we had to bring with us on our visits was a towel and then we could all go to the communal village bath house where all villagers, regardless of gender or age, took to the waters completely unclothed. His observation that we would not look out of place gave rise to a few ribald remarks on our way back to camp along the lines that perhaps we British could show the Japs a thing or two after all and please our AOC no end! We never did accept his offer.

Our shopkeeper friend also introduced us to the art of drinking the national brew of Sake which, apparently, had to be within a degree or two of body temperature to taste right. After mixing the spirit with water and another substance, it turned a milky white colour. He was more than generous in providing the rice based drink, so we returned his hospitality in the only way we could think of, and that was by gifts of bars of soap and cigarettes, etc. No way in the world did we regard this as trafficking, it was just mutual gifts on a very small scale, as far as we were concerned. This completed my education in national drinking habits, other than beer, I had noted that the majority of steady drinkers in Southern Africa went for Brandy, Egypt Ousu, India Gin, Malaya Whisky and now Sake in Japan. Gin was my favourite, even to this day.

On the flying side, trade suddenly picked up in June of 1946 when thousands of Korean workers who had been returned to their own country after the Japanese surrender, decided that Japan was a much better place to live and work in than their own country and were making strenuous efforts to return. The one and only method was by sea, by way of anything that came to hand from nothing much more than small fishing boats up to trading junks and inter island cargo ships for the short crossing. All ships were supposed to fly identification flags which were changed at frequent intervals. On our greatly increased number of sea patrols we sometimes spotted ships that flew the wrong flags and, occasionally, flew none at all. There was nothing much that we could do about it except submit a position report on return to base, had higher authority something more drastic in mind? At squadron level we suddenly received orders that patrols would, in future, be fully armed and all guns were to be tested forthwith. No reason was ever given for these orders, but we all set too with a will. In my case, I was given two Spitfires to test on the first day without any specific instructions about where to fire, other than that it would have to be out at sea. About three miles offshore from our bathing beach I had often noticed a lone rock which I thought would prove ideal as a ground target. This rock protrusion was very small, but I did a low level inspection to confirm that the most likely situation existed, that is to say no one was on the rock or near it. Having confirmed that, I carried out a steepish ground attack run and was quite pleased with the results, and that I had picked a specific target rather than random shooting out to sea. The aircraft for my second gun testing flight of the day was not quite ready when I landed back at Miho, so it was about one hour later before my next take off and I thought I would speed things up by going straight in on the rock. The safety catch was off and my thumb on the firing button when I approached the ideal range for firing. As I pressed the button I suddenly spotted a lone figure sitting on the rock fishing. It was both my, and the fisherman's lucky day as one 20mm gun fired and the other did not, which swung the aircraft so much that he was in no danger. I climbed up and circled around and was mighty pleased to see a rowing boat making rapid progress towards the shoreline. The defective gun was soon rectified and I was up and away again very quickly, but not back to the rock this time, or ever again!

Not only was June to prove our best month for flying in Japan, but also very significant for another reason. It had been decided that small groups of other ranks, supervised by an NCO, would spend a week off normal duties in Tokyo. Although it was to be called leave, that name did not quite fit the bill as the accommodation was to be in a British Army enclave in Tokyo, and at least two days of the five in that city would be given over to attending the International War Crimes Tribunal, as official British representatives. Needless to say, I was particularly pleased to be put in charge of the very first party from Miho to make such a memorable visit to the capital city of our recent enemy. After catching a train at Matsue, we headed south to connect with the main South central line which took us through the historic towns and cities of Kobe, Osaka, Nagoya and Yokohama, before reaching our destination of Tokyo. The mainline stretch was a real eye opener in that the rail system was far in advance of anything yet achieved in the UK. It was very fast, clean and comfortable, with American type sleeping accommodation for all, with one long corridor and two tier bunks on each side. One of the finest sights I ever saw from a train window was Mount Fuji, with its peak pointing through an early morning cloud layer.

Our base in Tokyo was with the "Dorsets", at their occupied barracks at Risue, which was on a commuter line, just minutes from the city centre. The attendance at the war crimes trial was very interesting, being conducted in English with all the accused sitting impassively with headsets on listening to the Japanese translations. On both days, a prisoner seated directly behind Tojo, the Japanese war minister and number one criminal, leaned forward and slapped Tojo on his bald head. As no one took the slightest bit of notice, including Tojo himself, it must have been a regular occurrence. We managed a few hours looking around the city centre after the trial was adjourned for the day, and made full use of the remaining free days at our disposal. On two of them we fell in with an American Army private who claimed that he was also on a spot of leave, or Furlough, as he called it. We found it very difficult to come to terms with the fact that he had his own Jeep and insisted on driving our party here, there and everywhere. The Emperor's own building, looking like a massive shrine with a moat, was very impressive, as was the Japanese Parliament, or Diet, which was very modern, having been built in 1936 and escaping bomb damage during the war. We were taken aback that on showing interest in that building we were suddenly besieged by a bevy of reporters, two of whom spoke excellent English. After giving us a conducted tour of their Parliament, which was actually in session, they asked us how it compared with the British system. We had to admit that it looked very much like our own Westminster House of Commons. In fact, privately, we were very surprised that they also seemed to have an opposition with the nearest thing to a shouting match that one could get to in the Orient going on at the time of our visit.

The return rail journey to our Miho base was just as pleasant and efficient as the outbound one, which left a permanent impression of how things should be carried out, plus a lingering dissatisfaction with British railways. On return I was to receive the one and only complaint from our tame Japanese professor. Apparently, one of our airmen had adopted a very truculent attitude towards the local labour force, right from the start, and during the week that I had been away he had even threatened physical violence. That was the very last thing we needed, as everything up to now had worked out far better than expected. When I caught up with him he admitted all and tried to plead a case of mitigation in that his sister, a nurse, had been raped in Hong Kong by the Japanese. I explained that he was not in a position, like the rest of us, to act as judge and jury in any shape or form, and, from what I had seen in Tokyo the previous week, every effort was being made to bring all war criminals to justice. This did not pacify him in the least and he went on to say what I was already thinking, that it would be most unlikely that the individual responsible for the outrage against his sister would be identifiable four years later. However, his attitude continued to be such that I was forced to issue verbal orders that, if broken, would certainly lead to charges being brought against him, that seemed to calm him down, for the time being at least.

One strange full squadron formation flight occurred during this period when we were tasked with carrying out a dummy dive bombing attack on HMS Bermuda, a Royal Navy Cruiser, operating in the Inland Sea. That would have been straight forward enough, but why on earth was it that we had to formate, line astern, off the New Zealand Corsair Squadron from Iwakuni, with one of the Australian Mustang squadrons from Bofu formatting in line astern to us for the approach to the target area? The Corsairs had played their part well during the war however we found that their normal cruise speed was so low that we in the Spitfires had to induce extra drag to keep a reasonable amount of throttle on for formation flying. This extra drag was provided by opening our twin radiator shutters. Although the attack was carried out successfully by each squadron in turn, this would not have been a good idea in a war situation. Three squadrons of any one particular type attacking at the same time would have been a better bet. Quite a few RN cruisers with names starting with the letter B were around at that time, so it seems that it is highly likely that HMS Belfast, now permanently moored in the Thames at Tower Bridge, was a sister ship to the Bermuda.

Another mass formation that comes to mind took place when our Wing Commander Flying, a post that I had not previously come across, decided to lead a full wing show of strength over Kure, which went off quite well, until the landing back at base, when it took 30 minutes to land the 32 Spitfires that had taken part, which did not best please W C Topham DSO DFC, who was related to the Aintree race course family. Having flown No 2 to the Wing Leader and, therefore, second to land, I had become a spectator, not all that far away from our leader. Some of the aircraft had gone around several times because aircraft landing ahead had taken their time in clearing the runway.

Another formation trip over Kure was a very tragic affair indeed. It was over the British War Graves Cemetery in that city at the time of the internment of one of our most popular officers. Flying Officer O'Conner Quick, a born and bred Rhodesian from Bulawayo, who had joined No XI Squadron from No 1315 flight at Iwakuni just two months before his untimely death. He had fallen foul of a disease called Japanese encephalitis and from feeling unwell one morning he was to die within 48 hours. In the intervening period he was flown by Dakota to the Military Hospital at Iwakuni. It was a sad way to earn a compliment, but our new Flight Commander, Flight Lieutenant Ian Forbes DFC said, he had heard that I was quite a good formation pilot and I would be his No 2 in the five ship formation that he would lead on the flypast of the funeral. The jabs that we all received later from our resident Princess Mary's Nursing Service Nurse, to counter that nasty illness, knocked us all for six.

August of 1946 proved to be a disaster as regards flying, with non-stop interruptions for one thing or another. We had to contend with both an aviation fuel shortage followed later with fuel contamination which entailed draining all aircraft fuel tanks for cleaning, a couple of typhoon warnings which meant dismantling our tented flight office accommodation and re-erecting same when the predicted storms failed to appear and, most annoying of all, the breakdown of our one and only fire tender on at least two occasions. Why on earth we did not have a back up was beyond our comprehension. The Wing Commander flying took advantage of one of those non-flying days to hold a wing parade on the aircraft parking area in front of the hangars and it turned out to be one of the biggest shambles of all time as regards parades it was utterly embarrassing, raw recruits could have done better. On another non-flying day somebody came up with a much better way of keeping up morale, it was a full day out to a fishing village called Mihonoseki, which boasted one of the best Shinto shrines in the prefecture. It was after taking a good look around the shrine that we were nearly conned by a very old shrew of a woman who was mad keen on selling us fans. When fully deployed they showed a magnificent view of Mount Fuji, just as I had seen from the Tokyo bound train, but as she very slowly closed the fan she was displaying it began to change from Mount Fuji to one of the most obscene figures one could ever imagine. Looking at our stunned faces she went into shrieks of laughter, bordering on hysteria. Not content with that, she then produced a small drinking glass and filled it with what looked like Sake, and invited one of our group to drink up, which he did in fine wild west style. It was only when the old girl pointed to the bottom of the glass that all was revealed- another obscene figure. Our professor back at base sheepishly confirmed that he had come across both in his time, but talked more about the drinking glass than the fan. He said the Japanese, like the British, did not like to see empty glasses and normally the scene would have been of a temple or mountain, and not obscene at all, but it became visible when the glass was empty of it's milky water/Sake, the hostess would quickly top up glasses when noticing images appearing. This explained everything to a certain degree. It was during this conversation that I finally asked him why he had often mentioned that the Japanese did not care much about the western habit of some men wearing moustaches. It appeared that in Japan it was deemed that men who think that they are good looking grow them to try and make themselves look better still. An interesting theory, when you come to think about it!

The overseas tours for the RAF had, since the end of the war, gradually reduced to 3 1/2 years from the pre-war ones of six or seven, and now it was being brought down to 3 years from setting sail to landing back in the UK. In theory, pilots like myself, who had left the UK for their training in Southern Africa in 1943 would be home in time for Christmas at the latest. In fact, I was to beat the deadline by six weeks, or so, due to the fact that not many troopships actually made it out to Japan, usually returning to the UK from the Middle East, Bombay or Singapore.

One final event before leaving Miho and No XI Squadron, was a message from the professor that two of the elderly bat women would consider it a great honour if we departing NCOs would grace one of their humble homes with an evening visit. The professor also added that if we accepted he would also be there for interpretations. Before accepting, I asked him would our visit cause the ladies any trouble with the rest of the village. He reassured me that although there would be jealousy, there would be no trouble. It turned out to be a jolly evening with all sitting around on the floor minus shoes, drinking Sake in a very relaxed atmosphere. Although since leaving England most of us had served in six or seven different countries, it was only in Southern Rhodesia, and now Japan, that we had been entertained in a private house.

The end of our time in Miho came quite suddenly when, about 8 NCO pilots, four from each RAF Squadron, plus others, were told that we would be leaving for the transit camp at Kure docks within the week. Both Squadrons would be left with less than 10 pilots each, including their respective COs but, apparently, the 3 year rule for overseas service was sacrosanct. The usual send off from outside SHQ was a mini version of Ginger Lacey's, with all Mess staff and sundry others waving farewells.

On arrival at Kure we were given the name of the troopship that we would be taking passage all the way back to the UK, it was to be the Mataroa, a pre-war meat ship on the New Zealand run. We were given not only a departure date and time, but the added snippet that our voyage would be one day longer than first expected because our first port of call would be Shanghai, and not Singapore, as usual. This was to pick up a WAAF F/Sgt, and a few other personnel from the staging post there who were tour ex. This suited us fine, Shanghai being one of the best known ports in the world at that time. This type of information was in stark contrast to the cloak and dagger nonsense of WWII when, on occasions, Khaki drill had been issued to aircrew going to Canada, and not the tropics, just to fool the enemy. Even in peace time, things can go astray and our ship arrived 24 hours late. The first thing we noticed as we boarded was a F/Sgt WAAF leaning over the ship's rails. Yes, there had been a change of plan and we would not now be seeing China after all. The advanced notice of which ship we would be returning in proved to be very useful as it gave us time to write to England with all the details. At that time the Daily Express printed lists of all returning troopships with the expected port of disembarkation. This was updated during the voyage and was a real morale booster for families awaiting the return of husbands, sons or even daughters.

The Mataroa was a vast improvement on the Orbita that we had left the UK on, mainly due to the fact that we were now NCOs and treated accordingly. No hammocks this time, but bunks, albeit stacked three or four upwards, and ample room at mess tables. This accommodation was in one of the pre-war meat holds, with the bonus being that the temperature was kept to a steady level, even in the tropics. A small part of a particular mess deck had been partitioned off by way of slung ropes, with blankets hanging down to ensure some kind of privacy. Behind these makeshift curtains, there lived for the first leg of our voyage as far as Singapore, 20 or so Japanese male civilians who were never to be seen on deck, even to take exercise. It soon became known that they were all from the legal world of Japan on their way to do what they could in the defence of their fellow countrymen standing trial for war crimes in Singapore. No sooner had we dropped anchor in Singapore Roads than a special launch came alongside to disembark these gentlemen and, as we viewed the proceedings, we were all surprised that every single one of them stood facing our ship, bowing continuously as the launch pulled away. It felt strange to be back in Singapore, being so close, yet so far, from the various service clubs that we used to haunt, but without any chance of being allowed ashore.

Heading South from Japan the ship had been far from full but that was all to change from now on. At our SNCO level we had a large influx of naval Chief Petty Officers (CPOs) from the Royal Navy's Pacific Fleet. A few that we became friendly with had served on a submarine depot ship by the name of HMS Maidstone, which had been based in Eastern Australia for some time. They were certainly going to miss their rum ration for the next five weeks, if nothing else. Their tales of a submariner's life as given to them from various ship's crews that they serviced enthralled us for many hours during the voyage. I have not met many pilots who would go down in a sub for 10 minutes, let alone weeks at a time against the enemy.

The second stage of our voyage home was probably the longest sector: Singapore to Aden direct, and also particularly boring with very little sign of land or other ships, but at least we were heading in the right direction. The sight of Aden from the sea was by now, almost three years after our wartime approach, almost a distant memory for people of our young-ish age. This time, it was not only the ship that was to take on fuel, because a padre travelling with us was proud of the fact that he had managed to arrange a run ashore for all passengers. This was great news, particularly so because we had on board a pre-war SNCO who had served some time there and was more than happy to act as a guide around the few square miles of this barren outpost of Empire. No sooner had we landed from our tender than he had whistled up a taxi and shouted at the driver "Crater", it was only a short ride into the middle of what was a long extinct volcano, hence it's name. On arrival at his well remembered drinking den, he refused to pay the Arab driver, which we thought was asking for trouble, however he told him he would get more than double the normal rate after he had reported back 5 hours hence, it was certainly one way of making sure of returning to the quay in time for boarding. It worked perfectly, apart from the actual boarding.

We had been allowed all of six hours ashore, and with five of them taken up with steady drinking of bottled beer after a three week period of enforced abstinence, it was not everyone who made steady progress up the ship's steep gangway after leaving the tender. In fact two of our group started pushing and pulling which ended in several over-balancing over the safety rail and falling into the water about 20' below. They were soon picked up by the tender, and very few people even saw the incident except, of course, the padre, who up until that point had quite a smile of satisfaction on his face as he welcomed his captive flock back on board.

The short third leg up the Red Sea was pleasant enough in dead calm conditions. After arriving at Suez, little seemed to have changed, with one or two ships at anchor, either awaiting northbound entry to the canal or picking up extra supplies after exiting southbound. Small RAF picket boats were still scurrying about between ships and shore, and when an airman crewing a picket came aboard Mataroa from another ship, I asked him if the southbound ship he had just left was bound for Bombay or Singapore. "Neither, Flight", was his crisp reply, "Durban in fact".

"Durban", I replied, with some questioning in my voice. "I thought that all South Africans would be home by now". "Yes they are, cleared off within weeks of the war ending. No, this lot are off to re-open training schools in Rhodesia, even some lads from here have been roped in to join 'em, and they don't like it one little bit. Thought they were going home, didn't they". Was I going mad, I thought my flying days would be over when I arrived in England, and I might have to revert to my ground trade for the remainder of my RAF service, such was the surplus of aircrew at war's end. However, if the RAF's future policy was to be training x number of pilots per year to keep an even age spread surely they could all have been catered for in the UK, with the large number of airfields now available? This was my very first taste of the barking madness that swept through the RAF for the first decade post WWII.

Arab traders, who had been well known over the years by generations of British servicemen for their crafty trading, were also now aboard, trying to drive hard bargains, including money exchanges. Were the passengers on our ship going to be the first ever to turn the tables on them? Just before we left Japan, a new set of Yen bank notes had been issued and we had been told that any still in our possession were now null and void. However, most of us had retained our old notes as souvenirs and one chap thought he would try it on. After the Arab had consulted his little book, he duly handed over some sterling, no doubt well below the going rate, that opened the flood gates and for the first time the boot was on the other foot.

Sailing up the Suez Canal brought back many memories, particularly so as we made the mandatory stop in the Great Bitter Lake, near to our Spitfire training base of RAF Fayid. No Italian battleships this time having, in all probability, returned to their own fleet.

The fourth and final leg of our 41 days on the Mataroa was to be a non stop passage right back to Southampton from Port Said. The first sighting of England was the Isle of Wight as we made what seemed slow progress towards Southampton docks. Moored just opposite our eventual berth was that old faithful, the four funneled Mauritania, nice to know she had survived the war. The disembarkation was very slick indeed, mainly due to the fact that all passengers had been invited to retrieve their deep sea baggage from a forward hold the day before docking. For the RAF, a special train had been laid on to take us to RAF Burtonwood, a transit camp near Warrington, which was only thirty miles or so from my home town of Southport.

Within minutes of clearing the built up area of Southampton a whistling noise was heard in the sky and we all rushed to the train windows just in time to catch sight, for our very first time, a jet propelled aircraft. It was a twin boomed Vampire, an aircraft which was to play such an important part in my life in future years. Burtonwood were also on the ball and the very next day after arrival we were on our way home for four weeks leave and, for most of us, it was the parting of the ways. Being a serving airman and contracted until the age of 30 I was put at the disposal of the then Fighter Command at RAF Bentley Priory, which looked rather promising in that it just might mean a flying posting with a fighter squadron after all. However, I would not know my future for certain for another month.

The journey home from Warrington took only an hour or so, which led to a mid afternoon trudge from Ainsdale station with a kitbag over one shoulder and a suitcase in the other hand. Passing a local church on the way, and noting a wedding crowd gathered outside, I thought it was an excuse to take a short breather and see if it was one of my school mates who had taken the plunge. It was not the bridegroom that I instantly recognised but the bride. It was a younger sister of our local barber, called Forshaw, and I got the sweetest of smiles from young Alice as she settled into the bridal car. A very nice start to my homecoming.

I discovered virtually all my school friends had survived the war, including Les Blunt who had completed a tour of bomber operations as a Flight Engineer, which made him a very lucky chap indeed. At school he had stated a preference for the Merchant Navy, so there had been a change of plan along the way.

CHAPTER 14
Acklington, towing targets and meeting Betty

The four weeks at home soon slipped away, and now it was time to make my way down to Bentley Priory for an interview regarding my immediate future. A squadron leader gave a quick review of the situation, which indicated that for officers in the day fighter world, a Squadron posting could be guaranteed, but there was a surplus of NCO pilots at the present time, although the situation was changing by the minute with demobilization still in full swing. He went on to say that as I was a regular airman with still some time to serve he could arrange a posting to the German island of Sylt to

Betty, taken shortly before we met

tow targets at an armament practice camp. My mind went into overdrive, it would be a double whammies to have served in the occupation of both Japan and Germany, but it would also commit me to another three full years overseas, and I might miss out on a squadron posting during that time. I asked, rather tentatively, if any similar posting in the UK was available. He said he fully understood my reluctance to go overseas again so soon and he would fit me in at Accrington which, being near my home, suited me fine. It was after a clerk started filling in a rail warrant from Kings Cross that I

Miles Master

interjected and said shouldn't that be Euston, that I eventually found out that Kings Cross was correct and I was going to No 2 APS at Acklington, Northumberland. It was to be an ideal posting, in the event, in that I was to meet my wife to be there, Miss Betty Elliott, who shot me down in flames in more ways than one, but more of that to come.

APSs were a way of life for pre-war fighter squadrons when they held annual camps away from their normal base stations to indulge in intensive air firing against both live targets, in the form of towed drogues, or flags

Miles Martinet

and air to ground attacks against fixed targets on sectioned off beaches. For obvious reasons, the closer to the sea for air to air firing and it's shoreline for ground targets the better. The average climactic conditions for given areas was also another factor in the siting of these stations, with the east coast normally being the preferred location. In that context, RAF Acklington was an obvious choice for an APS. During WWII it had been a base for both day and night fighter squadrons defending the north east of England, and being located close to Durridge Bay was ideal for firing practice with it's two headlands impossible to misidentify. The aircraft in use for target towing was the Miles Martinet, but because no dual control versions of that type had ever been built, a couple of Miles Masters were used for dual checks prior to going solo on that type. In the event, the check on the Master only lasted 30 mins, followed by 30 mins solo and then it was off on the Martinet.

Both types proved to be remarkably easy to fly with very little swing on take off or landing compared with the Harvard. I soon found out that when towing a Drouge, the drag was such that fairly high power settings were the norm which, in turn, led to high cylinder head temperatures that required the engine gills to be opened up accordingly. That was also a drag inducing device, so it became a mini vicious circle that required a fine balancing act on the part of the pilot. The Mercury engine did not like constant high power settings one little bit and, with details of up to two hours or so, the windscreens were often spattered in engine oil droplets which reduced forward visibility no end. At least one pilot resorted to using a small stick, covered in four by two, well known in the rifle world as cloth for cleaning gun barrels, and, after reducing speed drastically and opening his cockpit hood, cleared a small patch of Windscreen before landing. The drouge operator in the back seat of the Martinet was, more often than not, an aircrew SNCO awaiting demob, with almost all of them having flown as gunners in Bomber Command. Some had actually spent time in POW camps in Germany, so it was not all that surprising that they lived life to the full when off duty. As is usual in such cases, the other side of the coin was that when airborne they were highly professional at all times. Their job in life was to launch the drogue after the aircraft had been levelled off at the required height for the detail, the pilot would, by that time, have reduced speed to a safe minimum after which the operator would gradually reel out the cable to about 1,000' astern. The maximum cable length carried was 7,000', but that was used only for ack ack firing. The operator was invaluable in keeping a good look out and informing the pilot if any attacking aircraft did not conform to the rules in breaking away after reaching the 30° angle off line during a firing run. Some time later, when Tempest fighter aircraft had replaced Martinets for towing duties, and carried only a pilot, an attacking pilot at Sylt was so carried away during one such run that he managed to score a few hits on the towing aircraft, and as both pilots were members of the Sgts' Mess, there was quite a punch up later that evening. After the firing session the Drouge would be wound in to about 20' or 30' astern, and taken back to base where the operator would sever the cable during a low level run across the dropping zone on the airfield. This saved the cable and drouge getting tangled up together during drops.

Squadrons came and went, and no two seemed alike, especially off duty. I seem to remember that it was No 92 which decided that all their pilots, officers and NCOs would wear bowler hats with civilian clothes. I don't know if this was a reaction to the RAF reverting to the pre-war tradition that required all officers to wear some form of headdress when in mufti. Another squadron thought it was the done thing for their pilots to own an Alsatian dog each. With all Squadrons having more pilots than aircraft, some of those travelling to Acklington by road bought their pets with them which caused quite a few problems during their visit.

The towing of targets in itself would have become particularly boring if there had not been the odd distractions, and they seemed to turn up at regular intervals. One being to use the Master, in addition to dual checks, for air to ground firing practice by staff pilots, this proved highly popular and was a type of flying I always relished, despite my let off in Japan.

Christmas leave was soon upon us, and with Acklington being a non-oprational station, virtually all staff aircrew managed two weeks away from it all, never realising what awaited our return. The worst winter of the century was about to break, which prevented any flying until late in January of 1947. Most of our time was spent out on the runways, trying to clear away the snow, no sooner had we made a little progress then down it came again. A rum ration was provided in both the mornings and afternoons, which just managed to keep us going in the amazingly low temperatures, with a wind chill factor of goodness knows what. After a few days we noticed that it was always the senior air traffic control officer (SATCO) who appeared with the rum and also partook of a wee dram himself with we labourers, but with about five different gangs at work we couldn't help but admire his stamina! It was not only the clearing of snow that we grounded aircrew were employed on, because, although we were surrounded with coal mines, our station stocks of that indispensable commodity were running down rapidly due to most roads being impassable for miles around. A chap in our group, with a vast amount of local knowledge, opined that if we opened up the short back road to our nearest beach we would find plenty of coal for the taking. In fact, many locals had never bought coal in their lives. Not far out to sea a coal seam had been uncovered by tidal action over the years and during stormy weather a fair amount of coal was washed ashore in the bay. It proved to be a very productive week indeed and we managed to supply enough of the black stuff to keep the station going until official supplies arrived.

After a very short spell of flying, the storms struck again and it was back to the old routine. During one short break, some Vampire aircraft had arrived and it was one of their pilots who had a brilliant idea. If we could clear two small tracks, that fitted the Vampires' wheel base, out to and along the main runway he could start up and blow away the snow with his jet exhaust. Not only did it blow the snow straight backwards, but also melted it so that shortly afterwards, in sub zero temperatures, it formed a solid sheet of ice several inches thick. This took some weeks to melt after the thaw had arrived and I think we were the last RAF airfield in England to resume normal operations. History books tell us that the idea had some merit in that at another station a Vampire Goblin engine had been used for that purpose, but not pointing downwards and backwards as fitted to the Vampire. In fact, it was fitted to a contraption towed by a lorry, and on a swivel which allowed it to be swung from side to side to blast the snow/ water off the sides of runways before it re-froze. It had proved to be most effective and full marks to whoever had thought of that one. Even after the weather had improved enough for us on the coastal plains to start flying again, the villages in the North Pennines and Cheviots were still taking a battering from the elements, with many still cut off by road, and their cattle starving. So it came to pass that the Martinet was put to a use that even it's designer would never have dreamt of. With a big aperture in the floor for the releasing of drouges, why not drop bales of hay out of it? Our contribution was a drop in the ocean with the finding of any particular village difficult in snow storms, let alone Farmer Bloggs' farm after his plea for special attention.

Our social life had gone on apace and on two occasions after we had drunk the Sgts' Mess cellar dry, we still got by. A rail branch line used for colliery traffic only, passed through Acklington airfield to a coal pit near the coastline, skirting the village of Broomhill on it's way. Right next to the line in that village stood a public house officially named "The Greyhound", but known to all the locals and the RAF as "The Trap". We soon discovered that although the rail lines were often under about three feet of snow, the higher embankments had been kept clear by the high winds, so walking the two miles or so to that pub presented no real problems. The landlord and landlady, being short of their normal passing trade, were more than happy to serve our needs, and with the threat of the local bobby appearing from the next village just after closing time, now virtually null and void, we had quite a few late night sessions there.

Every now and again during that dreadful winter, the weather relented long enough for the roads to be cleared and it was during these random spells that food supplies and mail arrived so, in those respects at least, all was not lost. The spells of improving weather became more and more frequent and eventually one person in particular was welcomed back with open arms. She was Gladys Parker of Ashington who managed the station cinema which made her very popular with the troops. For NCO Aircrew, however, going to the cinema on or off base was not really our scene. As Gladys was an honorary member of the Sgt's mess we often met her socially when her chores for the evening were over. One night she suggested inviting two of her girlfriends to the mess for a few drinks. We all agreed this was a good idea, so Gladys was told to go ahead and arrange a date. She chose a certain Sunday evening which suited most of our NCO tug pilots and rear crew operators as many of us would be attending a wedding on the Saturday of one of our most senior NCO pilots.

Warrant Officer 'Taff' Jones was to marry a charming young WAAF from the station who came from the Newcastle area. Taff had been a Typhoon pilot in Normandy, and, therefore, was very lucky to have survived the war. I well remember many of the guests attending from our towing flight, not least another Warrant Officer Pilot called 'Wacko' Cox, who was always leading the charge when we were off duty. He had flown a full tour as an air gunner before conversion to piloting. Like myself, he became a long serving member of the RAF and I last saw 'Wacko' as a Commissioned Air Traffic Control Officer at RAF Abingdon in the mid sixties. Our reunion turned out to be quite an occasion. Yet another ex Typhoon/Tempest pilot in our group attending Taff's wedding was 'Fireman' Jack Brannon, who acquired his nickname not only from the fact that he had served in the Tyneside Fire Brigade before joining the

RAF, but also for his propensity for demonstrating the Fireman's lift on any ususpecting person, be it male or female, after he had a few drinks.

Although we should have returned to camp late that Saturday night after the wedding, it was almost 24 hours later that we eventually staggered in the mess. The hospitality and generosity of the people from the Tyne area is well known and the brides' family insisted we stay overnight for an extra day of celebrations. Gladys and her guests for the evening were already installed when our group burst through the ante room door. The ladies could not completely hide expressions of something between curiosity and surprise. We must, I admit have looked a sorry bunch after almost 3 days of drinking and without a great deal of sleep. Some inmates of the mess thought it was most unlikely that any of us would make a lasting impression on our young guests, who were very good looking and well dressed. Perhaps they had accepted Gladys' invitation out of pure curiosity, having probably heard some strange stories from their hostess.

It was about a week before the visitation that Gladys had been present when, even by our standards things got out of control. One of our rear crew members was not only the proud possessor of a high powered motorbike, but had actually been a wall of death rider pre war, and decided to give us a demonstration of his abilities. After all furnishings had been piled up in the centre of the ante room he roared around on his bike at quite a remarkable speed for the space available, while the rest of us cowered in the four corners of the fume filled room. It was during this demonstration that an immaculately dressed warrant officer entered the room. He had just been posted in to take over the post of station warrant officer (SWO) and therefore, in charge of all discipline on the camp. His face was quite a picture, and it was not improved when a civilian from the works and bricks department, who lived in the mess, asked him if he had a problem, "Had he never seen bike racing in a mess before?"

To go back to our retreat from Taff's wedding reception and its aftermath, I had eventually slumped in a chair at the far end of the ante-room away from the bar when I caught sight of one of the guests who was a real stunner, I thought I would chance my arm and wander over. Gladys was on hand to make the introductions to Miss Betty Elliott and her life long friend Isabel Reid. Betty and I seemed to get on quite well together for a first meeting. She seemed quite interested in what aircraft types I had flown, which was not always the case in post war England. When I proudly said Spitfires, in the far east. I was startled when she said, "I don't suppose they were fitted with gyro gunsights out there were they?"

"In fact," I was quick to reply, "I was on the first unit in India to fly Spitfires with them fitted." Again I was surprised when Betty said, "In that case you may have used a gunsight that I had tested." It transpired that Miss Betty Elliott and now my wife of 56 years standing. Had, during WWII, been an Inspector of Gyro Gunsights with the firm of Reyrolles who had made the gun sights for the RAF. So began our courtship. I did eventually persuade Betty to enter The Trap Inn at Broomhill, her first visit to a pub! During and after the war her parents had forbidden her from ever entering a pub. She did confess to me later however that on occasions she had been entertained in the Cocktail Bar at the Eldon Grill, Newcastle. Most probably by aircrew who were not NCOs!

It was not all beer and skittles, of course, and with the weather improving by the day, our flying hours increased dramatically. It was on one towing trip for air to air firing that I actually saw the wake of bullets disappearing into the distance. I thought it must have been a one off with the position of the sun, humidity on the day, and the point at which the attacking pilot had stopped firing, which had given rise to the sighting. Some years later, when I had taken up long range rifle shooting as a hobby, I found it was all to do with eye level. Over ranges of 400 yards or more, if you sat on an ammo box behind somebody firing, and moved your head up and down, you would eventually find the eye level that coincided with the zenith of the bullet's trajectory and see the supersonic bow wave before it dipped down out of sight towards the target. Over the years I have often wondered if what I saw on the range at Acklington indicated that the bullets had been far too close for comfort.

During the Spring of 1947, two one off trips came my way in quick succession, and I mention them because I thought it very strange at the time that I should be collecting an extra Martinet for the Station one minute and taking another one away for scrap the next, both trips proved to be of interest for very different reasons. The first flight was as a passenger in the Station's Airspeed Oxford, with the OC flying at the controls, for the short hop across the high ground between Northumberland and Cumberland, to land at the MU at RAF Kirkbride. As the Oxford circled around for the landing, I could hardly take it all in. Below were hundreds of aircraft awaiting their fate, parked in every conceivable piece of land and some even on fields that had obviously belonged to the local farmers until recent times. After taxying towards the control tower and stopping, with the engines still running, I was given the thumbs up to vacate the aircraft. The boss must have had more important things to do back at base than hang around awaiting my own departure. I managed to splutter, "what if the Martinet is not ready, Sir?" "I'm sure they can produce another one from that lot" was Sir's riposte, but he did add an afterthought which was, "don't forget it must be one with low hours". So the cat was out of the bag. Why should Acklington lose a Martinet while it was on a major inspection when many unused ones were still available? A more likely explanation, as it later turned out, was that OC Flying was one of the few who already knew that the days of the Martinet were numbered, for towing air to air targets for fighter aircraft at least. This was due to it's low speed in the jet age that had already dawned for fighter squadrons. In fact, Acklington was to use high speed Tempests towing unmanned gliders in the not too distant future.

As Acklington's Martinet was not yet ready and the concept of 'taking another away" was just not on as far as Kirkbride were concerned, even if it meant me having to stay the night. It was a tempting thought, even though I hadn't brought any night stopping kit with me. The delay was to last about three hours, but in the end I wished it had been longer because I was given carte blanche to poke my nose into any corner of their massive aircraft graveyard. Some of the aircraft types, particularly American ones, I had never set eyes on before, and I soon felt like a small boy in a sweet shop. I well remember clambering up into the cockpit of a Mitchell bomber only to be confronted by a Mrs Blackbird sitting on her nest, in the top area of the control column. She cocked her head and gave me a look which seemed to say "and what do you want"? I beat a hasty retreat, after all there were hundreds of other aircraft to view.

Shortly after that lovely away day, I was to take a Martinet to an MU at RAF Shawbury, in Salop, for scrapping. "Wacco" Cox was to fly down in another Martinet and I would return as his passenger in the rear crew position. Civil aviation had not yet recovered from the war years, so we both just drew a straight line on our maps and off we went. The flying conditions could not have been better with superb visibility throughout. The route took us more or less over Manchester and then towards the famous Runcorn suspension bridge over the Mersey, with Burtonwood Camp, where I had spent my first night back in the UK a few months ago, within sight. The landing stage of Liverpool waterfront was also visible, from where I had embarked for South Africa, three years prior to that. The idyllic situation was too good to last, and it was about 10 miles after passing the Manchester ship canal that the engine started playing up. A bit of rough running to start with, followed by the odd backfire which increased in frequency and intensity. It soon became a case of "so near yet so far" as I looked around for a suitable field for a precautionary landing. However, in the distance the unmistakable shape of an airfield came into view and, with a quick check of my map, I concluded that it must be the abandoned airfield of Tilstock, only about fifteen miles short of Shawbury, my destination. The devil was beginning to drive now, but with a reduction in power, which in itself meant a slow descent, the engine seemed happier with itself, but not so on the few occasions that I tried normal cruise power again. Tilstock was getting ever closer and, with a slow descent, well within reach, so I radioed "Wacco" Cox, in the other aircraft, to request he inform Shawbury of my intention to make a landing at Tilstock. The landing was uneventful, but with a completely deserted airfield what was my next move I asked myself? Stay with the aircraft, or make off to the nearest house that might, or might not, have a telephone? The situation became academic with the high speed arrival, down the runway I had just landed on, of four army officers in a Land Rover. They were more than helpful, and having both seen my descent, and heard the coughing engine, guessed that it was more than likely that I would be putting down on Tilstock old airfield. I now had to stay put with my aircraft after the Army officers said they would contact RAF Shawbury by way of the nearest phone, to inform them that both I and the Martinet were safe and well. It seemed to be no time at all before a civilian team from the MU arrived and, after I had asked if they intended to fix the engine, they declared that it was not worth the effort. All they intended to do was take the wings off and then load the lot onto a Queen Mary type lorry. It turned out that the propeller might be of some use later, but the engine would be sent off to the local scrap metal merchant and the wooden fuselage and wings burnt. A small van soon followed to take me to Shawbury and the waiting "Wacco" Cox and his Martinet. Unlike the RAF of the 1950s and ever since, no pilot's report was required about my precautionary landing, and the incident hardly got a mention back at base.

CHAPTER 15
Horsham-St-Faith's and Oxfords

I think the Sqdn Ldr who had interviewed returning fighter pilots from overseas at Bentley Priory, to whom I had requested a Squadron posting, must have put my name on a waiting list, because I received a posting to No 64 Squadron at RAF Linton-on-Ouse to fly Hornets in the early summer of 1947. It was sad to be leaving RAF Acklington, especially after meeting my future wife, Betty, but with the main east coast rail line passing through York and Morpeth, her local village, it seemed at the time that we could still meet most weekends. However, after arrival at Linton the first thing I heard was that with the Squadron Mosquito being off line, awaiting spares, it might be some time before I could be given a twin engined conversion course which was a pre-requisite for the flying of the D H Hornet which, like the Spitfire and Martinet, did not have a dual control version. After my experience of seeing hundreds of virtually unused aircraft at both Kirkbride and Shawbury I thought to myself "why on earth don't they get another dual control Mosquito from an MU somewhere". When I mentioned the concept to one of the senior pilots on the Squadron, I was told, quite firmly, that they had already tried and found out that dual Mossies were in very short supply. I found it very difficult to accept that situation at the time, but a book "Aircraft of the Royal Air Force since 1918" records that the Mosquito trainers, and a night fighter version, were just about the only two British built wartime aircraft ever to be put back into production after the end of the hostilities, such was the shortage that had developed by 1947. Some units in the post war chaos could have too many pilots on strength one day and, about a month or so later, suffer a shortage due to the demobilization programme, and it was because of that situation that I never managed to fly the fastest piston engined fighter that the RAF ever operated.

After hanging around Linton-on-Ouse for a couple of weeks or so without any sign of the Squadron Mosquito becoming serviceable, I was on the move again to plug a gap on No 695 Squadron, based at RAF Horsham St Faith's, on the outskirts of Norwich. Before leaving Linton-on-Ouse, the CO, a Sqdn Ldr Shaw gave me a short interview to explain the situation in detail and expressed the hope that I would return to the day fighter world one day, but it was not to be. It was well known on No 64 Squadron that Sqdn Ldr Shaw had survived all of WWII in the service, and having also been involved in the Spanish Civil War as a pilot in the mid to late 1930s, was a very experienced pilot. However, no one seemed to know which side he had flown with in Spain! On leaving Linton it was goodbye to two former NCO pilots who I had known on No XI Squadron in Japan and had preceded me back to the UK. One "Junior" Everitt became, after demob, a well known dentist in nearby York, and the other, Leo Hook, stayed on in the RAF, but it was to be 30 odd years later before our paths crossed again when I landed the RAF's BBMF Lancaster at Linton for a Canadian Squadron reunion. Leo, by that time, was the station's chief ground instructor, after a long and varied flying career, which had included experimental flying at Boscombe Down. He also took root in York after demob.

Although Norwich was about three times the distance to Northumberland and Betty than Linton, we stayed in touch, although the visits had to be less frequent than either of us would have liked. No 695 Squadron would have been the highest numbered ever in the RAF but for a strange occurrence in Malta at the height of the battle for that island. 1435 flight, flying Beaufighters changed to Spitfires and with an ever increasing number of aircraft on strength declared itself a Squadron! The Air Ministry actually recognised that number as a Squadron twelve months later, despite the fact that it was well outside the usual numbering system for RAF Squadrons. No 695 Squadron was officially an army co-operation squadron, although it provided targets, both live and non firing, for all three services. It was equipped with a mixed bag of aircraft which all pilots on strength had to be qualified on. For live firing, target towing Martinets were still in use for an Army ack-ack range near the Wash and for the Royal Navy, who usually used pom poms at Sheerness. Army searchlight work was catered for by the Squadron's twin engined Airspeed Oxfords, with Spitfire Mk 16s being provided for various ground radar establishments. Also on strength was a couple of Harvards for refresher flying, and a single Vultee Vengeance, which I just missed out on because it was soon to be sent for scrap under the lease lend deal. Pilots on No

695 did not exactly regard themselves as the poor relations to the four Meteor squadrons also based at St Faiths, but we were certainly vastly outnumbered in both the Officers' and Sgt's Mess.

There is at least one turning point in every pilot's flying career that is highly significant as to his future employment. In my case the first was the mandatory conversion to the Oxford which henceforth labelled me as a fully qualified multi-engined piston pilot, but that was hardly correct in a true sense. This was because the Oxford's Cheetah engines were fitted with fixed pitched propellers which meant that they could not be fully shut down in an emergency. All the pilot could do to reduce the vast amount of drag that is part and parcel of a windmilling engine in such situations was to increase power on the live engine, to full if necessary, and make for the nearest suitable airfield, leaving the lowering of the undercarriage with it's extra drag until on final approach. My conversion to the Oxford was remarkably brief, and consisted of one flight of 1 1/2 hours only, which included a return flight to our permanent detachment at RAF Wattisham in Suffolk, which took up most of the detail. However, the Oxford was a very forgiving aircraft, with any possible swing on landing best countered by using the wheeler technique. That is putting the two main wheels on the runway when still in the flying attitude and allowing the tail wheel to settle at it's leisure. I really enjoyed my first taste of twin engine flying, especially the searchlight co-operation night details, although these flights could not operate from our base airfield because of noise complaints from the local population. This was despite the recent war when such anti-military attitudes were unheard of. In our case, the solution was simple, we took the Oxford over to RAF Coltishall, which was six miles away, in late afternoon, and returned by road after completing the night detail. These night searchlight flights were only flown either on cloudless nights, or when the base was near or above 10,000' which meant little or no turbulence. It was the first time that I had taken to the skies after dark since my Spitfire OTU in Egypt, just over two years before, yet I still found it to be a most agreeable and relaxing form of flying. Our task was to fly straight and level, at a specified altitude, over a given position at random intervals, without taking any evasive action when picked up by the lights. It was a bit startling when first coned by a searchlight, the light intensity in the cockpit being far greater than imagined, and regaining of normal night vision when leaving the beam took quite some time.

Of course, the aircraft had to be collected the following morning, but that was of no consequence, in fact it was excuse enough for a short sightseeing tour of the Norfolk Broads, always a pleasant sight, before landing back at Horsham. Another exercise that was always popular with pilots was flying one of the Spitfires for ground radars. We were just given the height to fly, usually about 10,000', and the number of runs required between two points. I could hardly believe it when I was given one of these details which called for four runs between Regent's Park and the De Havilland works at Hatfield. As we had to be on course at the start point, it meant manoeuvring the Spitfire over the Westminster/ Buckingham Palace area of Central London, but nobody thought that would be a problem, not so long as the engine kept turning was my own view. Such a trip, which lasted for two hours, just about the fuel limit, would be unthinkable these days, but the very limited civilian traffic, unpressurised aircraft the norm, rarely reached 10,000' in those immediate post war years.

A one off Spitfire trip came my way when the experimental firing range at Llanbeder in the Cardigan Bay area of North wales, asked No 695 Squadron to provide a plane for a full day of trials on some system or other. I could visualise a good days flying as I set off early in the morning of a lovely summer's day. However, as I approached the Welsh mountains from the east, it became obvious that it was not to be when I saw them covered in cloud with the tops going up to a great height. As I had been airborne for about an hour or so, more fuel would be required from some airfield or other and having just passed over RAF Shawbury that was the obvious choice. After landing I reflected how ironic it was that I was now at Shawbury when I should have been somewhere else, yet just two months ago I had set off from Acklington for this very station, but fell ten miles short due to engine problems.

I found the flying of No 695 Squadron's bubble canopy Mk XVI Spitfires (fitted with the American built Packard Merlin) very interesting and often mentally compared them with the British Merlin and Griffon powered Spitfires that I had already flown. Although not everybody agrees with me, I thought the American version was both smoother and sweeter running than the Rolls Royce product. Over the years I have admired the Americans when it came to aircraft and their power units. Although they often got it wrong to start with, just as occurred with their first attempt with the Merlin, they never let up until they came up with a workable answer, which is far from the case with many other countries. However, they were far too generous when they provided a full tool kit with each Packard Merlin built, and with the Lancaster Mk III being powered with that engine, there was certainly no shortage of engine tools on many units!

The towing of targets for the army for Ack Ack practice was a very sedate affair indeed, with longish runs off the North Norfolk coast, between the villages of Wells and Stiffky, flying at about 8,000'. Although there were many gun emplacements on the shoreline, only one gun ever fired at any one time so that there could be no misunderstanding as to whom had done what as regards accuracy. Due to the fact that the gunners were using a radar device all our targets (drouges), had been reinforced with a kind of wire netting device to give a blip on their screens. To ensure that the blip being fired at was from the drogue and not the towing aircraft, an officer was always positioned behind the gun due to fire. This came in very useful indeed one day when I was just about to start another run and noticed a Wellington aircraft flying along the same line, and at the same level, in front of me at about towing distance. I pulled away very quickly indeed, not wishing to be clobbered by friendly fire two years after the war ended! That was not the end of the matter, because I was warned by radio from the army range that they had picked up five or six

Airspeed Oxford

more aircraft approaching as per the first Wellington. Needless to say, there was a big to do about this incident, and a black mark was eventually placed against the RAF Navigation school at Middleton St George, now Teeside Airport, for planning such a route for their student navigators for that particular day's training programme. The firing range was clearly marked on all charts as to be "deemed to be active at all times". Why no one had picked that up was beyond comprehension. The army radio referred to was always manned by ATS girls who sounded a lively lot at times, although their phraseology was not always as per the book, and often included the immortal phrase of "Over and out", as in aviation and police films. "Over", by the way, means that you were expecting a reply, and "out" that the interchange of chat was finished.

I could never approach the firing range at Wells and Stiffky without thinking about the Stiffky parish priest of the mid 1930s who hit the headlines of the national newspapers for all the wrong reasons. Reports of goings on with some of the ladies in his flock duly led to his de-frocking and he turned to lion taming as a means of earning a living, but it did not last all that long because he met his end in a lion's den on the sea front at Skegness!

St Faith's was somewhat unique in the fighter world in that it was almost part and parcel of the ancient city of Norwich, which did not bode well for it's long term future, due to ever increasing noise complaints. It was one of the first RAF stations to close as a result of the "Sands Axe" of the 1950s. However, it was destined to flourish as a civil airport, and became another of my old airfields that I had the privilege of landing the RAF's last Lancaster in later years. One such landing there will forever remain in my memory due to the very unusual nature of the trip that I had just completed, but more of that later.

With being so close to the city centre, we were spoilt for choice as regards off duty leisure activities, starting with a good local pub, only about three hundred yards from the main gate and, opposite that, a speedway track with a first class team in those days. A regular bus service into the city centre passed a famous, in RAF terms, dance hall but that was one pastime that I never indulged in. Like all ancient cities, Norwich had more than it's fair share of public houses, catering for all tastes, with the Bell Hotel being the favourite with NCO aircrew from Horsham's five squadrons. As for my own particular passion for football, Norwich City's ground was just a stroll from the city centre, which took care of every other Saturday afternoon during the season. Ever since those far off days

I have followed the ups and downs of "the Canaries", who still sport the yellow strip I so well remember. Life on the squadron itself was very pleasant and as laid back as it was possible to be on an RAF Squadron under an excellent Flight Commander in Flt Lt Key and a Squadron boss of the old school, Sqdn Ldr Jordan. They were both full of good ideas and one in particular boosted morale no end during the very hot summer of 1947 when they managed to persuade all of our many customers that they did not need our services on one particular working day, so that the entire squadron, regardless of rank, could take off for a full day by the sea at Great Yarmouth- needless to say, it was a huge success.

Yet another excellent innovation was the introduction of the odd clay pigeon shoot, in the old bomb dump area on our base. One or two who had tried it before suggested that the best time to fire was when the target was just reaching the highest point of it's trajectory, when it was running out of forward speed and, therefore, needing far less deflection (angle off). I thought that might be too easy an option so I decided to have a go and shoot early in it's flight with plenty of deflection. However, it was ages before I made a score, and that only came after I had laid off about twice the amount of deflection that I had first thought necessary. I have thought ever since that if only clay pigeon shooting had been part and parcel of a fighter pilot's training during WWII extra kills would have been recorded. Many of the aces of that time have recorded in their memoirs that at the start of their first fighter tours they had often fired at too great a range and without enough deflection before adjusting both and gaining victories.

For many people in this country, other than for those who actually lived through it, it is extremely difficult to come to terms with the fact that after six full years of wartime austerity, it was to be another nine years before the rationing of food, and other commodities, such as clothing, finally ended. In that context, there were no such things as coffee bars in every nook and cranny as there is today. The wartime tradition of the NAAFI, or Sally Army van appearing twice per day to vend liquid refreshments with the odd bun, was still very much in vogue, and the highlight of the day! On the morning run at Horsham you could almost set your watch by it's precise arrival, but if no visual sighting was made all was not lost because a massive Irish Wolfhound knew the route of the van better than some of the drivers, and galloped about 300 yards ahead making loud barking noises which could be heard for up to a quarter of a mile away. One of our WAAF wireless mechanics had, eventually, to send one of her mates out for her char and wads, because the dog had obviously fallen madly in love with her and on one occasion sent her flying, complete with tea mug, when it leapt up and put one massive paw on each of her shoulders. The dog really missed her when she stopped using the facility, and gave plaintive looks towards her crewroom before tucking in to the tit bits given by others. For the RAF, at least, food seemed to be in shorter supply than in the war years, and many stations resorted to pig farms, kept going by the cookhouse swill bins to increase supply. Unlike today, it was still legal to use swill for that purpose. The WAAF Sqdn Ldr in charge of the Pig farm at St Faith's went one better than most other stations and started a smallholding for vegetables. Labour was no problem with stations closing down all over the place, plus the onset of national service, which was just beginning. Two Polish NCO aircrew also helped out as far as the Sgts' Mess was concerned during the mushroom season, by getting up at the crack of dawn and setting off for the middle of the airfield. If they failed to fill one kit bag each of this delicacy, it was considered to be a bad morning's work.

The Squadron detachment at RAF Wattisham, in Suffolk, was primarily to cater for the needs of Royal Navy pom-pom gunners based at Sheerness. Some members of our Squadron much preferred the tranquility of the RAF station in the middle of nowhere, rather than being next to a bustling city like Norwich, so there was a hard core of volunteers who were more than happy to stay at RAF Wattisham as long as required. I would certainly have been one of them but for the fact that it would have stopped my visits to Northumberland to see Betty. However, the time came for me to be based there for a couple of months and I found it quite interesting to tow targets at a relatively low level, compared with the army's requirements. It certainly was different in that the Army only used one gun per run, so accuracy could be assessed, the RN had different ideas, and let loose with every gun on line at the same time, which would make it virtually impossible to allocate praise or otherwise. The chap in the back cockpit of my aircraft never seemed too happy with this situation and perhaps I was lucky in not having the same view as he had!

One interesting Spitfire trip I made from Wattisham was also over the Navy's Sheerness range when I was told to carry out dummy low level attacks against their gun positions, and pretend it was a warship! As our commander at Wattisham was not around as departure time approached, I took it upon myself to give the Navy a ring and try and establish minimum heights to fly, etc. I thought I was speaking to an officer at Sheerness at that time, but had my doubts later. He seemed a little off-hand and in reply to my question about minimum heights for the attack replied, "as low as you like mate", so I took him at his word. Yes, minimum heights were introduced shortly after my trip.

It was about this time that the RAF fell in line with the rest of the flying world and replaced miles per hour airspeed indicators in aircraft with ones calibrated in knots. As world charts are in knots it was a long overdue move. It caused a few landing accidents to start with, due to over running of runways when some pilots still used the same indicated speed instead of a reduced one after the change over, which did not occur overnight. Many units having a mixed bag to start with, did not help matters one little bit. A very serious situation nearly developed during WWII when an aircraft carrier captain told the RAF that he would launch the RAF's fighters aboard his ship when he reached a distance of X miles from their destination because of probable enemy action in that area. The RAF assumed, wrongly, that the X number was in miles when in fact, the RN had used the chart measurement, which was in knots. Quite a big difference over a long distance.

CHAPTER 16
North to Leeming

One stroke of luck came my way in early 1948, when the night fighter OCU (228) at RAF Leeming in North Yorkshire decided to include air to air firing in their basic syllabus and, therefore, required extra staff pilots for this increased commitment. They already had on strength quite a few Martinets, which acted as flying targets for trainee radar operators who, with their instructors, flew in modified Wellington bombers fitted with airbourne interception radar. The first NCO pilot "specially selected" for a move north was not at all impressed, particularly so because he had only recently married and was living in local accommodation. I became an instant friend of his when I said I would gladly take his place because it was so much closer to the North East and Betty. It was the best move that I ever made as I was able to see Betty every weekend, our romance developed to the point that we became engaged, although our marriage was to take place over a year later.

Just before leaving St Faith's, two important changes in the RAF structure took place. The first was mostly to do with aircrew below commissioned rank. The upshot was that the revered rank of Sgt Pilot, writ large in the annals of the RAF, particularly during the Battle of Britain, was to be lost for all time. In fact, no SNCO pilots or navigators would ever wear stripes to indicate rank ever again. All Sgt Pilots became, overnight, Pilot Twos (P2) which meant that instead of the usual three stripes of a Sergeant, known throughout the military of the entire world, would henceforth wear a badge which consisted of two crossed laurel leaves with two stars in between. This meant absolutely nothing to anyone outside of the RAF. F/Sgt Pilots became Pilot Ones (P1) and Warrant Officer Pilots Master Pilots, with other aircrew following suit, eg Master navigator, etc. The scheme also envisaged that there would be a separate mess on each station for all aircrew of any rank, but thankfully that bit of nonsense soon fell by the wayside, but not before I had been involved in a bizarre situation at my new Station of Leeming. Before going into that never to be forgotten night, I had better explain that in addition to the three new ranks there were also three new grades which no one could equate to any of the normal rank structure of the RAF. They started at Aircrew Cadets (Laurel leaves with no stars), which indicated under training. After being awarded wings, cadets became Pilot Fours with four stars, and after passing an advanced course, usually on jets, they became Pilot Threes, with three stars. They finally reached the status of Pilot Two, if not already commissioned, after completing an OCU course. Thus at Leeming we had one or two Pilot and Navigator Threes passing through and, with no special mess yet provided for them, they became members of the Sergeants' Mess, although if any had fallen foul of the disciplinary system it was far from clear as to what would happen as regards punishment; confinement to camp or jankers as it was known in the RAF was not an option for Corporals and above, but just where did Pilot and Navigator Threes fit in? I found out soon enough when one day I was the station Orderly Sergeant although I was, in fact, a P2.

During a lull in doing the rounds that evening I thought a couple of half pints in the mess would not go amiss, and it was there that I fell in with a student P3. He seemed just as interested in what the Martinet was like to fly as I was on his thoughts about the night fighter Mosquito. The time was fast approaching when I was due to undertake my last chore of the evening which was to inspect the defaulters parade outside the guardroom. I took my leave, saying I would be back shortly and he indicated that he also was off but would likewise be back. About twenty minutes later, after a quick wash and brush up, I was quite pleased to see as I approached the Guardroom that the orderly Corporal had the five or six Janker Wallahs, all wearing full webbing kit, nicely lined up for my inspection. He brought them to attention and I started the routine from the nearest end to my approach. All was going well until I stood in front of one of the miscreants and noticed that he had a right smirk on his face, and then it struck me like a bolt from the blue. It was none other than the pilot that I had been sharing a drink with half an hour before, and would be doing so again very shortly. Just what was the RAF coming to, was an instant thought. Flying one of the finest aircraft in the world one minute and stood like a naughty little boy the next. Something had to change, but why oh why had the system of ranks to be changed in the first place?

The other massive change that had occurred just before I left St Faith's was far more logical, and most certainly to the benefit of the service. It was called the three pronged system which introduced three distinct wings to all flying stations, namely; flying, engineering and administration. Each with a Wing Commander in charge and a Group Captain in command of the station. Over the years flying wing has become Operations Wing and Engineering Wing changed to Technical Wing, but the basic structures remain intact, having stood the test of time.

The flying of the Martinet as a pure target aircraft was a little onerous at times, particularly so in certain climactic conditions, when important decisions had to be made by the pilot alone. Although the Wellingtons were stuffed full of navigators, staff and trainees, they were all in the blacked out rear compartment, without any outside visual reference as to actual position and cloud conditions, so it was left to the Martinet pilot to ensure that both aircraft were kept clear of other airfields within a specified area, and out of cloud. The last factor was of immense importance because student radar operators in the back of the Wellington had not only to call for changes of heading to intercept the Martinet, but also request speed increases, or reductions, to bring the Wellington to the correct simulated firing range. Sometimes speed reductions were left far too late and the Wellington would go sailing past the Martinet on one side or other and the procedure would start all over again. With the best will in the world it was almost inevitable that on a few occasions both aircraft would find themselves in cloud, but prompt action by both aircraft captains took care of the fleeting danger during my time at Leeming although, with hindsight, perhaps it was an accident just waiting to happen, which duly occurred on 13th August 1951. With the RAF losing about 200 aircrew per year at that time, the accident might have gone down as just another statistic but for a remarkable incident after the Wellington and Martinet had collided. As was normal in those days, were Air Training Corps Cadets to be given flights on every conceivable occasion during their summer camps on stations that had suitable aircraft for that purpose. Space was limited on the Wellingtons but room was usually made available on each detail for one cadet to be carried. The cadet, like all aircrew aboard, other than the pilot, had been fitted with a parachute harness of the type that the actual parachute is only clipped on to the front of the harness just before use. It was at the time of the collision that a Flt Lt J A Quinton DFC, a navigator undergoing conversion to night fighters found himself in the rear of the aircraft, along with the ATC cadet as the aircraft broke up and started to fall to the ground. The cadet, sole survivor of the accident, later related that there was only one parachute stored in that area of the aircraft and that Flt Lt Quinton had taken it out of it's stowage, clipped it onto the cadet's harness, pointed his hand to the rip cord and then to a hole in the fuselage. For that act of self sacrifice a posthumous George Cross was awarded to the late Flt Lt Quinton.

With RAF Leeming being mainly a twin piston station, an Oxford aircraft was provided as a flying hack, so I was able to keep my twin flying time ticking over nicely. One trip in particular was of interest, although it had nothing whatsoever to do with flying as such.

Both the Police and local authority realised that something had to be done about the A1 road (which at that time ran alongside the main runway), such was the upsurge in traffic, and asked if the station could possibly provide aerial photographs of a ten mile stretch in our area, to include the village of Leeming which would have to be by-passed one day. It seemed unlikely that we could do much about it, because the photographs required would certainly have to be taken from the vertical position. It was at that point that one of our NCO staff pilots remarked that a metal frame in the perspex nose of our Oxford looked as if it had been fitted for camera work at some time or other. The photographic section did not have a suitable camera to fit the frame, but they tracked one down within a week. The developed pictures appeared, to our untrained eyes, quite remarkable, and they certainly impressed the authorities who called for more on other occasions.

As one might expect on a night fighter OCU, our lords and masters had all been involved in that black art, and had served with great distinction during the war. Our immediate boss was Squadron Leader "Sticks" Gregory, who was probably the highest decorated rear crew member to have served in the RAF, sporting a DSO, DFC and DFM. He had flown as Radar Operator to Wing Commander "Bob" Braham, one of the top scoring night fighter aces of WWII, ranking alongside "Cats Eyes" Cunningham. "Sticks" Gregory, by the way, had brought his well known nickname with him from civilian life, having played the drums in a dance band in his native North East. The Wing Commander Flying also had a very distinguished night fighter career behind him, having flown under what must have been very difficult conditions during the siege of Malta, and in many other places. Wing Commander Powell-Sheddon was also the holder of the DSO and DFC. He had been accepted into the pre-war RAF for pilot training despite having a slight stammer. Not surprisingly, it had got steadily worse during the stress of war and it was now causing quite a problem, especially when he went flying, but he always stuck to it and got messages out eventually; we certainly knew when he was aloft and watched our Ps and Qs accordingly. During my NCO pilot days he was the only Senior Officer who ever saw fit to give NCO aircrew phone calls to put them in the picture on personnel matters. About two weeks prior to one such call, a round robin had been sent from HQ Fighter Command asking for lists of all pilots with Spitfire experience. The WingCo's call was to let me know that I could now forget about it, because they had rounded up as many pilots as they needed to ferry Spitfires out to Greece to reinforce their Air Force, who were doing battle with communist rebels. He thought it very strange that only he and myself had flown Spitfires on the entire station. I thought it strange too, but was more struck by the courtesy of an officer of his rank in making such calls to people well below his station.

The towing of targets for air to air firing off the Yorkshire coast got off to a very slow start indeed due, in the main, to the fact that quite a lot of work had to be put in by the ground engineers to bring the airbourne winches back up to standard after being neglected for the last few years or so. Providing rear crew operators was now a problem too, with the pool of redundant air gunners rapidly drying up as demobilization took it's toll. Although many ground crew were eager to take on this task, I had to fight a one man battle with the Station Accounts department to ensure that they received some flying pay for their efforts, which took two or three weeks to resolve. However, when we eventually got it under way it provided a nice diversion from being chased all over the sky by the Wellingtons.

Only one serious question mark was raised against our method of operations, and that was when I was detailed for a towing sortie on a Wednesday afternoon, which was as near as one could get to sacrilege in those days, because in theory, everybody was supposed to be involved in sport, even if it was only as a spectator. As luck would have it, the station rugby ground was on one side of a short, little used runway, and our unmarked, adopted dropping zone was on the other side. The Station Commander was a spectator to what was a rather important rugby game, and the next day demanded to know which idiot had flown so low the previous afternoon just to drop a target? The reply from our boss that the pilot (me), was using the standard operating procedures did not fully satisfy the Group Captain, and his final blast was that the engine noise alone could so easily have upset the players' concentration- talk about frightening the animals!

The very high accident rate, for peacetime that is, continued on both operational and training stations with many attributed to loss of control when flying in cloud. This resulted in the introduction of an Instrument Rating System which graded pilots according to both ability and experience, and placed stricter limitations on the lesser qualified as to what weather conditions they could operate in. To get the scheme up and running, our own Group Headquarters, No 12 at RAF Newton near Nottingham, turned one of their front line fighter squadrons into an Instrument Training Unit using Harvard and Oxford aircraft. The Squadron chosen for the dubious honour was No 41, based at RAF Church Fenton near York, and still operating Spitfires until it's dramatic change of role. At Leeming I was primarily a single engined pilot and was sent down as such to take the course with No 41 on the Harvard. The idea was that on each course there would be four pilots flying the Harvard and four flying the Oxford. The theory was that the four on Oxfords would be drawn from the twin piston world of Mosquitoes and Hornets and the four for the Harvard from Spitfires and Vampires plus, of course, the dear old Martinet and one or two others. It goes almost without saying that five single engined pilots and only three twin pilots turned up for the course. I leapt in and let it be known that I was current on Oxfords which resolved the problem and also built up my twin hours to somewhere near a respectable total for future years.

In the aftermath of WWII not much of the old school of the pre-war flying club attitude to aviation survived, and those blooded on the hectic lifestyle of operational flying remained hyper-active to the nth degree, running around inventing work when none was required and making changes for the sake of change. What had started as a perfectly sensible concept of improving all pilots' flying ability in cloud and poor visibility suddenly became known as "all weather flying" and it literally became just that. In the days of coal burning fires in most households, the Vale of York, shielded by the Pennines and Cleveland Hills, was notorious in the RAF for poor visibility which could last for weeks on end under certain conditions, with little or no flying possible. The ethos of all weather flying, however, was taken to extremes during our course and the take offs and landings on some occasions were under conditions which would have been unthinkable before that time, or ever since for that matter. We only had precision approach radar (PAR) for landings and often touched down without being able to see the far end of the runway which meant, at least, mist conditions (2,200') and possibly Fog (1,100'). Only the slow speed of aircraft such as the Oxford and Harvard made it possible for us to operate on some of the days that flying took place during that hectic course. No 41 Squadron returned to Fighter Command's front line, about a year later being re-equipped with the DH Hornet, the aircraft that I had hoped to fly at Linton-on-Ouse.

Another "brilliant" idea thought up by the fighter top brass was to make use of a surplus to requirements airbourne lifeboat for courses on sea survival. Located in a small fishing harbour on the North Sea coast, so that students could experience rough sea conditions? Of course not, it had to be near a fighter station so Horsham St Faith's and the dead calm of the Norfolk Broads was specially selected and thoroughly enjoyed by all who managed a full week of pure pleasure. If only all RAF courses had been so pleasant! Apart from life on the Broads during the day I was able, in the evenings, to catch up on the news and gossip from my friends on 695 Squadron. One of my drinking pals, Jimmy, had managed to get in on the Spitfires to Greece trip and said it had been a jolly good outing. He also informed me that the Martinet was on it's way out, and would soon be replaced by the Bristol Beaufighter for target towing. If we had been looking at tea leaves in the bottom of cups, and not pint glasses, the omens would have looked far from good for that project. Both Jimmy and "Dutch" Holland, a very popular officer, were killed during conversion to that aircraft type. Another item of news from 695 was chilling. The ground F/Sgt in charge of the Technical airmen had applied to extend his time in the RAF, and after being turned down put an end to his own life behind the door of his room in the Sergeants' Mess. Having known the Chief so well, I could hardly believe it possible.

On return to Leeming it was back into the old routine for both flying and the limited social life available. Things improved no end when one of the NCO staff navigators named Ginger Rhodes produced a motor cycle which extended our radius of action in the evenings and eventually led us to settle on "The Nags Head" in the village of Pickhill or "Eddie Shine's Place" in Marton-cum-Grafton, some miles further south. Eddie had survived the war as a Lancaster rear gunner, and, after demob, taken up as a publican although his main interest was in motor cars to the extent that ale was dispensed from mini petrol pumps with nozzles activated by hand grips. His chief barmaid was his niece called Rusty, due to her reddish hair, who delighted in regaling customers in uniform with tales of the perils and dangers of her nine to five job as a waitress in one of Harrogates top restaurants. Although Eddie had long gone, Betty and I did visit that pub about 45 years later when our hosts on that occasion joan and digby Lamb took us there thinking that neither of us knew about the place. It certainly brought back happy memories. Pickhill, being closer to Leeming, had most of our trade- to the extent that Ginger and I were both roped into the village cricket team on a number of occasions. They could only provide one pad for the chap batting and one afternoon I received a full toss that should have been sent for six, but missed it completely and thought that my kneecap without the padding had been shattered. It was not quite so bad, and luckily it was the last game of the summer anyway.

In the days before television and other distractions, the village pub was certainly the centre of the universe for villages such as Pickhill, perched in the middle of nowhere, and the "Nag's Head" lived up to that concept. It was frequented by the biggest cross section of society one could ever imagine, helped on it's way by the fact that it was unique in having only one bar. We certainly had a squire and also a city slicker import who thought he also was a squire, but that cut no ice at all with the locals and they certainly knew how to deal with people like that in their own way. It turned out that one ever present farm hand, who was immensely popular with all and sundry, actually lived in the barn of his employer how he managed to remain so band box clean at all times was a complete mystery, to all.

One little group who frequented the Nags Head were from the Land Army and they certainly lived up to expectations. All ruddy faced, back slapping types who could down a pint with the best of us, and, often having arrived straight off the fields still in their working breeches, were certainly ready for a nogging or two. They pulled our legs at times, making snide remarks about being "Brylcream Boys" etc, which kept us on our toes.

Riding pillion to Ginger outbound on our evening visits to the "Nags Head" was sedate enough, but the returns could get a bit hair raising at times in these days before drink driving laws. We had only one mishap, however, and that was just inside RAF property and very nearly outside the main Guardroom, long after the defaulters parade had finished, thank goodness. Before the main runway at Leeming was extended, a side road off the A1 came very close to the camp entrance at the Guardroom, and it was whilst trying to negotiate the steepish bend off this public road at too high a speed that the bike went skidding sideways, leaving Ginger and myself to lick our wounds.

I lost track of Ginger Rhodes after leaving Leeming until his name appeared in the press in the 1950s when he lost his life in a Canberra air crash in North Lincolnshire. I have often wondered If he was laid to rest in his home village of Kirk Smeaton in Yorkshire, or in a military cemetery.

It would appear that the place of internment of RAF personnel killed both in peace and war over the UK was left to the discretion of the next of kin. I well remember changing trains at Southport's Chapel Street station, when returning to Manchester at the end of my last wartime leave in England, and seeing a coffin draped in the Union flag being transferred to a waiting hearse. Naturally, everyone stood still during the passage of the coffin with the doffing of hats, or salutes from those in uniform. All present were no doubt wondering if it was somebody they had known, I learnt later that it had, indeed, been one of my ex-classmates. This was very much on my mind after a fatal Mosquito crash at RAF Leeming, when I and other NCO aircrew had been detailed to form a party to take the coffin of one of the two victims to Northallerton railway station to load into a goods wagon. Surely, we all thought, road transport would have been far more appropriate, no matter what distance was involved, but ours was not to reason why. Our arrival at the station, in the back of a 5 ton lorry, was a classic case of mis-timing. Passengers awaiting a main line train thronging the Southbound platform became known to us only after we had entered it with the RAF ensign draped coffin on our shoulders, to proceed along it's entire length to a minor platform used for local trains and the odd goods wagon. The contrast between the onlookers at Southport station and this was marked. At Southport all onlookers had looked grim faced but seemed to accept death as part and parcel of WWII. Now many of the would be passengers looked particularly distressed, with many women wiping away tears. Perhaps they thought it was a life wasted now that the war was over, or perhaps they may have known of or been war widows themselves of aircrew who had failed to return.

Another NCO pilot from Acklington had arrived at Leeming to boost our tally of towing pilots and it was none other than "Fireman" Brannon. I did not see a great deal of "Fireman" off duty as he had managed to find accommodation in the lovely town of Thirsk for his wife and family. In any event, his time at Leeming was to be very short lived. Although there is an old adage in service life that one should never volunteer for anything, Fireman was not actually around when our Sqdn Ldr "Sticks" Gregory asked after the morning Met briefing if any pilot had flown

Tempests. It looked very much like a nil return until one of our NCO gang piped up that although he had not himself flown that type he thought "Fireman" had. Poor old "Fireman" was off within the week, posted to the Canal Zone of Egypt. There had been plenty of trouble in that area ever since the war ended, with the RAF involved against both the Israeli and Egyptian Air Forces at one time or another. One well documented incident involved Spitfires against Spitfires which, under normal circumstances it would have been impossible to recognise friend from foe in a dog fight, except that on that occasion the Egyptian Air Force obliged by flying straight and level at a sedate speed, which allowed the RAF Spitfires to draw alongside to identify national markings before dropping astern and shooting them down! We heard that Tempests eventually were involved in that area but never a word from "Fireman" from the day he left.

The very rapid rundown of the Royal Air Force from over 1 million men at it's peak in WWII, came to a juddering halt at about the 200,000 mark in 1948. This was due, in part, to the onset of the Cold War, starting with the Russian blockade of Berlin, which stretched the RAF's Transport resources to the limit and, in addition to the normal Transport Squadrons, even necessitated the use of Coastal Command's flying boats. Another important factor was the introduction of National Service, and with the Army being unable, or unwilling, to cope with the numbers involved for a full two years, the RAF had to cater for what many thought was more than it's fair share. The RAF trained some of these conscripts to "Wings" level, which meant that they returned to civilian life before even reaching a Squadron. A vast waste of public money, but I'm the first to admit that it kept me, and many others, in employment doing what we liked best-flying aeroplanes.

My time at Leeming was not to last long because a sudden panic to re-build the RAF again to about 300,000 men, meant that the number of Flying Training School was to more than double over quite a short period of time, with a corresponding increase in qualified flying instructors. When a call for volunteers for the Central Flying School Instructor Course arrived, it seemed an excellent opportunity to extend ones flying life to the distant horizon. This particularly applied to those of us who had only Squadron experience on day fighters, as we had passed our sell by date, which was still set at about the mid-twenties by the RAF although in the Korean war the Americans found that fighter pilots reached their peak at about the age of 38. In any event, the policy of using only Commissioned pilots in Fighter Command, wherever possible, had gathered pace with a new C in C now in place.

A strange twist to the Officer/NCO pilot saga took place when one night a new NCO pilot appeared in the Sergeants' Mess at Leeming, who, when I had last seen him, had been a Flight Lieutenant at Saint Faith's and very keen to make the RAF his career, but had been turned down for a Short Service Commission. After a few months in civvy street he had agreed to re-join as an NCO pilot and, luckily, had taken demotion in his stride however justice was done within the year when he returned to his rightful rank of Flt Lt.

Unbeknown to the rank and file at the time, all pilots gaining their wings after 1950 would automatically be commissioned at that point, and all serving NCO pilots actively encouraged to apply for a commission to try and square the circle. However, some dug their toes in and decided to see their time out in the Sergeant's Mess, all becoming Master Pilots on time promotion, in a shortish timescale. I think many thought that they were quite happy to remain big fish in a small pond. They may have had a point but they rapidly became an endangered species, with many being shunted into Air Traffic Control and other non-flying appointments with just one or two managing to continue flying, mainly in the flying training and staff pilot worlds.

One aspect of the CFS course, that may have had some influence on my volunteering for it, was the fact that the last part was known as "Type Flying", which meant flying a variety of war surplus aircraft plus a real carrot, a jet propelled aircraft in the form of a DH Vampire. Not all that many pilots in the RAF in the late 1940s had actually flown a jet, other than those already on Meteor and Vampire front line squadrons, and I was extremely keen to see what it was all about. I was a little surprised that after having put my name forward I learned that an interview before a board of senior officers was required at RAF Little Rissington, prior to final approval. Over the years I never met or heard of anyone failing it. However, a couple of days away from North Yorkshire to such a beautiful part of the world as the Cotswolds would certainly not go amiss. Although the rail journey south was somewhat tedious, the MT run between Kingham station and Little Rissington was a wonderful experience, particularly so when I first saw the village of Burton-on-the-Water, just before reaching RAF Little Rissington. It is still, arguably, the finest of the many picturesque villages in that area, despite the inevitable commercialization that has taken place over the years. The interview seemed to go fairly well and at the end I had been given a broad outline of things to come, if selected. The first two months would be spent at RAF South Cerney, nr Cirencester, and the final four months at Rissington with the greatly anticipated type flying taking place there. I was told that they would be in touch after all interviews had been completed, not knowing at the time that failure was almost unknown, I sweated it out for a few weeks before a posting notice came through to join No 109 course at CFS in early 1949.

During the two month wait before leaving RAF Leeming I used up one more of my nine lives through nobody's fault in particular. It was during a radio controlled descent through cloud, without area radar, when the ground controller could only give headings to steer, followed by a timed "descend in safe area", after passing overhead his station. It was whilst descending in cloud, and turning back towards Leeming, that an Anson flashed across my bows at remarkably close quarters, it's slipstream nearly turning my Martinet upside down. It turned out to be carrying out exactly the same procedure at another station, RAF Middleton St George. In later days, with secondary radar being the norm, that type of incident should not occur. However, overlapping let down areas for two different stations should never have been countenanced in the first place, and I understand a compromise was reached between the two stations as a result of the near miss.

CHAPTER 17
CFS course

Leaving Leeming saw the end of an interesting, but mundane, period in my flying life between front line fighters and the start of instructing others on how to fly aircraft if I managed to pass the CFS course. On reporting to RAF South Cerney I was struck by the diversity of backgrounds represented by our group of would be instructors. They came from every single corner of the RAF's flying spectrum; Flying boats, day and night fighters, transporters, bomber barons, staff pilots, the lot. It certainly led to some interesting stories, especially on out nights in downtown Cirencester. The number of NCO pilots on our course necessitated dormitory accommodation in Barrack blocks to start with, until the senior course moved up the road to Little Rissington. This did not please those of us who had become used to the comforts of mess

Auster 77

living. South Cerney was still a grass airfield which could have curtailed our flying considerably during the January and February part of the course, except for the fact that we had use of a satellite airfield called Blakehill Farm, complete with Tarmac runway. After noticing an Auster aircraft in our hangar which never seemed to move, I asked my instructor, Flt Lt Wheeler, if it ever flew and I was quite startled when he said "I'll arrange a trip in it for you later in the day". I found it quite a delight to handle and was particularly impressed with the view from the cockpit, being the very first high wing aircraft I had ever flown.

The two months at South Cerney soon rolled by, but I did manage to make several flights over North Cerney, and the adjacent World War One airstrip of Rendcome which, via my RFC/RAF Uncle Harry, had influenced my future life in aviation. Looking down on the still discernible, and later restored, airfield one did not need to have much imagination to picture the scene of the bi-plane days of the WWI era. The move to Little Rissington was to the highest airfield, at 750',used by the RAF in the UK. I mention that because it played quite a part in when we could, and could not, fly safely. On some days students who had found local accommodation for their wives did not turn up for the first details because in the valleys they had awoken to a scene of dense fog, although we at Rissington could look down on the low clouds, with flying definitely on. The other side of that coin, of course, was that they sometimes set off in high spirits and good visibility only to drive into low cloud as they climbed the hill towards the airfield. You cannot win them all, especially in aviation.

Our social life could not have been better, with the super village of Burton-on-the-Water well within walking distance, at the bottom of a steepish hill, clambering back up was another matter. A hotel called the "Old New Inn" soon became our favourite watering hole, not least because Mr Morris, the hotel landlord, was particularly well disposed to the RAF, be they commissioned or otherwise- although the tradition of separate bars for officers and the rest still prevailed. I was so pleased on a recent visit to the Cotswolds to note that the descendents of Mr Morris are still running that hotel. One major attraction at the rear of the main building is a stone scale model of the village, which had been crafted in years gone by, and proved so popular that it attracted many visitors from all over the UK and beyond.

Although the flying at CFS became very hectic indeed, we still managed to fit in all of the type flying that had become part of the CFS course. This included flying the Harvard, Tiger Moth, Prentice, Spitfire, Mosquito III, Vampire III and Lancaster. Including the Auster, which I had just flown for the hell of it at South Cerney, the final tally became eight different aircraft types, a number that anyone joining the RAF of today is unlikely to acquire in his entire time in the Service. The most exciting and pleasurable to fly was, without doubt, the DH Mosquito. It's ability to loop with one engine shut down was quite remarkable for those days and that, combined with the best control co-ordination I was to come across ever again, made it the most popular of the 34 RAF types I flew during my 44 years in the RAF.

However, it was the prospect of flying a jet propelled aircraft for the very first time that had been uppermost in my mind until that day actually arrived. To say it was one of the biggest disappointments of my flying life would be an understatement. Handling was so simple it was almost beyond belief, no swings on take off or landing, and hardly any rudder at any stage. My view was shared throughout our age group at that time, although older, senior officers had formed a very different opinion to the extent that the concept of all through jet training was thought to be imperative and was introduced in the mid 1950s. This was not only at vast expense, but also to the detriment of the all important aspect of airmanship. Many countries continued with the well proven Harvard virtually to the end of that types viable flying life 30 or more years later. When one considers that virtually all the students on 109 course had never flown a tricycle undercarriage aircraft before, nor used pressurisation and that the main runway at Rissington was less than the RAf's standard 2000 yards, it must have been a simple aircraft to handle otherwise it's accident free record at CFS would not have remained intact. Another important point was that no dual version had been built at that time so, literally, you were on your own from the word go except that, in my particular case, it did not quite work out like that.

I well remember that I was under the wing of one of the senior instructors, a very down to earth Yorkshire man by the name of Flt Lt Joe Croshaw, for my first jet flight, which was to be in a Vampire Mk III. He not only escorted me out to the aircraft and, unexpectedly, carried out both the outside and inside checks, but even strapped me in before starting the engine. He pointed towards the exhaust gas temperature gauge as he slowly opened the high pressure cock. The flight was a big anti-climax and it was only after landing and taxying into dispersal that a difficulty arose, and that was how to stop the blasted engine! All piston engines in the RAF had two magneto switches with some having mixture cut out levers as well. Both could stop the engine with the mixture lever the preferred method when fitted, but what was the preferred method for a jet engine? During the 30 minutes or so that I had managed to get my hands on a copy of the pilots' notes for the Vampire earlier in the day I had written down all the important speeds such as take off, climb and landing, plus emergency procedures but I just could not recall the method for stopping the gas turbine type. Pull the high pressure cock as per starting, or should it be the low pressure one for stopping? I was pondering on which cock to pull first when I felt the control column moving violently from side to side. A quick look out of the cockpit revealed Joe Croshaw waggling the ailerons violently to attract my attention and, with the palm of one hand moving across his throat, the traditional sign from ground crew to a pilot to cut engines. I had just decided to pull the correct lever when I thought, better safe than sorry, and beckoned Joe over and shouted to him to stop the engine for me. He gave a look fit to kill before doing so and I last saw him stomping off into the distance shaking his head. So now I had actually joined the jet set club without having started or stopped a jet engine. Reference to one of my old log books confirms that the trip was exactly seven days before my wedding day, which was a saga in itself from RAF Little Rissington's point of view, and it also records that I had flown the open cockpit Tiger Moth the same morning, prior to my Vampire experience. Rags to riches, or was it the other way around? The latter I suspect, although they both came from the world famous stable of De Havilland. During my Type flying on the Lancaster I marvelled at it's lightness of control when airbourne, not unlike the Tiger Moth in fact, although it's reputation for swinging, like most tail wheeled aircraft of it's size, was very much on my mind on each trip. I never thought that one day I might be employed flying a similar aircraft in the form of the HP Hastings, with it's more vicious swing, but that came to pass ten years later.

Another new type I flew at Little Rissington was a Percival Prentice, which had just begun to replace the Tiger Moth as the RAF's basic trainer. Many of the dyed in the wool instructors on the CFS staff thought it was a retrograde step, because it was so easy to land compared with the Tiger, and might well prove detrimental to students absorbing basic airmanship. For myself, the thought of flying the Tiger Moth with it's open cockpit,

de Havilland Vampire

in winter months was not particularly appealing: the Prentice by contrast had an enclosed cockpit, radio, full instrumentation and side by side seating. However, not many aircraft are built absolutely faultless from the word go and the Prencice was no exception. Spin recovery, which took some time, was one major problem and, like most other aircraft, a normal spin can eventually develop into a flat spin if left in that state for too long a period, when recovery becomes, sometimes, impossible. In the early days the Prentice was a classic example of this. It duly happened to one Prentice and the two pilots abandoned their aircraft by walking along the wings, one on each side, before jumping and activating their chutes, but not before giving each other a quick look to make sure that both had vacated the cockpit safely. This fault called for modifications which resulted in the turned up wing tips, which gave the aircraft an ungainly look. One minor defect, that no one could explain, was that some Prentice aircraft would suffer from aileron flutter if it dived to more than about 115 knots during aerobatics whilst many did not. It was about a 50/50 split and by checking the serial numbers on the aircraft, we soon established that the batch built by the parent Percival company at Luton, fluttered at high speeds, yet those built under licence by Blackburns, at their Brough plant on the Humber, did not. A very strange business even by aviation standards.

One bit of nonsense inflicted on the manufacturers of the Prentice, plus the Balliol and Athena later, was that a third seat was called for in the Air Ministry specification to be located to the rear of the two side by side pilot seats up front, so that a non-participating extra student could be carried. I tried it once during a map reading exercise and came to the same conclusion as all the other instructors of the day- an utter waste of time.

A touch of irony crept into the course when my turn came to fly the Spitfire in that a very young member of CFS staff, without even asking if I had ever flown a Spit before, launched into one of the most detailed briefings one could ever imagine and then asked a number of questions and seemed quite pleased that I had given the correct replies, even saying that I had obviously done my homework and read the Pilots' Notes thoroughly. "But not for many years" read my balloon caption. He, like Joe Crowshaw, escorted me out to the aircraft and warned me to watch the Glycol temperature gauge as it was a warmish day. My balloon caption changed to "Nothing like Egypt, Singapore, or even Japan in mid summer". Being a lowly NCO pilot I managed to keep my mouth shut and went off and enjoyed myself, convinced that this was to be my very last trip in a single Merlin powered aircraft. In fact, I was to fly two more, but one can never see into the future. The Spitfire flight was completely uneventful, and perhaps it showed as I signed the authorization sheet at the end of the detail. The young eager Beaver was awaiting my arrival, and no doubt looking for the big smile of a pilot who had just completed his first flight in one of the world's most famous aircraft. After a long quizzical look he blurted out, "You haven't bent it have you"? Before I could stop myself I replied, "No, not this time", and made a rapid exit, leaving him slightly open mouthed.

Like many other people, I tend to put things off until the last minute and it was just as well that Betty my wife to be kept reminding me to have the Banns read in the local church on the mandatory three consecutive

Sundays. However, trying to catch the Vicar proved to be on a par with finding Lord Lucan in later years. He seemed to have more Parishes under his care than you could poke a big stick at. It took several attempts before I eventually caught up with him and by that time the expression "up hill and down dale" had taken on a whole new meaning as my means of transport was a borrowed bicycle, which I hardly ever had to pedal because I was usually free wheeling down hill or pushing it up another. I eventually made contact with him after several close calls, such as "you've just missed him", or "he called earlier to say he had been forced to change his plans for the day". And it was after deciding, in desperation, to lay in wait for him outside his own church one evening that we finally met. However, that was not the end of the matter because he noted that although neither Betty, nor myself, were members of one of his numerous flocks around the Cotswolds, he really should give us a couple of half hour, face to face sessions on marriage. I think it would be called counselling in todays jargon. However, after pointing out that my bride to be lived more than 300 miles away, he reluctantly gave it a miss. It was with a great deal of relief when I rang Betty as soon as I returned to Rissington with the good news and was able to point out that we still had a few weeks to spare before the deadline, but that did not quite turn out to be true because we soon started flying most of the daylight hours and getting time off to chase a Vicar around the countryside would not have been looked upon with any favour whatsoever. After about two weeks of this over intensive flying, everybody was getting a little punch drunk, to the extent that one officer I had flown with on the five a.m. shift found himself lumbered with me again on the 9 am detail, and as we circled the village that he lived in with his wife, he idly said over the intercom "I wonder if she's got my tea ready yet"? "I suppose you mean your breakfast, Sir"? was the only thing I could think of saying. Should any pilot have been called upon to fly at such strange hours day by day?

Each course had quite a few students from foreign Air Forces and I well remember one from the Thai Air Force, with a surname that was just about unpronounceable by Anglo Saxons, and it was just as well that he settled for a small part of it which stood for both his Christian and Surname. The name used by all and sundry was "Pan", and whilst flying with another co-student on a practice "patter" detail that we heard on the radio, the plaintive cry of "Pan Prang". Air Traffic Control seemed completely mystified and after many "Say again" calls from the tower, and replies of "Pan Prang", we felt obliged to butt in and say "The pilot calling you sounds to be ok, but you should contact the Squadron dealing with 109 course for details of the flight and mention that a Thai officer is thought to be the pilot". Pan was found safe and well in a field near the A40, thank goodness.

The panic to turn out ever more instructors for the expanding number of Flying Schools continued apace, despite the ending of the Berlin Blockade, and it was decided to increase the flow by slightly reducing the length of the course by replacing the number of different aircraft in the type flight to just one, and that was to be the newly introduced to service dual control Meteor VII, which was to equip a number of Advanced Flying Schools. The era of pilots flying jets for the first time without the benefit of dual instruction on type was drawing to a close, or so I thought at that time. The introduction of the Meteor to CFS at Little Rissington, which was now becoming a marginal airfield for modern aircraft, due to it's limited runway lengths, did not go completely according to plan. One total write off of a Meteor T did have a lighter side to it. Not only did the two instructors flying it manage a safe parachute exit and descent, but also landed in close proximity to each other near a country lane. Having joined forces and, with their rolled up parachutes, they stood on the roadside awaiting any possible motor traffic that might come by. It almost goes without saying that it was the proverbial two little old ladies who drew up in their Austin Seven, having passed the burning wreckage of the Meteor. When the two, lucky to be alive, officers asked if it was possible to cadge a lift, they got a very stern "certainly not", followed by a right dressing down about despoiling the countryside with burning debris. It cannot have been often that two CFS members of staff were left completely speechless at the same time!

My own instructor at Rissington seemed to have been allocated to more secondary duties than he could cope with, which led, in turn, to my co-student and myself often being shunted sideways and flying with numerous other instructors. I always thought it was my lucky day when I found myself flying with Flt lt Graham Hulse, a remarkable officer who many thought would go to the very top in the RAF. He had the rare ability of getting on with staff and students alike, regardless of rank or background. He also had that difficult to describe presence which singled him out in any company. With his fighter background, the call for RAF volunteer pilots to go out to Korea to fight alongside the Americans at the start of that conflict, must have sounded like a bugle call which he duly answered. Tragically, he became one of the forty or so Commonwealth pilots who became killed in action (KIA) victims. This was deemed to be an absolute tragedy by all who had known him in the Service.

Another tragic death of those on strength at CFS at that time was no less a person than the Commandant himself, Group Captain Stephenson, although it did not take place until he had given up command and was flying a high performance jet of the USAF in America. My first sight of the Commandant was a bit of a shaker although, as it turned out, not a one off occurrence. On a Wednesday afternoon which was, until after the speeding up of instructor output, reserved for sport of one sort or another, I was leaving the Sergeants' Mess for another couple of flying details when I spotted the Commandant's car in the far distance with the bonnet flag flying. On these occasions one instinctively straightens one's self up and gets into a more measured stride, ready to give an eyes right, or left, as the case may be, with a smart salute. With the oncoming staff car only about 30 yards away I noted the scrambled egg on the driver's service hat indicated that the Group Captain himself was actually at the wheel, almost unheard of in those days with service chauffeurs being the norm. However, the biggest shock was yet to come, when, as the Station Commander returned the salute I couldn't help but notice that his service hat was the only item of RAF uniform that he was wearing. No, he was not starkers, or even wearing swimming trunks, but for an ex-Brat like myself it was almost as bad, he was in riding dress and on his way to a local point to point meeting. I suppose being top gun, or top dog can have it's privileges as well as responsibilities!

Before the hectic, almost panic, rate of flying for students had set in, we managed a day visit to the Bristol Aeroplane Company at nearby Filton. In aviation they say if an Aeroplane looks right it will fly right, but the reason for our visit, to view the mighty Bristol Brabazon, shortly before it's first ever flight, was to prove the exception to that rule. It looked lovely, but became a complete flop, flying only 400 hours in four years of flight testing, before going to the scrap yard. If it had ever entered commercial service it would have been a ground engineers nightmare with eight Centaurus Radial Engines, completely enclosed in the wings, driving four sets of contra rotating propellers, it almost beggared belief. It had a maximum weight of 290,000lbs with a wing span of 230' and a maximum cruising speed of 250 mph, which was nothing to write home about, even in those days, and all to take just 80 passengers non-stop across the Atlantic. A viable passenger fee would have been astronomical. However, it was probably a conception that was no worse than the Short Princess Flying Boat which also failed to enter commercial service. Many people just could not accept that the days of the flying boat were over and yet Short Brothers even managed to produce a single engined flying boat fighter in the post war era, an idea which was completely incomprehensible to anybody who had flown, or worked, in the fighter world. That type was also a failure.

Back at Little Rissington a personal bombshell was about to burst over my head in that the course was suddenly reduced by four whole weeks, which meant that it was to terminate on the weekend after I was due to return to work at the end of our honeymoon. After I had approached the Squadron Leader in charge, pointing out the short time interval between my return to work and the new course ending date, he just said, "Better just take the weekend off", and walked away, for the first, and last, time in the RAF I felt like jacking it all in. Our pre-booked honeymoon was to take in seven days in Paris and over £500 had already been paid for travel arrangements and hotel accommodation and was non returnable. It was with steam coming out of my ears that I approached my Flt Lt Instructor and asked for an interview with the Chief Flying Instructor. He obviously asked me to spell out my gripe before trying to arrange anything, which I duly did and he soon took on a look of utter dismay. He said that I had only two more trips plus the final test and they could almost certainly be fitted in during the last remaining week of the course, after my return. Unless my leave pass was returned as not granted,

Our wedding day

he would, if in my position, just carry on and not treat the Squadron Leader's remark as a direct order. So it was that I went off as planned to Northumberland to a well organised wedding and reception, which went down well with both the Elliott and Jackson families, followed by our first night in the Turks Head Hotel in Newcastle upon Tyne. The next day we took the train south to London and then a new adventure in travel, as far as my bride and I were concerned, was the night sleeper to Paris in the days when all passenger carriages were shunted onto a cross channel ferry. That pre-war mode of travel did not last all that long after WWII, so we were particularly lucky to sample it before it's demise in the early 1950s. Our hotel in Paris was the St Petersburg and located in a central position which meant that most of the sight seeing attractions were within walking distance. The food was superb and plentiful which was something of a shock because in England severe rationing was still in force and was to remain so until 1953 or so. After a few days our waiter said "You have had steak for the last three nights, surely you would like a change"? "Not just yet", said Betty and I in unison.

The return rail journey was a repeat of the outbound leg, except that we made our way to the "Old New Inn" in Burton-on-the-water for a week in the Cotswolds, although I would be flying during the following week days to finish the course. Our first night in the hotel was a Sunday and I was fully expecting at least one or two of the ten NCO pilots on our course to be in the bar, sooner or later, for some leg pulling about honeymoons in Paris, etc, but not one was to be seen. However, one pilot from the junior course eventually arrived on the scene and said "Where have you been Jacko, they've been looking all over the place for you, your course left on Friday, they brought it forward another week and our course will be off soon by all accounts". The instructor shortage was really beginning to bite, it seemed.

I returned to work the following day, as planned, to find a near deserted crew room with only two members of our course there. They had been retained for some extra training, having not quite lived up to expectations on their final test, so I was not completely alone, and flew with both of them as a "pretend" student whilst they practiced their patter on a few occasions. One, a Squadron Leader, I thought to be particularly good and could not begin to understand what the problem was, but then I was no expert. Perhaps there was more to it than met the eye. I was soon informed that the Wing Commander Flying would be dropping by to have a word with me about my 'leave', and I concluded that if he was calling on me, and not the reverse, he might have already heard the full story from my own instructor and did not want to make too much out of the situation, which proved to be the case. The upshot was a little amusing in that I had positioned myself near an open window in our crew room which gave a good view of the control tower and the CFI's office therein. The Wing Commander, whose surname was Keen, known throughout CFS as "Keen by name and nature", deigned to use the RAF car that he was entitled to, and preferred to ride a bicycle at high speed around the various squadrons under his command. Some thought that he was trying to save some petrol, and others that it was his way of keeping fit. Having noted that he was not averse to taking a Lancaster away for a long weekend on occasions, I think physical exercise was the likely reason. It was not long before I sighted his approach to our hangar at an even faster speed than normal and, after throwing his cycle against the hangar wall, asked a pilot, who just happened to be returning from a trip with his parachute slung over his shoulder, if his name was Jackson by any chance? I had one of the biggest shocks of my life when the pilot, who I had never seen before, said, "Yes, Sir, that's right". The CFI then launched into a spiel about the exigencies of the service and how could anybody think of going on a honeymoon to Paris in the middle of a CFS course, etc. The other Jackson kept tight lipped until the Wing Commander had finished and then said "I've been married for four years, Sir, and have two children, wait till I tell my wife this one". I couldn't stand it any longer and shouted "I think you're looking for me, Sir". I thought the incident with the married officer by the name of Jackson outside the hangar might have acted like a red flag to a bull, however it soon proved otherwise. By the time he entered our crew room he appeared, if anything, a little deflated by the incident outside. He asked me to go over the events leading up to my marriage and then suddenly changed the subject completely and asked one or two pointed questions about the course as it was, and my thoughts on the impending reduction of type flying to the Meteor VII only. The two other remaining officers of No 109 course, plus the odd instructor who happened to enter the crew room did double takes at the sight of their Wing Commander sitting alongside an NCO pilot, indulging in what might have appeared to be idle chat. It certainly added to my own slight discomfiture at the time.

Although I was fully employed during the day, finishing my CFS course, my wife, Betty, enjoyed her week in the Cotswolds as much as Paris. She took the local bus into Cheltenham, a ladies shopping paradise, on several days, and in the evenings in the "Old New Inn" we met many interesting people, both local and visitors and met two very famous entertainment personalities of that age who happened to be guests in the hotel during our short stay.

The first was Wilfred Pickles, a particularly well known broadcaster who had lived in my own small village of Ainsdale, near Southport, before his career suddenly took off. The second was my own favourite comic, Al Reed, who fully lived up to expectations.

A final twist to my time at Little Rissington came after passing my final handling test, when I was asked if I was interested in going out to Southern Rhodesia again to instruct. I would have been delighted to take this posting however, I thought that Betty would need time to adjust to service life in the UK before an overseas posting. A co-student of mine, Flt Lt Jack Holt, of flying boat fame, had already taken up a similar offer and came back at the end of his tour married to one of the Meikels' daughters. Meikels being a vast hotel empire with it's Salisbury branch a well known watering hole for RAF types.

CHAPTER 18
Flying Instructor

My actual posting was to No 6 FTS at RAF Tern Hill in Shropshire, a much underrated part of England as far as scenic beauty is concerned. Ternhill had started life as an RFC Flying Training Station in 1916 and it's origins, as recorded in a book called "Action Stations Vol. 3", is a somewhat romantic story and worth repeating. It is recorded that in 1906, only three years after the first flight by a heavier than air aircraft, piloted by the Wright brothers, a certain Major Atcherley, father of the famous twin brothers who both rose to air rank in the RAF, force landed in a hot air balloon on the site and suggested it's potential to the war office. During WWI an airfield was duly built there and after the training of many pilots on Avro 504s and Sopwith Camels, disbanded in 1919. However, a brand new RAF station was built on the same site in 1934. From 1936 to 1976 it remained in continuous use as a Flying Training Station. In addition, it housed elements of both day and night fighter squadrons during 1940 and 1941 for the defence of Liverpool and surrounding areas. The station was unique in layout with barrack blocks built on differing levels on a gently sloping hill. On the opposite side of that hill stood an old manor house, which was used as an annex to the Sgts' Mess. It was in this house that I and other NCO Pilot Instructors were lucky enough to be billeted, completely out of sight of all other areas of the camp. We even managed to persuade the two girls who ran the NAAFI van to make calls on Wednesday afternoons when trade on the rest of the station was a little slack, because of sporting activities.

I eventually found accommodation for Betty and myself in the local village of Market Drayton, which we both found to be particularly relaxing. We soon became quite friendly with the owner of the "Corbet Arms Hotel" in the Market Square, who was Mr Tom Stallard. After leaving Ternhill in 1951 it was to be another 18 years before our paths crossed again and it was to be quite an historic occasion in British aviation terms that brought that second meeting about. I was stationed at RAF Brize Norton, undergoing the Short Belfast Ground School at the time, and managed- with some of our course and Betty- to take a half day off to motor over to RAF Fairford to witness the first ever landing of a British built Concorde, which was due to arrive there after an initial take off from Filton airfield near Bristol. I think that Pilot Brian Trubshaw would be the first to admit that it was not one of his better landings, but it was reported later that a malfunction of the radio altimeter was a prime cause. Another incident at Fairford also remained in my memory, it was the one and only time over many ensuing years that I saw the RAF's Red Arrows aerobatic team put on a well below par performance. They arrived overhead with only six aircraft and that, being an even number, gave the formation a lop sided appearance. Added to this, two of the aircraft had not yet been painted in thir trademark red. The display itself lacked cohesion and it came as no surprise when Ray Hannah was re-called to be their leader again. Later that after noon, Betty thought it might be a good idea to take tea in the well known village of Bibury, which we had not, until then, had a chance to visit. It was in the main hotel of "Bibury Court" that we met up with Tom Stallard, the owner, again. There was instant recognition on both sides and after a great deal of chat about the old days in Market Drayton, he asked what brought us to his hotel. When we said the Concorde landing at Fairford he said, "Oh, that lot". It turned out that a fairly senior member of British Aircraft Corporation had been to see Tom, looking for accommodation for Brian Trubshaw and his crew, plus a few others during the time that Concorde would be at Fairford, but had started to quibble over the costs, and finally said he would have to check with upper management before agreeing terms. By that time, however, Tom Stallard had received an offer from an American tour company for the entire season that he could not possibly turn down.

The system of training pilots in the RAF had changed dramatically since the war, in that basic (elementary) and advanced (service flying training) would amalgamate and a potential pilot would henceforth only fly from one airfield, but on two aircraft types, before gaining his wings. At one stage of the scheme, a student was to fly with the same instructor during both stages, but this proved to be unworkable and, in any event, not thought to be a particularly good idea. Not many pilots fail to pick up one or two bad habits over the years, to say nothing of some ex bomber and transport pilots not being too keen on aerobatics anymore!

My first taste of instructing was on the first basic stage flying the Percival Prentice, although I had only managed to fly that type for less than three hours at CFS. However, it was a particularly easy and gentle aircraft to handle and I could well see that some U/T pilots might cope with it quite well, but later find the Harvard something of a handful, with it's well known swing on landing and hefty wing drop if allowed to stall before touchdown. The Prentice was also my first, apart from half an hour in the Auster, side by side seating single engined aircraft. This arrangement was part of the specification issued by the Air Ministry and had the full support of the examining wing of CFS. My own view was that it had it's drawbacks, not least when a student was on his first solo and found a large empty space next to him at a time of high tension. The tandem seating, employed on virtually all training aircraft in the RAF until the introduction of this Percival type, made one feel, in my opinion, more part and parcel of the aircraft with both instructor and student sitting on the nose to tail centre line, with each shoulder virtually touching the canopy. The tradition of side by side seating was to continue for another thirty years before the present day Short Tucarno, not only reverted to the old tandem arrangement, but also re-introduced the propeller, albeit attached to a gas turbine, finally putting paid to another theory of the early 1950s that all pilots must be trained on pure jet aircraft from the very beginning. I, and many other instructors, had dismissed that particular concept immediately after first flights in the Vampire which proved to be far too simple to handle to make a good trainer.

When the Tucarno was first introduced, many of the older generation of pilots were incredulous that although the aircraft was to be built by Short Brothers in Belfast, it's origins lay in Brazil- what on earth had happened to our aircraft industry, which had built Spitfires, Hurricanes and Lancasters during very difficult times? Many new aircraft types can claim some sort of innovation or other and the Percival Prentice was no exception. The item concerned was a novel method of teaching instrument flying, always referred to as IF, and it was a monumental improvement on the only method I had come across hitherto. It was one of the few benefits of side by side seating and was called "Two stage amber". It consisted of the placing of amber coloured screens on the inside of the normal perspex cockpit windscreens. When the time came for the student to fly by reference to the "Standard Blind Flying Panel" only, which was originally thought of by the British aircraft industry and fitted to nearly all UK built aircraft, be they Sunderland Flying Boats, bombers, fighters or trainers and the envy of all, even the Americans, who tended to fit bits and pieces all over the plane, and not necessarily in the same place, even on one type of aircraft. The student would don goggles of a violet colour, which prevented him seeing through the amber screen, but left sight of the inside of the cockpit clear. A tube from the goggles was allowed to dangle a few inches outside the cockpit to ventilate the inside of his goggles to prevent misting up. The instructor, of course, could see the outside world through the amber screens as normal and keep a good look out for any conflicting traffic. A good look out in tandem seat aircraft, however, could only be catered for by the instructor flying in the front seat during IF sessions and the student taking his place in the rear and pulling down over his head the canvas hood provided, and always referred to as "Flying under the hood". It was also thought possible that "two stage amber" could be used for teaching night flying if special lights were laid out on the ground to represent a flare path, however I never heard of this actually taking place.

Our students at Tern Hill came under three distinct headings. Firstly, we had young chaps, virtually just out of school, who had always wanted to join the RAF as pilots and were more than happy to sign on for four years or so as part of their commitment. The RAF wanted to have a certain percentage of their pilots from a particular year of birth so that they did not finish up with a number of old, or young, pilots in the long term, so these entrants were particularly valuable. The second segment took some understanding in that they were all re-mustering to piloting from other aircrew trades and were called SEGs. That stood for Signallers, Flight Engineers and Air Gunners and with all being of WWII vintage it placed them, in 1949, and later, in a fairly high age bracket for learning to fly service aircraft. Many made the grade but some became accident prone with one or two known fatalities after gaining their wings. Why we didn't retain the hundreds of pilots trained d·.ring the war who had no wish to leave the service I do not know. The third and last bunch of students passing through the Flying Training Schools of the late forties and early fifties seemed to be something of a nonsense from a national point of view, considering that the UK was almost bankrupt as a result of the recent war. All these students were conscripts called up for National Service for two years, by the time they had gained their wings, and later converted to jets, it was time for them to return to civilian life and probably never fly again. Hardly a morale booster for instructors, but highly enjoyable for the students concerned.

Across the airfield from the main camp site stood a maintenance unit (MU) under separate command called RAF Stoke Heath, whose main task seemed to be the breaking up of war surplus aircraft and retrieving as much precious metal as possible for industry. It was always a sad sight to see as many as three Lancasters a day making their final landing, what a tale they could have told. Needless to say, their arrival called for some extra caution if airbourne at the time, due to their large circuits for landing, but that was a minor matter. In fact, for pure circuits and bumps sessions, many instructors much preferred our all grass satellite airfield at Chetwynd, to the South East. The old adage used by generations of Flying Instructors when teaching student pilots to land on grass took on a new lease of life. It was, that the time to flare the aircraft for landing was at the point that you could pick out blades of grass, as such, from a green surface- it seemed to work remarkably well for student pilots!

An abandoned airfield called Wheaton Aston, also under the control of Tern Hill, was located near Chetwyned and housed what were then called displaced persons (DPs), in this case Polish families trying to make the best of it in very primitive accommodation. One of the highlights of the day for those unfortunate people must have been the arrival each day of a general post office van to collect and deliver mail. The regular driver must have been a man of habit, because you could set your watch by his arrival on Wheaton's perimeter track to start his rounds. For ex-ground attack pilots it often proved to be a temptation that could not be resisted, and many head on dummy attacks took place. The driver had obviously got used to these stupid antics because he never veered off into a ploughed field, a la the Suez to Cairo road.

One piece of bad news that awaited newly fledged instructors at Tern Hill was that when we had completed our time on basic instruction on the Prentice, and moved to the advanced part on Harvards, air to ground attacks would no longer be taught. Having dropped practice bombs and fired .303 guns during air to ground attacks at CFS, we all thought that the pre-war, and WWII, tradition of giving U/T pilots tuition in that art was still part of pre-wings training, and felt a little aggrieved that it had been dropped from the syllabus. However, before moving to that stage, a little surprise awaited me.

It was in August of 1949, when I had been instructing on the Prentice for less than two months, that I was told I would be one of several pilots from No 6 FTS who would be taking part in the September Battle of Britain Day, and I would be expected to put on an aerobatic display at RAF

Sealand. The location suited me fine, having been stationed there twice during the war years, an aerobatic display, however, was another matter. In the case of aerobatics, I had always adhered to the rule of "never below 3000' above ground level", and had certainly never practiced a sequence of aeros orientated to a crowd line before. During air test and night flying tests (NFTs), I started to practice the black art, to me at least, of being an aerobatic display pilot in the Prentice which, although fitted with a 250 hp engine, was still a little short on power for a continuous session of aerobatics. I was a little lucky in that NFTs, an archaic daytime test on each aircraft that was due to fly the same evening, came thick and fast for NCO pilots and flying four such details at the end of a normal day's flying was not unusual. The concept of NFTs had started in the inter war years when night flying was a very rare event indeed, and cockpit lighting was rather primitive. The idea was to ensure that all lights worked and the aircraft was on top line as regards engine, instruments and radios. Despite vast improvements made in aircraft design and interior fittings, these nonsense flights had not only survived the war but continued into the 1950s. How many millions of gallons of fuel had been wasted over the years, to say nothing of the extra wear and tear on aircraft and engines? Traditions die hard, even in the junior service. However, waste not, want not, and I took full advantage of any air test or NFT on offer to work out an aerobatic sequence and gradually lowered the operating height. I had started to use an old airfield about ten miles to the south to simulate the pending Sealand air display and as luck would have it the visibility was so good during one practice that the Chief Flying instructor had caught sight of my aircraft and asked air traffic control to try and trace the idiot pilot who was doing low level aerobatics in the distance. As air traffic contained a large number of NCOs, they reported no success, but I had to stand a bit of leg pulling in the mess for the next few nights.

The CFI at that time was Wing Commander Stanley Grant DFC, who was very much of the old school. That is, very affable and sociable off duty, but a stickler for rules and regulations on duty. He even had a mention in one RAF history book in that context. It reported that during the darkest days of the air battle for Malta, which on occasions was just as intense, if not more so, than the Battle of Britain for the pilots involved, he was, when leading his squadron in a massive dog fight over the Island, still able to find time to press the radio transmit button to tell the rest of the defenders to cut out the chit chat! He was also the only uniformed person at Tern Hill who managed to wear the newly introduced beret properly, and that certainly took some doing, being made of particularly thick material for that type of headgear. He was often on the phone, complaining about someone or another looking as if they were wearing a barrage balloon and not service headdress. Who on earth had decided upon replacing the well liked glengarry? Probably the same person who had made a right mess of things in making alterations to the RAF officers No 1 uniform which, thankfully, were rescinded within two years of introduction. These alterations consisted of the removal of two side pockets on the tunic and also the waist belt, in addition the new tunic had two vents at the back and, holy of holies, the historic flat cloth RAF Wings had been replaced by ones that not only stood proud on the left breast, but also contained wire mesh striping to highlight them.

The Battle of Britain weekend duly arrived and it was with some satisfaction that I set sail northwards for RAF Sealand, my old stamping ground as an airframe fitter after leaving Halton and, shortly after that, the location of my Pilot Training School. So much had happened in the intervening six years to ponder on during the short transit flight. Of these six years, I had spent almost exactly half overseas, which had included over three months on four different ships, two being Royal Navy aircraft carriers and the other two dreaded troopships. After disembarking in Durban, South Africa, from the first trooper I was to pass through more than a dozen different countries and operate RAF aircraft from about half of them. Now here I was approaching the airfield from which I had first piloted an aircraft and was due to perform my first public air display as a fully qualified flying instructor, a proud moment indeed. I think the most nostalgic moment from a most memorable day occurred when I taxied my Prentice aircraft into dispersal and passed the old wooden building still in use as a "Watch Office"; the pre-WWII name for flying control. How many times had I marched past that building to and from work four times a day as an airman fitter I wondered?

It was quite startling to see so many different types of aircraft already lined up for inspection by the time I arrived and I wondered how the organisers of the Air Show had managed to achieve that feat. It soon became obvious when I met up with the pilots, almost all NCOs like myself. They all came from an RAF Ferry Pool at Harwarden, near Chester, carrying on the wartime task of the Air Transport Auxiliary who I used to "frat" with in Barlow's Bar as an airman. It was a bit hilarious at the end of the show when they all started to run to the line of aircraft to see who could be first airbourne for the five minute flight back to base. I heard at least one pilot shout that he had flown such and such an aircraft in but might try and fly another type back. They were all qualified on all types present, but it did seem a little unruly. I was reasonably pleased with my first performance and very flattered to receive a round of applause as I stepped from my aircraft. The magazine "Flight" duly reported that I had given a graceful, if leisurely, display of aerobatics. As far as I was concerned the leisurely bit came when I was struggling for altitude after every four manoeuvres or so. It had been a great day out but it was back to the grind come Monday morning.

During my basic flying instructional stint we had on the flight an officer pilot who was suddenly called away to carry out intensive flying trials on two new British training aircraft; the Bolton Paul Balliol and the Avro Athena, one of which was due to replace the Harvard in time. Instructors from other FTSs and the CFS also took part and finally declared they preferred the Balliol.

The Balliol had first flown with a Bristol Mercury piston engine and shortly afterwards with the Armstrong Siddeley Mamba turbo-prop engine, in fact the first single engined aircraft in the world to fly with a turbo prop. The brief history of the Balliol in RAF service was full of twists and turns. First it was decided that turbo-props might be too high tech for student pilots so a reversion to a piston powered version, fitted with the dear old Merlin was made as the final answer. However, only No 7 FTS at RAF Cottesmore and the RAF College at Cranwell ever used the Balliol for pilot training before the "Pilots must be trained on pure jets" brigade held sway, and the type finished it's days on other duties with the two seat Vampire trainer being it's replacement. It seems quite remarkable, looking back over half a century that in the Tucarno the RAF have a turbo prop trainer that they could have had all those years ago.

Before the Balliol entered general service one of the prototype aircraft started doing the rounds of all the Flying Training Schools so that as many flying instructors as possible could gain experience on it. It was a case of twice around the circuit and then off solo. I quite enjoyed the all important feel of the aircraft and also sitting behind a Merlin engine once again. About a week after it's arrival I was somewhat surprised that although CFS wanted this aircraft urgently so that they could get some practice in on synchronised aerobatics on type before displaying it at the forthcoming Farnborough Air Week, no one seemed particularly interested in the offer of a one way ferry trip to return it to

Little Rissington. Perhaps it was the thought of a return by rail, lugging a parachute that put many pilots off, but I jumped at the chance after the offer reached NCO level. One of my own students, OC Posey, expressed a very keen interest in flying down with me so I took him along for the ride and I needn't have worried about the return journey because another NCO pilot friend of mine by the name of "Rod" Burners managed to get his hands on a spare Prentice and picked us up for the return. Perhaps this was one of the very few times that the third seat had come in useful!

Bolton Paul Balliol

The flight down did not quite go according to plan when the left undercarriage wheel failed to retract after take off. I tried one or two selections of up and down with the same result so it was decision time, land back or proceed to Rissie as planned? I chose the latter, but with both wheels locked down all the way! The Flt Lt who came out to meet us after landing agreed wholeheartedly with my decision, saying CFS had more to gain by a quick technical fix than Tern Hill. Needless to say I followed the life of the Balliol with some interest and was pleased to read in aviation journals that the aerobatic display by two CFS Balliols at Farnborough had been particularly well received. On the other hand, it was very sad that a Boulton Paul test pilot had been killed when a Balliol he was testing broke up during high speed diving trials. Looking back at my Spitfire experience in Egypt I have often wondered if air brakes could have saved his life.

CFS did not always come out of Farnborough week smelling of roses, particularly so on the occasion when they mounted a mass formation of Harvard aircraft over the show and one of them managed to clip the tail wheel of the aircraft in front with it's propeller. Years later I heard this incident being recalled, but with a little embellishment, as is the wont in aviation. The story now ran that the victim did not feel the contact and the perpetrator failed to call him on the radio, resulting in the pilot landing back at base unaware that he was minus his tail wheel.

With quite a high proportion of flying instructors still being NCOs in those days, life was never dull in the Sergeants' Mess, and if we ever felt in need of a change there was a public house just across the road from the camp, much frequented by "other ranks" from both the MU at Stoke Heath and our own FTS. Among the NCO pilots, at least three of us continued on flying duties to the bitter end as specialist aircrew, up to the age of 60 in fact, and served on the same station at RAF Brize Norton in later years, with Norman Rose, who I had already met before Tern Hill when he was on one of the four Meteor squadrons at St Faith's, flying the Britannias and "Nobby" Hall and myself on Belfasts. During our time at Tern Hill, Norman had fallen in love with a newly arrived WAAF Sgt by the name of Dorothy and many of us were more than pleased to attend their wedding in the Manchester area some time later, both being highly popular Mess members.

We hardly ever saw our students, other than at the "flights", due to the fact that they were billeted in one of the barrack blocks and took their meals and recreation in a special area of the airmens' Mess. However, that all changed more or less overnight when they were moved into the Officers' Mess, lock, stock and barrel. Even a blind man could have read the signal that the days of NCO pilots were well and truly numbered, although it became a slow, lingering death in the event. Many of us took the plunge immediately and applied for commissions. Interviews took their usual torturous course and it was fairly well known that the interview with the Station Commander was the make or break point and if you could pass that it was most unlikely that the AOC at Group Headquarters would overrule one of his Station Commanders. Our Station Commander at that time was known to all as "Elsie", although it was all to do with his initials and nothing more. So eventually I was seated before Group Captain E.L.S. Ward and the interview began in the usual fashion. "Let's see", he said, "educational background? Ah, you are an ex-Halton apprentice then we can dispense with that one". "Which books do you read"?, was the next question and I could only splutter that I had just started on the "Just William series" before moving on to "Hornblower and then Ernest G Gann". "The usual stuff for a young chap like you, no doubt. You'll get round to more serious authors later", concluded that bit of the interview before he moved on to the next subject. I felt quite deflated as I left his office, but it was not long before I was informed that I should stand by for an interview with the AOC.

All instructors take an interest in the future lives of students who have passed their way and the names of some from my tour at Tern Hill cropped up time and time again over the years. First, we had Duncan Simpson who became a very famous Hawker test pilot and rose to the top as the No One Jump Jet pilot. Then there was John Elias, who accumulated more flying hours in RAF aircraft than any other pilot before or since; over 17,500 in fact. In John's case the tables were turned 25 years later when, once a year, he became my instructor for 5 hours each Spring on Shackletons before I started my annual stint as the Lancaster Display Pilot with the BBMF. Other students I well remember included John Waddingham who, after leaving the RAF, completed a long and distinguished career in civil aviation and now, after retirement, lives near me in Woodhall Spa. One became an aircraft designer and displayed one of his products at a Farnborough Airshow in the Mid 1970s. He was named Lockspeiger, son of Sir Ben Lockspeiger, a famous aeronautical engineer. His aircraft on display was a special type for agricultural work in Africa.

On the downside was the fact that at least three of the students who passed through our basic training flight in my time became fatal casualties of flying accidents, and two of the three happened to be ex-Brats. The first of these was OC Lane who, having just failed to make the grade as a pilot, opted for navigator training and, after qualifying as such, was killed in a Canberra flying accident. OC Rennie was the next to go whilst flying a Hunter aircraft from the Central Fighter Establishment (CFE) at RAF West Raynham. His older brother had already gained his wings under the SEG scheme at Tern Hill, prior to my arrival. The last of the trio was Andy Divine, and he was also killed in a Hunter aircraft. This last death was particularly sad in that I had been talking to Andy for the first time in over ten years just a week before his accident. It was while staging through Aden as a Hastings Captain that I bumped into him in the Mess there. He had nearly completed a full tour and was very much looking forward to his return to England, but it was not to be.

The second half of my stay on No 6 FTS was on the trusted Harvard which suited me fine, not only because of the more powerful engine and responsive controls, but also for the far greater flexibility and scope as regards pure flying that it offered. Our cross country navigation flights, for instance, took in far greater distances, proving to be more interesting to both student and instructor alike after basic training. An innovation for those days was the introduction of detachments to operational Stations for a full week of continued flying training and our first was to Leuchars near St Andrews, all of two full flying hours away. At the time of our arrival, Leuchars was in the process of changing from Coastal to Fighter Command, and No 120 Squadron, with Lancasters, and No 222 Squadron flying Meteors somehow managed to co-exist during the overlap. I would have thought that an influx of Harvards, often with student pilots at the controls, was the last thing that they needed. However, everybody made us welcome and it proved to be a welcome break for all. Back at Tern Hill, with less than two weeks to go before the next batch of Battle of Britain open days, which took place at over 50 different RAF stations at it's peak in the early 1950s, I was detailed to perform another solo aerobatic sequence, this time on the Harvard which was far more to my liking than the Prentice of the previous year. The course passing through our flight at that time had reached the aerobatic stage so I found plenty of time to indulge myself in working out a general plan for the forthcoming Air Day at RAF Wellesbourne Mountford and once again, it was a single away day. Flying down there in the morning, taking part in the show in the afternoon and returning to base in the early evening. The day itself went off quite well with the added bonus of meeting one of my wartime fellow students who had spent most of his life in India. Hugh Scanlon seemed to be missing his life on the sub-continent and had not really come to terms with the austerity of the immediate post war years in England. However, it was good to talk about what seemed to us at that age "Days long gone", particularly our epic train journey in India from Karachi to Poona via his home town.

In early October of 1950 notice of my impending interview with the AOC at his No 23 Group Headquarters at Leighton Buzzard came through, and as luck would have it another NCO pilot instructor was to be interviewed on the same day so it was considered that the use of a Harvard aircraft for two days away could be justified. RAF Cranfield turned out to be the nearest airfield to Group HQ that was prepared to accept a night stopping aircraft, otherwise everything turned out just fine with both of us given a broad hint that our next posting would be to an OCTU. However, life in the RAF at that time was particularly unpredictable with many Stations and Squadrons closing down whilst others, such as refresher training schools for aircrew re-joining the service or, in some cases, re-called much against their will from civilian life, expanding. In addition, there was always a steady flow of aircrew finishing ground tours in Air Traffic Control who needed retraining to a reasonable standard before returning to OCUs and then front line squadron service. It came about that No 1 RFS at RAF Finningley found themselves desperately short of instructors to cope with an ever increasing demand. I was one of five or six instructors plucked from various FTSs to plug the gap and although I mentioned to my Flight Commander at Tern Hill that my time at Finnnigley might well be limited due to a possible OCTU course, he replied that official confirmation of an OCTU course had not yet been received and even when it was I may have to wait up to a year before being called forward, such was the number of NCO pilots awaiting to cross the great divide. My total time instructing at Finningley? Exactly three weeks to the day! However, my log book records that it was a very hectic three weeks in the back seat of Harvards and I had even been promised the odd flight in Spitfires which were also based there along with Oxfords and Wellingtons.

One Sgt WAAF who had signed my arrival card at Finningley had asked if I was on a course or staff and I had obviously said "staff", was now, less than three weeks later, signing my clearance card and said "I thought you said staff when you arrived"? "Yes, I did", was my reply to which she retorted, "You didn't last long then, did you"? My final riposte of "I thought it was about time I was moving on", was met with a very frosty stare. How I would have loved to have reappeared with an arrival card as a Pilot Officer two months later!

CHAPTER 19
OCTU and then helping the Navy

The nine week OCTU course at RAF Spitalgate, near Grantham, which followed was a low point in my service career. In our intake, we ranged from eighteen year olds about to start their military careers as national service officers in various ground branches, through NCO aircrew who had been around a bit, to 40 something Technical Warrant Officers who were destined to finish their time in the Officers' Mess. Surely a long course for first timers in uniform, and a much shorter course for ex-SNCOs could have been introduced? No doubt it had all been thought about at one time or another and dismissed for some reason or other.

The RAF Regiment, which had not been invented until early WWII years, seemed to be controlling about 80% of the course, and to say that one or two of them were drunk with power would be something of an understatement. They gave us plenty of drill and time on the assault course, plus the usual yelling and shouting which might have impressed raw recruits but for most of us it was like the proverbial water off a ducks back. The other 20% of the course, however, made our time at OCTU well worthwhile, although it was mainly to do with admin and service etiquette which included the "do's and don't's" of life in the Officers' Mess.

RAF Spitalgate was one of at least three pre-war airfields in Lincolnshire which had remained "grass" only throughout WWII and, therefore, were most unlikely to become fully active operational flying stations ever again, although Spitalgate had somehow managed to obtain a Tiger Moth to keep the G D Pilots on staff in flying currency. I well remember the Tiger Moth's existence for two very differing reasons. Firstly, our immediate boss, Flt Lt Brown, was one of the keenest pilots of the aircraft and often took any officer cadet who could be spared on the odd trip. When my turn came around it was a full day away from it all to RAF Shawbury, which was most relaxing to say the least, and also, incidentally, my very last flight in an RAF aircraft with an open cockpit.

De Havilland Tiger Moth II

One fateful day another staff pilot, and it was certainly not our Flt Lt Brown, got a little carried away and beat up a column of marching cadets crossing the airfield to the assault course area with an RAF Regiment officer in charge. He flew so low that all the cadets fell flat on their faces, but not so the resolute Regiment officer, who continued his upright march before one of the Tiger's wheels clipped him, not fatally, but leaving him with serious injuries. Not so lucky was our ultimate boss on the OCTU, Wing Commander Fenton, who was killed in a later flying accident in the Isle of Man when an Anson aircraft impacted into high ground on the Island. He had been retained in the OCTU world for some time and it was in connection with one of it's many moves, this time from Millom in Cumberland to Jurby in the Isle of Man, that the accident occurred. One of the all too many tragedies of that era.

In the last week of our nine week course, all of our intake were told that we had passed and could now order our officer type hats, greatcoats and No 1 uniforms- now back to the original style thank goodness.

Betty attended the passing out parade, then she had returned home to look after her father while her mother visited her brother Christopher in Alberta, Canada, she had not seen him for six months. They had not met for over 40 years when, after leaving Oxford he decided to emigrate. I was able to travel north and join Betty most week-ends until her mother returned home. My first posting as an officer was a return to instructing, as expected, at the mainly Royal Navy Pilot Training School at RAF Syerston, near Newark. It turned out to be somewhat unusual in my own particular circumstances because of my rank of Pilot Officer, which did not have a Royal Navy equivalent. In their service the nearest to it was a midshipman, also known collectively as Middies or Snoties, who lived separate lives in a Mess called the Gun room when not on duty. However, as Syerston was still under RAF command this minor point only came to the fore during the periods when each course was detached to a full Naval Air Station for a week or more when special dispensation had to be granted before I was allowed to use the wardroom, so I never did see the inside of a Gunroom.

Supermarine Seafire

It felt good to be flying again and exactly where I had left off two months previously in the back seat of a Harvard aircraft. One aspect of operating from RAF Syerston was that the Royal Navy had installed a unique self help navigational device which I often thought would have been extremely useful on RAF Training Stations. It was a YG beacon which continuously transmitted in Morse code letters of the alphabet in various equal segments of the 360° of a circle. One only had to identify which segment one was in and then steer an appropriate heading for base.

Obviously, if the code changed, a left or right correction could be made until Syerston was sighted. Another bonus from the RN presence was that they kept a Seafire on charge for their pilots to keep current on, but one or two of us in the RAF did manage to get our hands on it from time to time. Not long after my departure, the Seafire was replaced by a Sea Fury, another type that I would have loved to have flown but missed out on.

The students passing through proved to be even more of a mixed bag than at Tern Hill, although none of them were RAF National Service pilots. On the RN side, we had students that ranged from Midshipmen right up to Lt Cmdrs. One Lt Cmdr, was the holder of the Victoria Cross. He was Lt Cmdr Place VC of Midget submarine fame. Also on his course was a particularly well known RAF navigator who, despite the fact that the RAF had already announced that Navigators would have equal opportunities for promotion and command as pilots in the future had still managed to persuade the RAF to re-train him as a pilot. He was Sqdn Ldr "Daisy" Sismore and I well remember at their passing out dinner they both got up together to give speeches. Obviously, the Lt Cmdr started the ball rolling by speaking first for a while when he suddenly gave way to the Sqdn Ldr to say a few words and so it rotated for 15 minutes or so. Much to everybody's surprise it worked out perfectly and had plainly been well rehearsed for some time before the event.

Another well remembered dining in night was one which had been laid on for the visit of the senior serving Naval Air Officer, at that time, Admiral Lamb, who had a long and distinguished Flying and service career behind him. His after dinner speech was by far the best that anyone could remember and brought forth the longest ovation decently possible in a Service Mess. Unlike most orations from very senior officers, it pulled no punches and dwelt in equal measure with the past achievements of both the Royal Navy and the Royal Air Force as well as the mistakes made, and the lessons that should be taken on board. Not many speeches have remained in my memory for any length of time, but that particular one certainly has.

In addition to the RN students we still had inputs of RAF Sgts converting to piloting, although with the end of WWII now being all of six years in the past, most were in their late twenties or, in some cases, early thirties, which limited the type of employment in the future for those that passed the course. This was due to the fact anyone over the age of 25 was considered too old to become a fighter pilot. One nonsensical let out was that a pilot with over 1,000 flying hours to his credit could still rejoin the fighter world up to the age of 30. Nonsensical? Very much so, because we had pilots in the RAF who had completed one or even two operational fighter tours during WWII and were still well short of 1,000 hours, although over 25 and under 30. They obviously, would have been an asset to any fighter squadron after finishing ground tours, or on re-joining the RAF from civilian life, as the case may have been. Quite a few of these ex Sgts did make names for themselves in the Transport and Bomber worlds later, although a few fell by the wayside, some in tragic accidents. Another problem in training older pilots was that ability, often being assumed on age, medals and ribbons worn, and rank, led to a few being made Flight, and even Squadron commanders, in double quick time, with many younger pilots under their command having far more experience in piloting of aircraft with acquired knowledge that only came with actual flying hours. This was not only an RAF problem because, as already stated, we had students from the Royal Navy up to the rank of Lt Cmdr. One of my students who already held the rank of Lieutenant when he started his course was four short years later, a flight commander at another FTS that I served on. He too, became a flying accident victim during a King's Cup air race some years later. The pilot with him, if he had lived, would later have become the Duke of Gloucester.

One particular SEG to pass our way was John Slater, who went on to give invaluable service to the RAF as a pilot. It was known that he had completed a full tour as rear crew in Bomber Command during WWII and was now in the process of attaining his long held ambition of becoming an RAF pilot. It was not long after gaining his wings that he found himself in action for real again during the Suez War. Some folklore grew up around his activities as a Canberra bomber pilot during that conflict. It was to the effect that, on the very first strike against Egyptian airfields, and having obtained the radio frequency of the airfield tower that he was tasked to attack, called them up on his bombing run to advise them to vacate the tower as soon as possible as he was about to bomb them. Although ten years later I was serving on the same Station as John in Singapore at RAF Changi when he was commanding the VIP squadron, I never plucked up the courage to ask him about the incident. In fact he was such a modest chap that it was not until I was invited as a guest to a No 617 Squadron re-union after I had left the RAF, that I met him again, not realising that he was a former member of the most famous RAF squadron of all time.

Yet another SEG who was to become a pilot, and a student of mine, was a Flt Lt "Bill" Goodridge who had probably flown on more bombing missions during WWII than any other crew member. It was in excess of 150 sorties during two tours in the middle east and one in England. He certainly lived life to the full, as one might expect, after all he had been through, and proved to be highly popular with staff and students alike. I eventually lost track of Bill when he was posted, yet again, to the Middle East, but this time round as an aircraft Captain flying Valetta transport aircraft.

Being a newly commissioned officer it was only a matter of time before I was lumbered with some mundane secondary duty or other and they don't come much more mundane than officer in charge of the blanket store. We had been told on my recent OCTU course that it was one of the very few secondary duties that aircrew officers of the General Duties Branch were not allowed to perform, and Air Ministry had issued an order to that effect. Whether this order had been issued because aircrew could be away from their base stations for longish periods, or that it was thought that they might not take the task of counting blankets and sheets every other week seriously enough, I never found out. Just in case readers might be beginning to think what on earth has running a blanket store to do with aviation I will just say that it did eventually lead to an unusual situation which my young Midshipman student thought was hilarious, as did the rest of the Gun Room when the story spread. The more senior members of the Naval Staff, however, thought I had been a bit caddish. Whichever, it all started to go wrong shortly after I had taken on that onerous task.

A steady loss of bedding became such that I changed the system of issue and return to the store, which was situated in one room of the ground level wing of a barrack block which was the nearest block to the secondary runway at Syerston. I decided that in future, no issues were to be made from that store outside of normal working hours, and to that end a sub store was established in the main guardroom to cater for airmen arriving in the middle of the night or at weekends. The sub store was stocked with a limited supply as not many airmen arrived during out of duty hours, although there was always the odd one.

About a month later I was on a night flying detail with my Midshipman student, and with a strongish north wind blowing we were using the short runway which started close to the Fosse Way and passed near to the back of the NAAFI and barrack blocks. During our second detail of the night for another session of circuits and bumps, we must have been the first out

228

of trap one because none of the other aircraft had even started engines as we taxied out. Taking a quick look towards the barrack block that housed the bedding store as we passed by I was amazed to see a light on in the store room and thought that the mystery of the missing blankets might well be solved at last if I acted quickly enough, so I asked my student to bring the aircraft to a halt and keep the engine revs to a minimum as I was getting out and would be back within a couple of minutes. He sounded surprised as he said in a funny voice, "Ok, Sir". After unstrapping quickly and vacating the rear seat of the Harvard, I ran like mad to the back of the store room and climbed onto a window sill to see if I could catch someone in the act. I needn't have bothered, because it was a very fed up looking RAF policeman, complete with armband, who was dishing out blankets to five or more airmen. He had obviously had a very busy night and run out of his limited stocks. As I jumped down I heard in the distance the second aircraft of the wave starting it's engine so I ran even faster on the way back- that was until I found myself flat on my face after tripping over two entangled bodies. As it was directly behind the NAAFI I didn't think it was unreasonable to assume that it was a NAAFI girl and one of her boyfriends. I do not know who was the most surprised, the two romantics when I said, "terribly sorry", and continued my mad dash to the Harvard, or myself. The detail of "touch and gos" continued until I said to the student. "I think we will just try one more standing start take off so make the next landing a full stop". "OK, Sir", he replied. The student was obviously resigned to the unusual by now and complied without further comment. After completing his checks as meticulously as ever I said, "I think we will just see if the landing lights are still working", was my next request, knowing full well that he would be thinking why on earth shouldn't they be, after performing perfectly well all night so far. It was the first time that I had ever seen the effects of these lights when pointed at a building less than 50 yards away. It was absolutely dramatic, and showed everything up far better than even a floodlit soccer or cricket match. I had also scored a bull's eye on the courting couple, with the airman, obviously, first on his feet. It was he who was something of a bounder because, without waiting for the young lady to get up, he was off into the distance very much like a startled rabbit, weaving all over the place whilst his ex-partner, one must assume, was still trying to re-arrange her clothing. When I told my Middie student that he could put the lights out now all I could hear was hysterical laughter from the front cockpit. A few nights later in our favourite watering hole in Newark, officially named "the White Hart" but in those days called "Sheila's Cottage" by all, my young student, having had a few, said "you remember the other night when we were flying (how could I ever forget), and you got out of the aircraft before we had even taken off, I thought at first you had gone for a nervous pee because of my performance on the previous night". "I seem to remember it" was my riposte which brought hilarious laughter from the Middie and his pals who had obviously heard the full story.

The name of the best pub in Newark had been re-named by the locals for two very different reasons. The first was that a racehorse of those times, which was almost as famous as Red Rum was to become in later years, was called Sheila's Cottage, and secondly, the unmarried daughter of the licensee, Mrs Kirrage, was named Sheila, and what a popular and pleasant young lady she was to all and sundry. Newark's "White Hart", along with the "Saracen's Head" in Lincoln and another "White Hart" in Boston, have often been quoted as being the three most frequented hostelries by Bomber Command aircrew in Lincolnshire. With Mrs Kirrage's son, David, away in the army during the war, mother and daughter must have hosted many young aircrew who were here today and gone tomorrow having partaken of their last drink on planet earth in their establishment. Sheila was certainly not dry eyed on the very few occasions that she mentioned the war years and could put a name to many who had gone off into the night never to be seen at her bar ever again.

The time came when the course I was instructing on was due to spend a week or so on a Naval Air Station and there was a great deal of speculation about which one it would be, particularly amongst the Naval Air Staff and students. I gathered from the reactions of our naval counterparts that we had drawn the short straw when it was announced that it was to be Anthorn on the South Bank of the Solway Firth, a rather remote area of the UK by any standards. It was, as customary in the RN, given as HMS (title) and in this case was known as HMS Nuthatch. In the RAF it would have been called a maintenance unit, but held the rather grand title of Aircraft Receipt and Dispatch Unit (ARDU) and although it had obviously played a prominent role during WWII, mainly bringing American built aircraft up to Fleet Air Arm standards, it now looked, like many other wartime built airfields, on it's last legs. Considering that the rundown of the Station was well under way it came as something of a surprise that it still sported two wardrooms and enough staff to provide a Wren stewardess behind every other seating place for dinner. A luxury indeed by RAF standards. The weather was particularly fine for flying during our short stay but pronounced as about average by the Naval Staff based there. In aviation terms, the UK must have just about the most variable weather, region by region, than any other country of comparable size.

Back at Syerston the steady plod continued, enlivened now and again by the composition of certain courses and, in that respect, one in particular often comes back to mind in that almost the entire course consisted of fully qualified RAF doctors, and what a lively bunch they turned out to be. They all mucked in socially and often enjoyed a night out in Newark drinking with the rest of us. One of my doctor students, David Urquart, dedicated his entire working life to "aviation medicine", finishing as a Group Captain on the staff of the RAF School of that name at Farnborough. Another, tragically, was killed at Farnborough flying a Meteor jet but his name lives on in the Air Force with the Fox-Linton memorial trophy being awarded annually. Yet another doctor dedicated his life to the Royal Air Force and during the time he was training for his wings, his caring attitude to others was well noted. It came as no surprise, therefore, that close on twenty years later, when Betty and myself were visiting a WAAF Officer friend in the RAF hospital at Wroughton that this ex student, and now the hospital commandant, should pop into the room to have a word with his WAAF officer patient well after the normal end of work hours. He had hardly changed, but was now Group Captain Riseley-Pritchard. He had a word with Betty however as I was in a corner in the early evening half light, he did not pick me out and I thought it was just as well because it was probably not the time, and certainly not the place, to bang on about the good old days at Syerston.

Another input of students came as something of a surprise, to me at least, because they were from the Indonesian Navy. It was just about five years prior to their arrival that the Spitfire Squadron that I was serving on in Singapore was flying patrols over the Dutch East Indies in the forlorn hope that we could induce local insurgents to keep their heads down whilst the British and Dutch armies endeavoured to restore Dutch rule to their lost empire. Surely I thought Indonesia, after gaining it's independence, could not already be thinking of operating aircraft carriers? It never came about, not surprisingly.

The Fleet Air Arm had one or two odd customs and I fell foul to one when I was asked to pick up a Harvard from Yeovilton Naval Air Station in Somerset. I had already completed two full instructional details that morning before I set sail in a Prentice aircraft I had managed to borrow

Percival Prentice

from one of the basic flights, along with a Ground School pilot who had jumped at the chance of getting away from it all for the afternoon. He would also be by himself for the return flight in the Prentice, which pleased him even more. With time not on our side it was a case of a quick coffee after landing before I signed for the Harvard and started the engine. It was certainly a little worrying when I asked for taxying instructions and was told to shut down immediately and report to Commander Flying, it was a Lt Cmdr in fact, but no matter. Had we flown through someone's airspace or what? On entering the Commander's office I was told in no uncertain terms that in the Fleet Air Arm flights extending to more than 40 nautical miles radius from ship called for a full briefing of the pilot concerned by the Commander Air, or his deputy. He then launched into a full Met. Briefing and departure procedure. Time was running out if I was to make it back to base that day, so I took the plunge and interjected that the Met. Briefing was very much along the lines that I had already received at Syerston, but in the event the weather had proved much better than expected on the flight down. "You mean to say you have just flown down and are returning on the same day"? was his reaction. "Yes, and I have already carried out two dual details with Royal Navy students before setting off and I'm rather pushed for time if you don't mind, Sir", was my final remark before taking my leave with an RN salute. Back on the flight line I told the Prentice pilot awaiting my departure to ensure I got away and that he had better start up and follow me before anyone else had any more bright ideas, and with a bit of luck the Tower would now assume we had both been briefed. We thought we might receive a phone call back at base but the Lt Cmdr must have given up on the RAF and their cavalier attitude to flying!

The only other solo away day that I managed during my time on the Naval FTS was very nostalgic indeed, for it was down to where it all began for me, and that was dear old Halton, a mecca for ex-brats even in those days. The Queen was in the first few months of her reign when she honoured that Station with a visit to present the first Queen's Colour to be awarded to an RAF station, which duly took place on 25th July 1952, with all ex-Brats having been invited to attend. RAF Halton, sporting only a smallish grass landing strip meant that not many arrived by air. However, whilst taxying to dispersal I noted with interest that one of the few visiting aircraft was also from Syerston. It had been flown in by a Flt Lt pilot from another flight, who I had never realised was also an ex Haltonian. As both of us had found some problems in persuading our respective Flight Commanders to release a Harvard for the day, we made a pact to keep quiet that two Harvards being used when only one would have fitted the bill. My landing had been a little emotional, thinking back to 12 years ago when I had made my very first RAF flight in the back of a Miles Magister from this very airfield.

After a most impressive Colour Parade, even by Halton standards, all guests were invited to stand outside the Officers' Mess to witness the Queen's departure from the Station. Security seemed to be far more relaxed in those days and many of us were virtually on the entrance steps for Her Majesty's farewell from what is highly likely the most palatial Officers' Mess that the RAF have ever known. The Mess started life as "Halton House", and was built on the French Chateau lines by Alfred de Rothschild when he took over the 1500 acres family estate in 1883 and, historically, shares the distinction along with Buckingham Palace, of being one of the first buildings in this country to install electric lighting. Halton House remained in private hands until the death of Alfred de Rothschild in 1918, when it was taken over by the Army and later the RAF, thanks to the efforts of Lord Trenchard, the father of the RAF. Although the mess had been out of bounds on that day for visiting officers, and probably for at least half the living in members as well, I resolved that one day I would have a look at the magnificent interior. On 31st October 1997, Betty and I, along with 1500 other ex-brats from all over the world, assembled at RAF Halton where the Queen presented a new colour to the station, and it might be right to point out at this time that only 9 Queens' colours have ever been presented to RAF formations, the last as long ago as 1969. However, the main reason for such a large turn out was that Her Majesty had also graciously consented to unveil a "Tribute" to the entire apprentice scheme which had terminated a few years earlier. The "Tribute" had been sited outside "Kermode Hall", the ground school for Halton apprentices. Another fantastic day for Betty and myself.

Although the flying accident rate amongst students during pilot training was kept fairly low, particularly in peacetime, we did suffer two fatal accidents during my time on No 22 SFTS, both being RN Midshipmen. The first was during a solo aerobatic detail, but whether the student was below his minimum authorised height when he got into an inadvertent spin, nobody will ever know. He impacted near a disused airfield in North Lincolnshire which was not within our normal operating area. The other student failed to return from a straightforward solo navigation exercise. As no reports of an aircraft accident were received, a few instructors were detailed to fly his planned route with students to double the look out scan. My log book records that I was aloft with Dr Dave Urquart for nearly two hours on what turned out to be a fruitless search. It was not until the next morning that a farmer found the wreckage in one of his fields, which was certainly not on the student's planned route. When we placed a line on the map between Syerston and the accident site it just so happened that it was on the direct route towards his much talked about home town! Sadly, this had happened all too frequently during the war years when for some young men it had certainly been a case of live for today for tomorrow you may die.

Syerston could get a little crowded at times but we were particularly lucky in having two relief landing grounds which took the strain at peak times. One was the all grass airfield of nearby RAF Newton, and the other was what is now known as Nottingham Airport but called Tollerton in those days, and was ideal with it's three Tarmac runways which catered rather well for varying wind conditions.

My final, and best remembered, period with the Royal Navy at Syerston included a two week detachment to St Merryn, near Padstow in Cornwall.

Not having visited that county before, I had often wondered if it could possibly be as scenic as people made it out to be. In the event, it more than lived up to expectations, and the site of St Merryn (HMS Vulture) could not have been, in that respect, located in a more idyllic situation, being on Cornwall's North Coast, close to the lovely fishing port of Padstow. St Merryn seemed to be suffering from a lack of trade at that time and our reception seemed to reflect that situation. Nothing was too much trouble, and one of our requests, on how we could manage the odd night out in Padstow without any of our own transport being available, was met with a prompt response. One of the staff officers said there would be no trouble in laying on a "Liberty Boat", a night bus in today's parlance, at a cost of about sixpence a head, which was about the cost of a pint of beer in those days, but we would have to ensure that the Coxswain (driver) was properly looked after in Padstow. One or two of us were wondering what on earth would we do with a hairy old matelot while we lived it up a little in downtown Padstow. We need not have worried unduly because when the boat pulled up alongside the wardroom one night, one or two of our Midshipmen's eyes popped out a little, to say nothing of those of us approaching the ripe old age of thirty. The Coxswain turned out to be a stunning young Wren in immaculate uniform, she paid us a compliment in volunteering to act as our driver on all subsequent nights ashore during our stay there.

Two other strange naval customs came to light at St Merryn, the first was when I was in the company of two resident officers who began to discuss if they should invite the ship's Captain into the wardroom for some special occasion or other, and seemed taken aback when I asked if a ship's Captain really needed an invitation to enter his own Wardroom. "Good God, yes", was the immediate reply. "He has his own quarters and staff, and is only allowed in here as a guest". In later years in the RAF I often thought it was a very good idea on some occasions, particularly so when a certain station commander gave a right dressing down to a visiting Flt Lt who had failed to stand on his entrance to the Mess Bar. As the visitor was facing the bar with his back to the sitting door, the visitor would certainly have needed eyes in the back of his head to see the self important grand entrance.

The second custom was completely foreign to the junior service from the start of the second war onwards, when bars had first been introduced to replace waiter service in the ante-room of each Officers' Mess. It was brought home to us shortly after our arrival when a Naval Officer approached a group of about seven or eight of us and asked each in turn what we wanted to drink, making due note on a bar chit. As most of our group were RAF we thought it was a very kind, if expensive, gesture on his part, that is until he went around the buoy, as they say in the Royal Navy, to ask each in turn what our bar numbers were. We had not even acquired a bar number at that time, however he said names would do nicely. The strictly "no treating" rule was obviously still in force.

A fantastic two weeks for instructors and students alike was rapidly coming to an end when a little mishap marred our visit. One of the RAF students, an SEG, managed to lift the undercarriage of his Harvard whilst taxying. He still gained his wings and I served under him, two Stations later, when he was a deputy flight commander at RAF Shawbury. Unfortunately, he was killed on his next posting when as a unit test pilot at the Central Flying School whilst flying a Gnat on a routine air test.

CHAPTER 20
Navigational Training School

My time at Syerston was coming to an end and after two tours on training student pilots to Wings standard I was certainly ready for a change, but what a change it turned out to be. I was now listed as a multi-engined pilot having flown both the Oxford and Mosquito, and this was certainly why I was on my way to become a staff pilot on Ansons and Wellingtons at one of the two remaining Navigational Training Schools in the UK, although for some strange reason the RAF were still sending U/T navigators to both Rhodesia and Canada. It was to No 6 ANS at RAF Lichfield that I was to spend just over 12 interesting months before that Station, known to the locals as Fradley, closed to operational flying and returned to it's original use of a Maintenance Unit. During the war it had acted as a Wellington Bomber OCU so accommodation was plentiful, although of the wooden hut variety. This was the very last RAF Station of wartime construction that I was to serve on, the remainder being of the solid pre-wartime type. No 6 ANS was mainly equipped with Ansons and Wellingtons with a few Valetta T3s, flying classrooms, with five astrodomes on the main fuselage.

I thought I would be employed initially on the Ansons and work my way up to Wellingtons and eventually the Valetta. Luckily I started off on Wellingtons, I say luckily because the Wellington was phased out long before the station ceased to be an ANS, and having worked on them as ground crew throughout 1942 I had always wanted to pilot one. I found that the dear old Wimpey was an absolute delight to fly and, much to my surprise, far less demanding than even the Oxford trainer. I knew the airframe side of the Wellington inside out, of course, but it was the first time that I had operated the Hercules engine and I, along with a couple of other new boys, went to Bristols on their engine course, the first of three "Makers" courses that I eventually took. It was absolutely superb, with just the right measure of what a pilot needs to know and enough technical insight to talk intelligently with ground engineers when recording defects. There was, understandably enough, some doom and gloom on the airfield when we paid a visit to see the mighty Brabazon in it's giant sized hangar, because everyone realised that it was not a goer and was, in fact, scrapped a year later. The engine side of Bristol's, however, was still on a high with their successes with the Hercules engine and later types, all using Sleeve Valves instead of Poppet valves which had been the norm in virtually every internal combustion engine hitherto. The internal sleeve valves not only went up and down, but with variable size cut outs in their casing made for extra efficiency in that the mix of petrol and air incoming, and exhaust gases outgoing, was far better regulated than had been possible in the past. A side issue was, that type of engine was much quieter than the poppet types and it was not surprising that the Beaufighter, fitted with two of these engines, was referred to by the Japanese army in Burma as "whispering death". The concept of this type of valve had been first thought of by a lady engineer called Miss Strickland, and was always referred to as Miss Strickland's orifice. Most unkind, I must admit.

Vickers Wellington

Having served only in the Royal Air Force until that time, I was not particularly well up on economics, but it was at Bristol's that I learnt my very first basic lesson. The Labour government of the early post war years had imposed some very hefty taxes, not least, the excess profits tax that reached a high of 95%. It was during yet another lavish lunch in a part of Bristol's Headquarters, reserved for top management and board members, that I protested that it must be costing the company a bomb with so much food and wine being supplied free of charge to we RAF mortals. "Don't you worry your head about that one", replied one of the very top men, "for every pound spent on you will cost us only sixpence and we think it is money well spent entertaining the RAF". He had a point, and no doubt most other big companies were doing the same, which sent one's mind into overdrive.

After returning to the job in hand at Lichfield one particular flight that I undertook in a Wellington, along with every other available aircraft of that type we could muster, was regarded as somewhat bizarre by any standards, a view shared by all pilots on the station from the Group Captain downwards, but orders had been received from group HQ that a raid on Cologne, in the Ruhr, as per second world war operating heights, etc, was to take place. We never saw any other aircraft during the flight so what had it all been about? A radar reporting exercise or what? We never did find out. Wellington's had, in fact, taken part in the world's first ever 1,000 bomber raid from Lichfield, just as per the OTU I had been serving on at RAF Pershore as ground crew on that fateful night, and in that respect it brought back memories of what the crews must have felt doing it for real and at night. However, it was now 10 years on, and the first jet Canberra bomber had already been in service for nearly a year with 101 Squadron at RAF Binbrook, so why had they not been tasked instead of Wellingtons?

My secondary duty at RAF Lichfield was a world away from the mundane one of I/C Blankets at Syerston. After completing a weeks Flight Safety course at the Air Ministry in London, I duly took over the appointment of Station Flight Safety Officer (SFSO) and found the task very interesting. I was involved with this aspect of aviation for my next four postings, covering many different types of aircraft. At Lichfield we had three major accidents in fairly quick succession, but, thank goodness, without any fatalities. Two involved the Wellington and in both cases I concluded that it was one of Barnes Wallace's best brainchilds that had saved the day for the crews. I refer to the geodetic construction of the fuselage which could take a great deal of punishment without disintegration. The pilot of the Wellington that managed to land in a farmer's field close to Lichfield had actually called "downwind to land" just before he called again to say he had crash landed but all the crew were safe. There are no prizes for concluding that the pilot had set the wrong altimeter setting when joining the circuit that very dark night. The second crash was far more serious in that it was something of a miracle that the entire crew were not killed in their accident. This time impact was with high ground in the Peak District when the pilot thought he was approaching base over the lowlands of the Trent valley. The Polish NCO pilot had realised just before the crash that all was not well and had converted a descent into a climb by applying full power with the result that the aircraft slithered up the side of a steepish hill, it was a close run thing. The pilot was the only crew member to suffer injuries necessitating hospital treatment, and he finished up in Burton-on-Trent General Hospital.

Even serious accidents can have a lighter side. It was part of my terms of reference to have photographs taken of every accident site whenever possible and things did not work out at all well from the very beginning of starting to comply with that diktat. The photographic section did not have an airman to spare to accompany me to the crash scene but, nevertheless, gave me a camera and some basic tuition. Next it was the Motor Transport section who could not possibly spare a vehicle let alone a driver for the day. The NCO in charge then came up with a possible solution. He had noted that if mileage was anything to go by the van placed at the disposal of the Wing Commander Flying, Wing Commander Percy Oldroyd, was not used much and he would give him a ring to get clearance for it's use on such an important mission as mine. He said that the Wing Commander always left the van keys in position and I could get on my way unless I heard otherwise. Sure enough, the keys were there in the van outside the tower, and I had already started the engine when there was a knock on the side window from a very puzzled looking Wing Commander Oldroyd. I obviously switched off and got out to be asked "where on earth was I thinking of going with the van without permission"? Obviously the WingCo had not been contacted by MT, but I assumed that after I had explained the situation I would be on my way. It was not to be, the Wing Commander said he had spoken to some of the survivors and it was an "open and shut case", and I needn't bother with photographs as it would be a complete waste of time. It goes, almost without saying, that the first thing the board of inquiry asked for was photographs of the accident scene. Because Percy Oldroyd was regarded as something of a dear old soul, old by our standards that is, I decided to take the flak and said I hadn't taken any because all the crew having survived, no doubt the reason for the accident would be regarded as an "open and shut" case at the end of their inquiry. That my opinion was not particularly well received was not very surprising.

Another twist to the inquiry was that Percy had asked me to have a word with the Polish Pilot in Burton Hospital before the board members arrived and convened the inquiry as he was the only crew member, so far, who had not given his version of events. I did not own a car at that time and it crossed my mind, for a split second only, to ask the Wing Commander for a loan of his van, but discretion prevailed and so it was that I took a bus both ways. During the ride to Burton, I was trying like mad to think if I had been given any coded messages for the pilot before the inquiry interviewed him, but drew a blank. After all, it was an open and shut case according to OC Flying. My appearance in an open ward in No 1 RAF uniform drew many curious glances from staff nurses and patients alike and our conversation, from a well bandaged Polish pilot, who did not speak English particularly well, seemed to make quite a few ears pop. Perhaps some of the other patients had not yet realised that he was an RAF pilot who had been involved in a very recent flying accident.

The final flying accident was when a visiting Meteor pilot, flying one of the early night fighter versions, failed to lift off on departure and crashed just across a canal at the end of the main runway. The RAFs knowledge of operating nose wheel type aircraft had been limited to American bombers, now all gone. The long nosed Meteor Mk VII trainer had, on a few occasions, failed to take off and it was later realised that if the nose was not lifted as soon as possible, negative lift could develop to prevent the nose lifting at all. If anyone should think that the RAF were slow on the uptake, it can be pointed out that one of BOACs earlier Comet aircraft suffered a similar fate at Calcutta after it had been in service for some little time before the accident.

All good things come to an end eventually, and it was a very sad day indeed when I made my very last Wellington flight on January 7th 1953. It was by no means the end for the dear old Wimpy as the other UK based ANS soldiered on with them a while longer, but it was certainly the beginning of the end for the ANS at Lichfield. The Wellington did not go out in a complete blaze of glory because at a Battle of Britain open day at RAF Middleton St George- now Teesside Airport- a Wellington was being put through it's paces along the crowd line when it's dinghy hatch, in the starboard engine nacelles, became detached and the dinghy became entangled around the elevator on that side of the aircraft. Control was lost and all five crew members were killed. It had been a black Saturday all round with 15 other RAF casualties that day. With the RAF losing, on average, 300 aircrew killed each year, something had to be done about the situation, not least of all because Sir Winston Churchill, now Prime Minister again, had started asking questions about the alarming statistics. Our Wellingtons were not flown out for storage, they were just towed across the airfield for the attention of a local scrap dealer and looked very forlorn as they were dismantled piece by piece.

Both Betty and I made some very good friends during our short stay at Lichfield and we all seemed to follow each other around the air force for many a year. "Taff" John, who had been awarded the DFM in the Far East as a Liberator pilot, went on to fly Hastings, like myself, and we both became instructors on that type at Thorney Island about 12 years later, and with Ray Hudson, unit test pilot at Lichfield, taking root in the local village of Emsworth, we often had a good laugh about our time at Lichfield, not least about Percy Oldroyd's renowned eyesight and his difficulty in picking up the runway after turning onto finals even in the best of visibilities, although we had all enjoyed serving under him. Being a married officer had certainly not been a bed of roses at that time and Taff, for instance, could only find lodgings in a local vicarage which, of course, had it's difficulties.

In that department I was a little more fortunate in finding a completely furnished house to rent in Hammerwich near Brownhills. Part of the deal was looking after a dog called "Winston" who wanted full attention all the time, and a black cat called "Butch" who we never saw except at meal times. The village was about twelve miles from the airfield but I managed to get by on public transport during normal hours, but when on night flying details it was a case of a bicycle made for one. The cost of living then was £31 per month rent against an income of £53 per month for a Flying Officer Pilot. There was certainly no chance of exceeding the £7.50 per month limit imposed on bar bills in those days for junior officers!

If I had thought that the Wellington was a very easy aircraft to handle I was in for another pleasant surprise when we on the Wellington flight transferred to Ansons for the aircraft virtually flew itself for most of the time, and that was just as well on long cross countries without an auto pilot. How bomber pilots managed 8 to 10 hour trips without a co-pilot

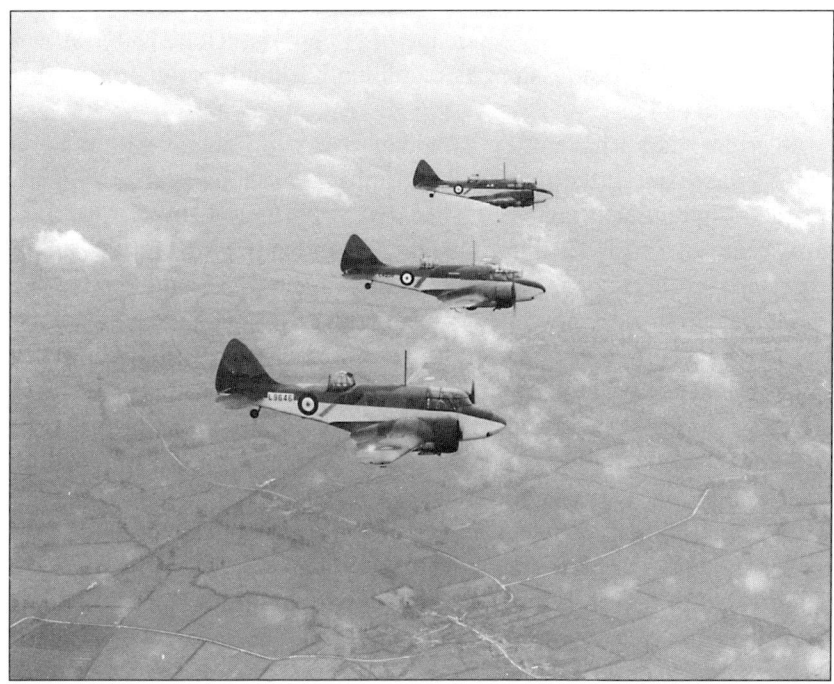

Avro Anson

beggars belief.

Our station commander at Lichfield was Group Captain Larkin, and that rank in peacetime indicated an age of about 35 to 40 plus which, in turn, meant that they were invariably of pre-war vintage by the early 1950s. Some had become accustomed to the more relaxed way of life during the war, whilst others wished to turn the clock back to the good old days. Group Captain Larkin was a mixture of both and having been awarded the DFC he had certainly not survived the war by being stuck on the North West Frontier, or some such place, for the duration. I think a bit of the old School came to the fore in the Officers' Mess one particular lunch time when most of us, including a certain F/O McCann, were reading the daily papers. Suddenly there was a mighty roar from the station commander when he shouted, "McCann, is this your engagement I'm reading about in the society column? I don't recall you introducing your fiancee to me for vetting. No officer was allowed to marry in my day without the intended being vetted, you know I don't know what the air force is coming to". We all tried to lift our papers a shade higher and suppress sniggers all round. F/O McCann also became a Hastings transport pilot in later years, and even after attaining the rank of Sqdn Ldr, was often referred to by his nickname of "Popo", which he had acquired when he was first commissioned as a pilot officer and his two initials just happened to be PO.

Over the years I have often wondered if Group Captain Larkin knew about a story doing the rounds about himself. It appears that during a top staff appointment in Italy he decided to fly himself in an Anson on an official visit to RAF Luqa, in Malta. On landing in Malta he fully expected a reception party plus staff car to meet him, and also that the two marshalling airmen would be in white overalls using red marshalling bats, as is the norm for important visitors of senior rank. What he actually saw was two scruffy looking airmen sauntering out and waving their arms around in a most disinterested manner to park his aircraft in an out of the way spot. As one might expect, the Group Captain was in a fine old fettle by this time, and really laid into the two marshallers after disembarking, while a third airman who had arrived on the scene stood looking on near the wing tip. It was a phone call from the Wing Commander flying to the Control Tower asking if there was any news on Group Captain Larkin's arrival that really set things in motion. An air traffic clerk was despatched by tower MT to check that it was not the Group Captain's aircraft that had already landed. The airman driver could have phrased his question better when he arrived at the aircraft and asked of the onlooker at the wing tip, "Is that Group Captain Larkin"? to which he got the unexpected reply, "Is he bloody hell as like, he's serious, I'd run off quick if I were you".

I was really enjoying my Anson flying, particularly so when we managed to fit in any pilot on a ground tour at the RAF recruiting base of Henesford, also on Cannock Chase. It was a delight to see the look on their faces when they got their hands on the controls again. I was to have my own wings clipped for a three week period in the summer of 1952 when I was detailed to take an Anson down to RAF Odiham where the Queen's Coronation Review of the Royal Air Force was to take place on the 18th July 1953 when 320 aircraft would be lined up for a mass inspection by Her Majesty and the Duke of Edinburgh, which would be followed by a formation fly past of 641 other aircraft. Not quite a 1000 aircraft but as near as damn it, and all being over, or on, one RAF airfield was quite something. Once again, I met Wing Commander Oldroyd just at the wrong moment, because two days after arriving at Odiham I was told by a Group Captain inspecting officer that I was the pilot of probably the worst kept aircraft that had arrived so far and I had better take it back to Lichfield for a complete re-spray of the mainly fabric covered aircraft. I must say our navigational trainer did stand out like a sore thumb when parked alongside other Ansons, mainly of the Mk 19 VIP variety. After landing back at base I bumped into Percy Oldroyd who, after doing a double take, said "I thought we'd sent you off to Odiham earlier in the week, what's going on?" I said that I did go but the aircraft had not passed their inspection and needed a paint job. "Oh, bloody hell, go and tell Tech Wing to get somebody to give it a touch up here and there and get back to Odiham", was his quick answer to the problem. He was somewhat annoyed when I said a Group Captain had said a full re-spray was required. Apparently Engineering wing worked a couple of 24 hour shifts to re-paint the Anson, but they could have taken a lot longer for all I cared because I had already tasted life at Odiham for a couple of days.

All visiting aircrew and ground crew below a certain rank, which certainly included me, had to sleep under canvass and take meals in a disused hangar. The only saving grace was that the delightful local village of Odiham, sporting many pubs, was well within walking distance of the airfield. However, three full weeks was not something to look forward to, and how on earth we managed to keep our uniforms fit for royal inspection, after many dummy runs, remains a mystery to this day, especially as we twice suffered waterlogging of the tented site during that period. After each waterlogging all tents were infested with earwigs to such an extent that an earwig club was born, complete with tie, but I never got around to buying one. Explaining the tie to curious strangers would have taken some doing. A full review of the Royal Air Force being connected with earwigs indeed!

I met two people from the past before the big day, the first going back eleven years when F/Sgt Bishop was my NCO boss at Pershore and he seemed to be genuinely pleased that one of his "boys" had made it to "Wings" plus a commission. The other was "Mack" McKenzie who had been on the same OCTU course two years previously, and was now the navigator of a B29, the Superfortress, which was parked on the row in front of our lines of also rans. After what seemed an eternity, the inspection day arrived and what a magnificent sight the mass fly past turned out to be, and I could not help but wonder how on earth the impeccable timing had been achieved with so many different types of aircraft flying at vastly differing speeds. Little did I think that 24 years later, I would be Captain of a Lancaster bomber with a Spitfire on one wing tip and a Hurricane on the other, trying to achieve the same during Her Majesty's Jubilee inspection of the Royal Air Force at RAF Finningley. In 1953 I did not think that I would still be flying with the RAF, even ten years later, let alone a quarter of a century on. The Queen and Duke duly inspected all of the ground based aircraft driving slowly by in the royal Land Rover, after which it was all anti climax, and we nearly had to suffer a bit of idiocy as regards getting the static display aircraft back to their bases.

A grand plan was published which only allowed so many aircraft per hour to depart, and in a set order by type. For instance, Mac and his B29 were slotted for day one after the inspection and our small Anson fleet, about six strong from six different Stations, on about day four. Thank goodness, I did not take up Mac's offer of a passenger flight to Marham in his aircraft after he had noticed my interest in that type. He said he could easily fix a rail warrant for my return to Odiham by stating urgent business, and I would be back by the end of the day and unlikely to be missed. The big offshoot of declining his offer was that I also departed on day one back to Lichfield. Not having anything better to do at Odiham after it was all over, most Anson pilots gathered to watch the departure of the B29s, when a pilot of another type on our line, also slotted for day four, said after noting how few aircraft were getting away per hour that he had had enough and was going to pack his kit and start up his aircraft and see what happened then. We all concluded that he would be told to shut down immediately and stood rather stunned as he taxied by with a big grin on his face, giving the thumbs up sign. It certainly opened the floodgates as we all dashed to pack our kit and get away as soon as possible. The air traffic controllers had a certain something in their voice which indicated that they, too, fully agreed with the mass exodus, instead of the programme initially thought of. What the cooks did with all the food they thought would be used that week remained a mystery.

Back at Lichfield I found that I had inherited some family money during my absence, and with Betty's full agreement, I took the plunge and bought our first car, a Ford Consul for all of £700; I suppose about £11,000 in today's values. My popularity shot up the Richter scale which was natural enough. Strange as it may seem, I did not have to pass a civilian driving test at that time having driven during the war years in the family Lanchester, so that was one big obstacle out of the way. On one occasion, being the owner of a car was a little amusing. I had been drinking in what was, at least in those days, the best bar in Lichfield, the saloon of the Angle Hotel, when I struck up a conversation with a fellow drinker who turned out to be an Army Major from the local barracks. At one point he said he had better be off to try and find a taxi, so I invited him to stay and have a few more when I would do the honours in my newly acquired car. Although we had already established that he was a Major and that I was a mere Flying Officer, he introduced me as a Squadron Leader when we took a few more drinks in the ante room of the Lichfield Officers' Mess. A bit of snobbery on the Major's part I suppose. It was a pleasant way to finish the evening with the few other inmates seeming to take an interest in talking to an RAF pilot. It also gave me an insight into what the social life must have been for RAF officers in the pre-war years, when they too had waiter service only.

I had really enjoyed life at RAF Lichfield, steadily building up my multi engine hours, which stood me in good stead later in my flying life with the RAF, and I had particularly enjoyed using the standard beam approach system for the first time in anger since training on that system in Rhodesia. As it turned out, it was to be the last time, as airfield radars gradually took over as the norm for guiding aircraft down to safe landings in marginal weather. The end came suddenly when our last course moved to RAF Hullavington to complete their training and a posting to RAF Shawbury quickly followed.

CHAPTER 21
RAF Shawbury

At that time RAF Shawbury, near Shrewsbury, was the home of the Central Navigation and Control School (CNCS) which had, with the sudden increase in airfield radars a vastly increased commitment to train air traffic controllers in the art of radar talk downs. This meant more staff pilots were required to flog around the visual circuit calling downwind, finals, etc time after time after time, in addition to flying for the U/T radar talk down controllers. Before our arrival of six or so extra pilots from Lichfield, the circuit at Shawbury had already become so cluttered that an old airfield to the North called Sleap had been re-activated for talk downs using a radar called ACR7, with which controllers could keep the pilot on the centre line of the landing runway and also measure his distance to run to the field, but it could not indicate if the pilot was at the correct height for the normal 3° descent. However it could inform him what height he should be at using the 300'/mile rule. The aircraft used for this task was the faithful old Annie (Anson), so a conversion course was not required for our input of staff pilots and our arrival was met with full approval all round. The Central Navigation School, sharing the Station with the Air Traffic School, was used for the training of instructors for NAV Schools, but with only one such school left in England by the spring of 1954, it's commitment had been drastically reduced over the recent years, although it retained quite a few Lincoln aircraft for that purpose.

On occasions we managed to get weekend trips, acting as second pilots, to Gibraltar. On our two free days off there we could either take a trip across the Spanish border, which was close to the Officers' Mess, to the town of La Linia, or even a day return on the ferry to Tangiers and visit it's famous Souk. Then again, if we tired of either, there was always our near relatives, the Babary Apes, up on the Rock who we could go and have a chat with after a few beers in the main street.

Avro Lincoln

With our prime objective being the training of Airtraffickers, as opposed to Navigators at Lichfield, it did not matter a jot what type of Anson we flew, and what a collection of different marks we wound up with, ranging from one very early Mk X through to the VIP C19, plus the very latest Nav trainer, the T21. The C19 still had all the trimmings of a VIP aircraft and was always very popular with senior officers when they wanted to go from A to B in some style. We quite enjoyed such trips as well, getting away from umpteen circuits per hour, or radar runs as the case may have been. For some reason or other, the number of radar runs had to be recorded at the end of each detail and committing the number to memory would have been an extra chore but for the fact that most of the fleet still had radio aerials fitted, although never used at Shawbury, with lead ball weights attached to the end of the cable, and all one had to do was flick one lead ball across after each run and then count them after landing. During radar runs the under training operator was called upon to say at a certain height, the minimum descent height, "make a check of your cockpit and land ahead visually". That was all very well until one day a very flustered WRAF officer was heard to call "Make a cock of your checkpit and crash ahead visually". Another cock up, not literally, was when the Station Commander decided to check the facilities for the WRAF U/T officers at our RAF Sleap satellite, and obviously took along the senior WRAF officer, always known as the WRAF "G" or Queen Bee, for the inspection. As luck would have it, the AOC rang RAF Shawbury for a word with the Station Commander whilst they were away. The adjutant took the call and informed the AOC that the CO had gone to Sleap with the WRAF "G". After the AOC had asked the adjutant to repeat what he had just said, he barked down the phone, "When the Station Commander returns from having gone to sleep with the WRAF "G", kindly tell him to give me a ring immediately". Word soon got around from on high that RAF Sleap was to be referred to in future as RAF Slape.

Another unfortunate incident with the same AOC and telephone calls occurred shortly after that. One day it was fairly early in the morning, by Station Headquarters standards that is, when an airman who had been told to report to SHQ at 0830 played on the safe side and turned up at about 0815 to find himself just about the only person on the premises. The key orderly having done his job of opening up all offices, had departed for a late breakfast. It was whilst standing patiently outside a Flt Lts office that the airman heard various telephone bells ringing. First the COs office, then the adjutant and so on until the one in the Flt Lts office rang and the airman couldn't resist the temptation any more and went in and asked the caller if he could help. A rather miffed voice asked if the Station Commander had arrived yet to which the airman replied "I've no idea mate, but I don't think so because I've heard his phone ringing". The AOC, full of rage repeated, "'I've no idea mate, do you realise who you are speaking to, I'm your Air Officer Commanding". At which point the airman had the final say of "Bloody good mate", before slamming the phone down and making a hasty exit through the back door of SHQ, returning about 20 minutes later, full of apologies to the Flt Lt for his late arrival. The airman, who was on National Service, kept his mouth shut for another month or so until his last day in the RAF when he confided to one or two of his friends the full story, which ended with his birds eye view of officers in SHQ running around like headless chickens from office to office, asking each other had they any knowledge of a phone call having been received from the AOC that morning. It had truly hit the fan, as they say.

The chances of being allocated a married quarter in the early 1950s was very slim indeed and so it was that I, and many others, lived in the Mess for some little time while we scouted around the local area for suitable accommodation to live out in. Life in the Mess varied wildly at that time, but what I did not expect was that two formal dinner nights per week was the norm for living in members at Shawbury, and what a farce they were with absolutely everyone concerned, officers and Mess staff alike, trying to end them as soon as possible. They would not have been possible on virtually any other flying station due to night flying commitments, but Shawbury hardly ever flew during the dark hours as my log book for that period records. After these very boring dinners, the race was invariably on to see who could get changed out of Mess Kit quickest, and get down to one of our favourite pubs in down town Shrewsbury, where we were certainly not spoilt for choice. However, it invariably fell to one of four. We had one called the "Old Post Office" which was a very down to earth public house, but with a landlord who thought the RAF could do no wrong. Next, there was the Boathouse and, as the name suggests, it was perched on a lovely stretch of the River Severn. Then came the saloons of two hotels, "The Crown" and "The Raven". The Crown, like all others, was supposed to stop serving drinks at 10.30pm, but it was legal to obtain them until 11.00pm if one was eating. Their obliging barmaids, if one was known to be RAF that is, did not bat an eyelid if at about 10.30 any of us asked for a pint of Worthington "E" and a plate with crumbs on, plus a rolled up napkin. Lastly, the Raven was an old coaching hotel, with a very nice cellar bar, on the old London to Holyhead route, and would certainly have been made into a listed building in later years, however it was demolished before then, much to the annoyance of no less a person than the Poet Laureate of the day Sir John Betjamen, who wrote stinging letters of disapproval to the national press about it's demise.

I eventually found accommodation for Betty and myself, which led to a more sober life, which was on the west bank of the River Severn, the same side as the Boat House pub, so an evening stroll down the hill was always possible. It was at Shawbury that Betty made her first ever aircraft flight. I had better begin by saying that our satellite airfield at RAF Sleap, or should I call it Slape, was only used for radar runs and we were never allowed to do "touch and gos" because the runway had fallen below acceptable standards for RAF aircraft and, in any event, it meant that fire cover was not required. However, with light aviation beginning to pick up again after the war years, a group of would be civilian pilots decided to form a flying group and successfully applied to the then Air Ministry to use that airfield for week end flying only. They certainly put the cart before the horse when they went out and purchased a war surplus Taylorcraft D High Wing Monoplane, without having any flying instructors yet available to start the flying training ball rolling. One or two of us , who had passed the CFS course, heard of their plight and gladly agreed to help out, however we had to wait a week or two before the CAA issued us with a civil pilot's licence. In the meantime, the Taylorcraft had arrived mid week and being unable to land at Sleap, due to our normal traffic using that field, had put down at Shawbury. The aircraft remained in one of our hangars until our licences arrived and then I had the honour of flying it out one weekend with Betty aboard for her very first flight and, also, my first solo on type, which was quite a double. Taking the aircraft out of Shawbury on a Sunday morning caused no trouble whatsoever as Shawbury, despite it's short runways, was a Master Diversion Airfield (MDA) which meant being open 24 hours a day with full emergency cover. The controllers, in fact, seemed to be glad to talk to somebody during their shift and one who was in the know even called "understand you are taking your wife to Sleap, Jacko". "Ah, very funny", was my riposte, although Betty had a big smile on her face as I glanced across the cockpit to see her reaction to the call. I understand that the flying club at Sleap is still going strong, although I doubt that they are using the Taylorcraft any more.

One morning I was somewhat surprised to be told that it was intended to make me an IRE, that is an Instrument Rating Examiner, which meant testing other pilots on their flying ability when under the hood or in cloud, and issuing them with a Master-Green, Green or White card allowing them to fly in varying conditions of poor visibility. The reason for my surprise was that, like most other flying stations, RAF Shawbury had it's own "Standards Flight" whose prime job was to do just that sort of thing and they were not conspicuously over worked as far as one could see. However, all would be revealed, as they say, and so it came about that after flying down to CFS at Rissington and returning with a pass, all in the same day, my Flight Commander was soon being asked by the Station Commander if I could be spared for a few hours so that he could fly with me whilst he brushed up on his I F and eventually take an I F exam. The Station Commander turned out to be an excellent pilot, but I soon had the impression that after he had flown with at least one of the "Standards" pilots that he was not too impressed with their attitude. The other side of the coin, of course, was that I suddenly became less popular with Standards than hitherto, but that's life for you.

Another twist of fortune soon followed when every pilot at Shawbury was asked if they had ever flown a Vampire jet. I had, of course, to admit to one trip only at CFS and that was five years in the past. That did not seem to matter because, unbeknown to most of us, the Air Traffic Control course at Shawbury was soon to enter the jet age and about ten staff pilots would be required to man the fleet of Vampire NF10s that would be arriving shortly. It seemed that the one jet trip of mine was reason enough to send me on my way to a full conversion course at No 206 Advanced Flying School at RAF Oakington, near Cambridge. This was to be followed by a makers course at the De Havilland factory at Hatfield. At Oakington the OC flying was Wing Commander Trent VC, the first VC I was ever to serve under. The school was equipped with the two seat TIIs. So there was to be no slap on the back and off you go this time round. In fact, we were given about three hours dual before solo and the total flying was to be about 25 hours with some night flying thrown in, although we never actually flew the Vampire at night at Shawbury. The De Havilland course at Hatfield was first class, and on a par with the Bristol Engine course at Filton. This time we had accommodation in a family run hotel virtually opposite the main gates of the DH factory, and what a happy time we had there in the evenings- spoilt rotten. I strongly recommended this hotel, which went under the name of the "Stone House", to many people over the years until one day an RAF friend of mine who had been on a day visit to DH's sadly reported that not only had the Stone House been raised to the ground, but that the A1 road now passed under Hatfield and not through it. Time marches on, but oh what a waste of a first class hotel.

It was during our course at the factory that I lost all faith in receiving information of importance by phone, because one morning a call from CFS, who were in the process of re-writing the Pilot's notes for the Vampire, was put through to our class room in the assumption that our lecturer would be taking the call. The lecturer, in fact, had not arrived at that time and one of our course members, not from Shawbury I might add, started answering questions and if he was not too sure about a point he would put his hand over the phone and ask around for information. This information given that day duly appeared in the next updated version of the Vampire handling notes but, luckily, none of it was life threatening.

Back at Shawbury the Vampire NF10s, now surplus to requirements in Fighter Command after the introduction of the Meteor Nightfighter, began to arrive, to teach controlled descents from high levels. They fully proved their worth but as soon as we started using them for radar approaches we received many complaints that our aircraft, being made mainly of wood, as per the Mosquito, did not show up at all well on the radar screens. Were we actually flying the very first generation of stealth aircraft, I now wonder? The solution, as is the case in many situations, was remarkably simple, we had the radar scanners, which had been removed from the perspex nose of the aircraft, replaced and all was well. For one reason or other, the newly formed Vampire flight was placed under the command of Sqdn Ldr Pinchbeck, who was already Commanding the Lincoln element of the staff navigators course. It seemed very strange to have a Squadron made up of 50% four engined bombers and 50% single jet night fighters, but everything worked out just fine. Sqdn Ldr Pinchbeck was a real character who always led from the front and one of his favourite stories was of how he once nearly got his nose brown when dealing with a senior officer. The full story was that when he was shot down and became a prisoner of war of the Germans, a fellow inmate at the camp a very senior officer by the name of "Hatti" Hyde, later Air Commodore, Commandant of CFS, was involved in an escape tunnel when our boss was following very close behind! Sqdn Ldr Pinchbeck was killed in a car accident after leaving Shawbury. Many years later I had the pleasure of meeting his son, who was running a top class hotel in Harrogate.

There was a wide cross section of pilots flying the Lincoln aircraft from a F/O Brown who looked so young that we called him Junior Brown, last seen as a Wing Commander at RAF Benson, to three WWII bomber barons, with more than one tour under their belts. In this department was a "Paddy" Jingles who sported the rank of Flight Sergeant although he was a commissioned officer when he was involved in the joint No 617 and 9 Sqdn successful attack on the battleship Tirpitz. He had, later in life, blotted his copy book somewhat after the war when he decided to make a dummy approach to land on a British Aircraft Carrier in his Lancaster with all checks complete which, of course, included the landing gear being down and locked. It would have been something of a jape but for the fact that the Royal Navy took it very seriously indeed and started to throw their on deck aircraft overboard until Paddy opened up his throttles and departed into the setting sun. Another of the trio was a Peter Bogis, who was coming to the end of his flying life with a unique accolade to his credit in that he was, during the war, entrusted with the Captaincy of a Stirling bomber, during his tour on No 15 Sqdn, named "McRoberts Reply". This aircraft had been presented to the RAF by Lady McRoberts to commemorate the loss of three sons in flying accidents. She also set up a rest centre called "Dounside" on the River Dee, not far from Balmoral, which I, and many others, are still privileged to use to this day. The last Bomber Baron was "Maxie" Chivers, who also sported a DFC along with the other two, and was probably the greatest extrovert that I ever met in the Service, and that is really saying something. We still see each other at Aircrew Association meetings once a year and, at the first one, it came as no surprise to learn that he had kept a Public House near RAF Northolt for some little time after retiring from the RAF.

On radar runs in the Vampire, when the overshoot height could be rather low, we took along look outs in the seat that had previously been occupied by the night fighter radar operator, to make sure all was well whilst we stuck religiously to our instruments and carried out the various commands issued by the U/T operators on the ground. The only requirement to act as look outs was that the person concerned was aircrew trained in one branch or other. This often led to some fairly senior officers acting as look outs just to experience a first ride in a jet aircraft. Those from the four engined piston world invariably commented on the lack of vibration and noise on their initiation to jet flying.

The RAF sported, at that time, a travelling team of instructors who taught the basics of ejector seat exits from doomed aircraft on a Martin-Baker practice rig. The word must have spread that we had recently started using Vampires because the team duly arrived with this rig, although the Vampire NF10 was never fitted with such seats. A classic horse and cart situation, but it was pointed out that sooner or later we were more than likely to fly an aircraft with one so were called upon to have a go anyway. I was about the second in the queue to be strapped into the seat and, after pulling the blind, shot up the gantry at what seemed to be an alarming rate. After being wound down I mentioned to the NCO in charge that it had been quite a hefty blow up the backside, to which he replied that we early birds had been the lucky ones, because we only shot up to about the half way point and later in the day, when it had really warmed up, it would be going to fairly near the top. I cannot think that that type of trainer is still in existence because todays seats, being far more powerful, invariably cause some back injury or other when used for real.

With still being an IRE examiner on Ansons, I was often flying what, to many pilots, even in the mid 1950s, was new fangled jets one minute and one of the oldest aircraft still flying in the RAF at that time the next. Both the Vampire and Anson were a pleasure to fly and I considered myself particularly lucky to do so. One particular story about the Anson that might interest pilots who had not flown that type, or other aviation enthusiasts as well for that matter, was that it was one of the very few aircraft types with a retractable undercarriage that could be landed wheels up without even damaging the paint work. Not only did this actually happen at Shawbury, but there was a very funny ending to the saga. An NCO pilot was slotted for a normal training detail for Air Traffickers when he was asked to take two WRAF airwomen along for air experience, which was not unusual in that type of aircraft. All went well until he selected the wheels down for landing when nothing happened. Needless to say, he went through all the emergency procedures including informing Air Traffic control, which had the usual result of every self appointed expert on the station making for the Tower to offer free advice. Luckily, it did not, on that occasion, distract the pilot too much, although there are many recorded cases when it did, with disastrous results. After it became apparent that a wheels up landing was the only option, the pilot shut one engine down completely and inched the two bladed prop round on the starter motor to the horizontal position so that it would not make contact with the runway on landing. He was pleasantly surprised to find how easy that had been, so decided to come in on finals on the high side and shut the other one down, and turned a powered approach into a glide approach and made a straight forward landing, the two blades on his last engine even stopped in the horizontal position for him! On the Anson, the wheels rotated freely in the engine nacelle even when retracted because they were not fully covered by closed doors. The pilot had no voice contact with the two girls down the rear and so, after rapidly switching everything off, he got quickly out of his seat and was more than surprised that when he arrived in the cabin area the girls had already opened the entrance door and were stood outside on the Tarmac. Before he could even say a word, they thanked him most profusely for an excellent first ever flight and then sauntered off across the grass towards the control tower! Shortly afterwards the usual mix of fire engine, ambulance and numerous staff cars arrived on the scene. The OC flying's later report to a fascinated group in the mess bar recorded that the NCO pilot was still looking in disbelief at the two disappearing airwomen, with his mouth wide open, when he arrived on the scene. He also recalled that when he had asked the pilots if the WRAFs had realised what was going on, he got the reply of, "No idea, Sir, never got a chance to ask before they made off".

Another stroke of luck at Shawbury, for me at least, was that a University Air Squadron arrived for their Summer Camp, now equipped with the recently introduced Chipmunk aircraft. It was while I was poking my nose into one out of pure interest, that I noted the pilot arriving, Flt Lt Lawson, who had been on the same CFS course as myself in 1949. "Like a flip in one"? Was his immediate question, and when I readily agreed he said, "we'll do it over the lunch hour". I thought it would be two or three times around the circuit but he said, "we'll make this a full stop so that you can have a go all by yourself". Little did I think that my last eighteen months in the Air Force, just short of 28 years later, would find me completing my RAF flying career on that type.

de Havilland Chipmunk

Two candidates for instrument flying tests that came my way were literally from Stations hundreds of miles apart. The first was an officer on the RAF Communications Flight based in Vienna, who had made the long trek back to the UK just to take the test in an Anson because that was one requirement before he could fly VIPs in that type of aircraft. The second was an officer who was based just a few hundred yards across the runway at the MU, also sharing our airfield; the same MU that I should have delivered a Martinet to for burning, but never quite made it. The test pilot at the MU flew so many different types in any one year that it would have been impossible for him to keep up a rating on each and every one so Maintenance Command had agreed that so long as he kept one type current that would do nicely. The MU test pilot was Flt Lt Jock Donaldson, a real man's man who I got on famously with, he even took me along on one or two air tests in Devons that the MU seemed to have in great numbers at that time. Like the Mosquito, Vampire and Chipmunk, this DH type was also a delight to handle, although the perfect aircraft never existed in my experience.

The tradition of a sports afternoon on Wednesdays was still the norm, made up for by working Saturday mornings, although many of us were just about approaching a certain age when we needed sports like a hole in the head. It was on one Wednesday that Jock and I both having landed late that morning, so late, in fact, that the Mess bar was just about to close when we arrived on the scene. Jock said "no problem, I know a pub about a mile away that will still be open" and so we set sail for the odd pint or two. I can still picture that pub now, with it's rear entrance which, for some reason or other, had a door that opened outwards. Well remembered because although the landlord was very friendly to us, he insisted on rules is rules and it was just on the 2:30 deadline when he called last orders. After we had finished our drinks, Jock, whose car we had arrived in, led the way out and it was when the door opened outwards that I spotted in the distance coming down the lane, the station commander taking his version of Wednesday afternoon sports. That consisted of taking his wife and dog for a walk! Jock had got several yards ahead into the car park during my "what do we do next" pondering and it was only after I heard Jock shouting "Come on Jacko, he won't let us have another drink you know". I opened the door an inch or so to check the situation and noted that the Station Commander had probably been too far away to hear Jock's call, but he did do a double take as he passed by, still outbound from the Camp, thank goodness. After I had eventually exited, we gave the CO another five minutes or so to clear the area before our own departure. Jock never heard a word about the incident, probably because his was in another Command to the rest of us at Shawbury.

On first commissioning, in 1951. I had been taken on for four years officer service with the possibility of an extra four years after that. With time fast running out I asked if anything had been heard about my request for another four years, which had not received any response so far, and with usual "It's in the pipeline somewhere" I replied to an advert in the "Flight" magazine for pilots to join a company that had recently been awarded a contract to take over target towing duties from the Army coop squadrons. Pilots would initially be flying Mosquito aircraft from the old RAF base at Little Snoring in Norfolk. This was, obviously, for operating off the North Norfolk coast as per my stint on No 695 Squadron at Horsham St Faiths. Both aircraft type and location suited me just fine, so I sent off my CV, such as it was at that time. I was taken aback to receive a telephone call a couple of days later asking if I could get out of the service any sooner than the actual four year point and start with the company in about three weeks time. I will never know if it became a trigger action or not, but shortly after I let it be known that I had been offered a civilian flying job, I was informed that I was to report to our Group HQs at Morton Hall, very near my next full flying Station of RAF Swinderby, near Lincoln. A board, consisting of a Group Captain and a Wing Commander had both been convened to give the nod, or otherwise, to officers wishing to extend their service. I was lucky in two respects, the first was that the Duncan Sandy's Axe, which wiped out about half the fighter squadrons in the RAF, did not fall until about a year later and, secondly, although I had only applied for a four year extension, the paper that I eventually received stated that I had been awarded a direct Commission Scheme "B" which, in effect, would give me 16 years of Commissioned service, taking me up to the age of 47 before retirement. The interview, in my opinion, had not gone at all well and I can recall questions and answers on two differing subjects. The first was did I think that the British should maintain a presence in strength in both the Middle East and Far East? The Far East was simple, the Americans, and ourselves to a far lesser degree, had been involved in the Korean war and the British were in the middle of the Malayan communist troubles so we had no real option there, but I thought in the longer term island bases, such as Gan and Cyprus, might be a better alternative to being on mainlands in force. The second topic was when I nearly got egg on my face when I favoured air to air missiles and rockets to machine guns and cannons. I think they thought I meant ground to air missiles for defence against all attacking aircraft by the look on their faces so I added, rather quickly, fired from aircraft of course, which was telling a little porky because, even in the mid fifties, not many active pilots could visualise fighter aircraft intercepting low flying fighter bombers at speeds near to mach one.

Not long after being accepted for further service, and nearing the end of my tour at RAF Shawbury, about the happiest station I ever served on, I was told that with the introduction of jet aircraft to the Advanced stage of pilot training I would soon be posted to one of the two Schools already using the Vampire TII at either RAF Swinderby or Oakington. The RAF College at Cranwell was still using piston types at that time, which seemed a little strange as they normally led the field in the flying world. What I did not expect was that I, and five other piston instructors, would be called upon to take the last part of the instructor's course all over again, particularly so in my case because I had chalked up several hundred hours on the Vampire at Shawbury. It seemed a little strange at first checking in at RAF Little Rissington as an officer after having taken the course there as an NCO pilot some years earlier, but it was to be the one and only station that I later served on in that context.

CHAPTER 22
Back to Rissington,
Hunters and with Vampires beyond

One big change, the second time round, was that the Commandant, now Air Commodore Paul, interviewed each and every instructor individually. During my interview I still don't know how I kept my face straight when he was going on a bit about how important it was to set an example to our future students, particularly in dress sense, as standards had slipped somewhat over recent years at about the same time that I lost eye contact with him and noticed that under the table his crossed ankles revealed that he was wearing two different coloured socks and neither one was the standard black called for when in uniform. I must point out that he was one of the most gallant bomber pilots to serve during WWII, having led from the front time and time again as a light daylight bomber leader. The exploits of those crews have never, in my opinion, received the recognition that they so richly deserved.

The social life of Little Rissington had changed little over the years and the Morris family, thank goodness, still ran the "Old New Inn" Hotel and gave me a warm welcome, as did many of the locals, who all seemed pleased to see an RAF regular return to the fold, even if it was for only two short months. On the course that our little group of five retreads were attached to, we stood out like sore thumbs, not least because we did not attend any Ground School lectures which was probably why with so much extra leisure time on our hands we became a little cliquish and tended to go around together. In our group we had two Jacksons, as if one wasn't enough, and so as to simplify the admin side of the flying programme we were referred to by our initials. The other one was known as W H and myself as K R. Unfortunately, not long after our respective postings, W H, who had been posted to Oakington, was killed when his Vampire was in a mid air collision with a Varsity aircraft. The Vampires at CFS, although brand new trainers, were still not fitted with ejector seats which I well remember because I and my instructor, would certainly have used them if they had been on one occasion.

It was during an aerobatic detail that my instructor, Flt Lt Harcourt, put the aircraft into a deliberate spin from the top of a loop, and asked me to talk him through a standard recovery. When the aircraft failed to respond, he took over control with no better luck, and it seemed an eternity, with an ever increasing rotational speed before the aircraft suddenly flicked out of the spin into the normal wings level situation.. Not much was said as we terminated the detail and returned to base. It was only after a slowly drunk cup of coffee that he started the inquest. He confirmed that I had, as required, the control column in exactly the wings level position with the stick well forward and full opposite rudder on against the rotational direction. The wings level selection was all important in the Vampire because the top of the control column, unlike virtually all other aircraft, was deliberately cranked to the left so that each pilot had a clear view of his direction indicator (DI). To this end, a strip of white paint was painted onto the flying control panel, to which the pilot could align his controls. In normal flight, the wings are automatically set in the wings level position by the slipstream passing over the ailerons but during spins the airspeed speed remains low throughout, and it is the pilot who selects the wings level position by positioning his aileron control in line with the white strip- or was it the man who had applied the white paint strip on the dashboard in the first place who had the final say? My instructor eventually concluded that we had been in an inverted spin and it was at the point when he had decided to take off full rudder that the sudden spin recovery had occurred. The RAF have never taught inverted spin recovery, nor flick rolls for that matter, so many pilots may not know that an inverted spin looks exactly like a normal one, and the only indication in the cockpit is that the turn indicator shows the true direction of rotation, and the rudder should be applied in the same direction at the visual impression of rotation. I, like many other pilots before and since my time, have failed to come to terms with this apparent contradiction, and it was only after Flt Lt Harcourt had produced a model aircraft and started placing chalk marks on the control surfaces that I understood the concept to my own satisfaction.

Type flying had been reduced to just one aircraft since the heady days of the late forties but what a type it was. The Hawker Hunter, no less, which had only been in service with front line fighter squadrons for just over a year before CFS managed to get their hands on one or two to let student instructors sample their first taste of supersonic flight. Like the Vampire before it, the dual version of type had not yet entered service so, once again, it was a pat on the back before going solo without the benefit of dual instruction. In addition to supersonic flight it was also a first for nearly all of our course flying an aircraft fitted with an ejector seat and, of more importance, powered controls, which invariably led to a bit of wing waggling just after take off until one got used to their high sensitivity.

The runways at Little Rissington were far too short for an aircraft with an approach speed of 135 kts, so all Hunter flying took place from RAF Kemble, some little distance away. The entire outfit appeared to be under the control of one man, and he was an aviation fanatic by the name of Flt Lt "Straw" Hall who was well known throughout the RAF in those days for his aerobatic skills. He had a jeep at his disposal and would take two or three would be Hunter pilots from the steps of the Mess each morning and return them in the evening, all being well, that is. My turn came on the 8th February, 1956, which I mention because it turned out to be a disaster day for the RAF in terms of Hunter flying which I will

Hawker Hunter

263

cover shortly. The weather did not look too promising as we left Little Rissington for Kemble at a very high rate of knots, Straw Hall's driving being just as dashing as his aerobatic displays. The cloud base started to lift gradually and after reaching about 1,000' above ground level our flying was declared to be "on", much to our surprise. I well remember that I was told that the tops would be less than 8,000' and that I would be up there like a flash after take off and, after making sure I was over the Bristol Channel, it would be ok to put the aircraft into a dive to achieve supersonic flight. In the event, the cloud tops were above 20,000', but otherwise the flight was a pure delight, despite having to climb and descend through cloud on instruments in an unfamiliar type of aircraft.

After landing I received a vague compliment in that "Straw" said I hadn't over corrected on the ailerons after take off to the extent that most other pilots had on their first flight in an aircraft fitted with powered controls. After lunch the weather started to deteriorate a little but Straw said I could probably squeeze in another trip before we called it a day. In fact, I was recalled to base after about 20 minutes due to a lowering cloud base and that was to be the end of Hunter flying for me. Arrival back at Rissington was just after bar opening time, and I was reliving my days flying with a pint or two when the bar steward switched on his radio to hear that the RAF had lost seven Hunters at, or approaching RAF Marham after diverting there from West Raynham due to bad weather. It sounded to me, at least, that the pilots were probably the victims of one or other of the many crazy ideas self inflicted on the RAF during the first ten years of peace following the end of WWII. The two most likely consisted of the concept of "All weather flying" and, secondly, "flying to the limits". Both claimed victims in one way or another, mostly in the all weather flying department when aircraft attempted landings in very poor visibilities. In the case of flying to the limits, some pilots were tasked with flights that lasted so long that the deemed safe fuel reserves were pretty low indeed, and particularly so at the Day Fighter Leaders School at RAF West Raynham. At RAF West Raynham, six pilots in the Markham disaster ejected after running out of fuel but one was at a very low altitude and was killed.

After asking my instructor what the big difference was between the Percival Prentice, which I had previously instructed on, and the latest Percival product, the Piston Provost, which seemed to have ousted it's predecessor in such a small time scale, he immediately laid on a dual trip plus solo. He agreed wholeheartedly with me when I said that,

Percival Provost

whenever possible, instructors should have some first hand knowledge of aircraft that their students had already flown. I found the Provost to be an ideal aircraft for instructional purposes, although many CFS Staff members thought that with a 550 HP engine it was far too powerful for a basic trainer. This did not prove to be the case, and students found little difficulty coping with the well known accident areas of take off and landing. I think that those who thought it too powerful had lost sight of the fact that swings on take off and landing are more to do with undercarriage width than engine power. For example, the Hurricane was easier to land than the Spitfire, and the P47 Thunderbolt easier still. This was also the case when comparing the Fokke Wulf 190 with it's very wide undercarriage and the Me 109. With the introduction of the Piston Provost the RAF reverted to the old system of splitting basic and advanced training by using different Stations. Even that system did not last all that long before the concept of all through jet training prevailed, aided and abetted by the CFS examining wing. Many instructors thought that there was little wrong in training student pilots on Chipmunks (a vast improvement on the dear old Tiger Moth) for basic flying, and either the Harvard or Piston Provost for advanced training before using the Vampire and Meteor for jet conversion, depending on whether the student was due to progress to the day fighter world or multi engined aircraft. In favour of this argument, it can be pointed out that some air forces still used the Harvard for pilot training into the 1980s with, no doubt, a vast saving of money. Apart from the money aspect, we might in the UK still have had a reasonable light aircraft industry but for the distraction of building so many military trainers in the post war years.

At the end of the two month abridge course there was a big discussion as to whether we should be on the end of course photograph of the one now passing out, because all our group had passed through the school in recent years. I failed to mention that it would be a first for me anyway, because I had, literally, been on "French leave" when my original course, No 109, had passed out in 1949. This last course had been very relaxing compared with the hectic days of the late forties and I had been particularly fortunate in having Flt Lt Harcourt as my instructor. He was a keen and dedicated young officer of the post war era and I visualised that he would shoot up the promotion ladder, but it was not to be, he was killed in a Hunter mid air collision not long after we had left.

My posting was to No 8 FTS at RAF Swinderby which had, the previous year, entered the jet age with the departure of Wellingtons and Varsities belonging to 201 AFS. The fleet at Swinderby was a mixed bag of Vampire TIIs two seat trainers and the single seat Vampire Mk 5s, used only for formation leading by instructors after a series of fatal accidents with that particular mark. The problem, similar to my own experience in the Spitfire, was recovery from high speed dives. The big difference, however, was that in this case it was the brute force required on the control column to recover from high speed dives that had caused the accidents. A special tribute must be paid at this point to a non-commissioned officer by the name of Master Pilot Evans. He had been tasked with putting all Vampire Mk 5s on Station strength into high speed dives and, equipped with an old type spring operated weighing machine, with a hook on the end, measured the force required to pull out of these dives from given speeds. I seem to remember that anything over 40lbs was deemed to be too dangerous and the aircraft was scrapped. "Taff" Evans had already become the first pilot, along with his student PO Jago, to carry out a double ejection from a Vampire. This was when they found themselves in an inverted spin which showed no signs of recovery, so sticking his neck out again on those air tests was even more praiseworthy. Eventually all Vampire Mk Vs were struck off charge as the production of TIIs gathered pace. All the new TIIs arriving, as opposed to those at CFS, had ejector seats fitted and that caused some problems for many instructors including myself. A wave of severe backaches developed after the introduction of these seats, and the medical world eventually announced that it was probably due to kidney pads not being incorporated into the design. Obviously, training could not be stopped while they were modified, so we had to grin and bear it for quite some time.

Another medical problem also arose with the use of ejector seats and, yet again, I was among the victims. Anybody with a sensitive rear end could endure up to about four trips per day, tightly strapped to a very hard seating arrangement but, beyond that, it could be pure agony and blood stained underwear was not unknown. The final, and most important problem arose with these seats now becoming standard on all new fighter type aircraft, was that not all pilots could fit into them and be assured of a safe ejection in an emergency. Although it had a great deal to do with the height of a pilot, that was not the complete story. For instance, two pilots both standing 6' tall, one might be judged to be ok and the other not so, it depended on the length of their backbone. We have all seen both men and women with short bodies and long legs and the reverse of course. For those student pilots with that problem who had already started the jet side of the course completed their training on Meteor T7s, which did not have ejector seats fitted.

I well remember when I was later flying the RAF's last Lancaster Bomber, that our AOC, after a final trip in it, saying that he was very disappointed that he could not get checked out on one of his Lightning fighters due to his height, and that he had spent most of his flying career on helicopters because of it. Air Vice Marshal Harding, later Air Chief Marshal Harding, Chief of the Defence Staff, stood about 6' 4" tall! He did, however, fly both a Spitfire and Hurricane that same day which completed quite a trio. There followed a handwritten letter of thanks which was deeply appreciated by all on the BBMF at that time.

Although the Vampire was a pressurised aircraft I found it particularly fatiguing on certain days/nights when high altitude sorties were called for, and I will never forget one night's activities when I processed four different students on their night height climbs, which called for climbing to 40,000' or more over London and then returning to base. I could not believe how tired I had become at the end of that particular night's flying, although it involved less than four hours of actual flying. Another particularly demanding detail in the same context was high level aerobatics which were carried out between 40,000' and 45,000'. At the top of some loops, the altimeter reading was in excess of 50,000' with the red cabin altitude warning light glowing. Not many lay persons can come to terms with the fact that an aircraft can reach higher levels after an energy dive than is possible with a normal climb. The technique is to climb as normal until the rate of climb indicator runs out of steam and after gaining maximum speed in level flight, dive the aircraft for a few thousand feet and then pull up into a steep climb. The energy built up in this dive is responsible for this phenomena. One exercise that I revelled in, although for the most part it was the student who was flying it, was practicing landing back at base after engine (simulated) failure at height, or flame out as it was called in the jet world. We only throttled back, of course, and did not actually shut down the engine. Due to it's extremely high lift/weight ratio, the aircraft would glide for mile after mile under the conditions and, providing you started the downwind leg at 2,000', instead of the normal 1,000' a safe landing was assured on a tight circuit. When above cloud this depends a lot on the ground controller who would "home" you to the overhead and then guide you into a descending circle to bring you into the downwind leg, position at the 2,000' point. All good stuff and the air/ground co-ordination at it's very best.

Betty and I moved into our first married quarter at Swinderby, and so began a very happy era for both of us. At the time only two wives on the 'patch' were able to drive and as there was only one bus from quarters into Lincoln per week they were very popular! So every Friday, Betty drove to Lincoln shopping with a car load of friends. Betty enjoyed her first taste of married quarters life, with all the wives mixing in together regardless of husbands rank or position. She, like all the younger wives thought the pre-war nonsense, which still lingered on of calling and leaving visiting cards at the station commanders residence, which could only be done during the afternoon on a particular day was a bit of a hoot! Not many wives of today's Air Force would conform, wearing a hat and gloves!

The time honoured coffee mornings in the mess and hosted by wives on the patch, soon turned into 'Sherry Mornings', and later still during my time, when more wives took to the road, finished in the 'Five Bells' at Bassingham. More than once I saw some officers, having arrived home for a quick lunch in the middle of a flying day, rushing from quarter to quarter looking for their wives. I soon came to accept that mine would be with either Lola Gegg, or Nella Troughton who have both remained life long friends.

One entire course of students came from the Iraqi Air Force and what a bunch of characters they turned out to be. During my time in Egypt I had often noticed that Arabs could be very annoyed with someone one minute and the best of friends the next. I must freely admit that some people have told me that I also have that trait! I did not think that I would ever fall fowl of the system but it did come to pass. I had flown with a student by the name of Kadhum, late one afternoon on a map reading exercise and, for one reason or another, he did not seem to be with it, bordering on disinterest. During the de-brief, I did not mince my words, but in the middle of it I was called away to a phone call in another office. It seemed quite incredible that on my return I found that Kadhum had disappeared. Wait till I catch up with him was going through my mind when I suddenly heard sobbing noises coming from a flying clothing locker. It was Kadhum, of course, and there was no consoling him, he said it was the end of the world for him, and if he failed the course and disgraced his country and family he would put an end to himself. I tried to calm him down, and said we would have another go tomorrow and I was sure that the trip would be much better than the last one.

The morrow came, but there was no sign of him as take off time approached and it was with many misgivings that I set off for his room in the Mess. After ascertaining his number at reception, I thought I would have a quick look at it from the outside to see if the curtains had been opened, and feared the worst when I noted that they were still firmly shut. However, a loud bang on his door eventually produced a grinning Kadhum who said "I must have slept in, how stupid of me, is the weather ok for our trip, Sir. I'll be down at the flights as soon as possible". It was almost predictable that the trip was well above average, and he acted as if the previous day had never occurred. He remained particularly well disposed to me throughout the rest of the course and even presented me with a Galabeya, a long nightshirt type of gown worn by Arab males, as a joke on the last day of his course. It came in useful a few weeks later during a riotous night in the mess.

It turned out that some of the young, unmarried, living in members had taken exception to the Officers' wives club virtually taking over the place one night for a fashion show conducted by a local firm. The firm, of course, had brought along a number of female dummies on which to drape their various products and then sent a van the next morning to retrieve same. The van driver did not seem to notice that one had gone missing, because nothing was ever heard about the misappropriation.

On the riotous night in question, it was produced from it's hiding place and various crude and lewd additions covering the missing parts, were painted on it. One very young officer suddenly had a brilliant idea, and asked if he could borrow my recently presented galabeya. Of course he could, and the next morning the Station Orderly Officer, arriving early for the ensign hoisting ceremony just outside the guardroom was horrified to find the dummy, dressed in the Galabeya, swinging gently from the flagpole. He was quick off the mark and managed to get it back to it's secret hiding place in the Mess before anyone of real authority arrived on the scene. I got my Galabeya back all right, but the bar rascals' next effort was just a little beyond the pale. In the dead of night, they took the again naked dummy to the Padre's married quarter, and finding the coal shed unlocked, virtually covered it with stove coke, except for one arm, which had red streaks painted on it, hanging loose from the pile. The officer living next to the Padre was startled the next night when he saw the Padre loading what appeared to be a naked lady into the boot of his car. A decent burial at last, we all concluded.

The passing out luncheon, to mark the end of our Iraqi course, had produced one light moment when our new Wing Commander Flying, Fred Symmonds DFC DFM, played host to the Iraqi Ambassador who had arrived from London to be the principal VIP guest. The Ambassador did not seem to be in good form at all, and who could blame him for it was in the month of Ramadan when, as is well known, Muslims do not partake of any food during daylight hours and, in any event, are teetotal throughout the year, in theory that is. He did not seem all that keen either when offered an orange juice so Wing Commander Fred took the steward to one side and whispered, "slip a vodka into the next one". Things soon brightened up, and when his Excellency took his leave, he told the Wing Commander how much he had enjoyed the day and said we seemed to have a far better orange juice than he was used to in London. Talk about wink, wink, nudge, nudge!

Our new OC Flying was a real ball of fire, and it is worth noting that during WWII he had been awarded the DFM as a navigator and, after pulling a few strings not only re-mustered to pilot, but had gone on to earn a DFC flying Mustang fighters. In the RAF of those days, there was often a cry of "Rhubarb, Rhubarb" if anybody complained too much, but Fred Symmonds took it one step further and had ties printed, decorated with bunches of Rhubarb on them, and solemnly presented persistent complainers with one. This normally took place in the Mess

Bar when the unfortunate offender was with his sniggering mates. It was also not unknown for complainants who lived in married quarters to come down to breakfast and find a stick of rhubarb in their letter boxes. OC Flying's reputation had preceded him and two stories from his last station became well known by the time of his arrival. The first was when he was President of the Mess Committee on that station and part of his appointment as such was to write in the "Suggestions and Complaints Book", a book that is part and parcel of all messes, a reasoned response to all entries made therein. After one WRAF officer had written that for afternoon tea, which was something of a ritual in those days, sugar tongs should be provided because she had noted that many male officers spent such a short time in their cloakroom that she thought it most unlikely that they had time to wash their hands, and this was a most unhygienic situation. Fred replied that he had personally been into the local town and purchased enough tongs to have one hung, attached to a piece of string above each and every stall in the gents toilet. It was on the same Station that a very senior WRAF officer visited during a round robin of all Stations in the Command to make sure that her "girls" were properly looked after, particularly regarding domestic arrangements. The fact that some WRAFS now helped out in the runway caravan flashing Aldis lamps and firing pistols, etc came out. She asked in a rather prim voice "and what happens when they wish to spend a penny?" to which Fred replied "the chaps go behind the van, but we do send a jeep out for the girls when they ring the tower." The senior WRAF retorted that she thought it might be a little embarrassing for the girls, and could not some other arrangements be made? Fred said he could probably find four poles somewhere, and make an enclosure by putting Hessian canvas around them. "Four poles and canvas" snorted the dear lady, who went on to say that what was really needed was some form of permanent erection. Most people around the conference table, including the Station Commander, heard Fred mutter "we already have too many of those on this Station".

Having just attained the rank of Flight Lieutenant I had no axe to grind as to who was appointed to become a Flight Commander or not, but even taking an impartial view I found it very strange indeed that of the six slots available three were taken by exchange officers. We had one from each of the following, The Royal Navy, the Royal Canadian Air Force, and the United States Air Force. All splendid chaps, of course, but I was just a little surprised that the USA officer was of the Mormon faith and, of course, stuck to the no drinking rules of his religion, although he did throw a massive party in the Mess on his departure. Both Betty and myself got on particularly well with the Canadian couple by the name of Bob and Rita Diamond and have a permanent reminder of them to this day in that on their departure they presented us with two beer tankards, one pint and one half pint, made in pottery by Denby Stoneware in a beautiful blue colouring with the RAF crest emblazoned in gold. The naval officer Commanding a flight was, as already mentioned, an ex-student of mine from Syerston days who was later killed in a King's Cup air race, with Prince William the eldest son of the Duke of Gloucester. Just to conclude the catalogue of our overseas commanders, one of the three squadron commanders was on secondment from the Royal New Zealand Air Force. Quite a collection, all with differing views on aviation.

One British officer who might well have been ideally suited to fill one of the command slots otherwise taken by exchange officers, was Flt Lt Tim Mills who along with his charming wife Molly made an ideal service couple. I well remember a rather hectic Saturday night in the mess bar when Fred Simmons thought it a good idea that all officers should have their trouser legs rolled up to their kneecaps when Tim and Molly walked into the bar with Tim's parents. It took a minute or two to register that Tim's father was none other than Air Chief Marshal Mills, who later became Black Rod in the Houses of Parliament. When one of our regular Sunday lunch timers said on leaving the bar, "see you in the Five Bells tomorrow then Jacko"?, that the Air Marshal interjected, "I might well join you". We thought nothing of it the next day, thinking that he was just being one of the lads for the night. The Five Bells pub was in the village of Bassingham, close to RAF Swinderby. Apart from the RAF, the pub was very popular with local farmers and two well known poachers. As luck would have it, it was shortly after the unexpected arrival of Tim and his parents, that one of the poachers started to regale us with his previous night's activities when he had, apparently, managed to bag a couple of pheasants by shining a torch in their eyes while they roosted in a tree. All the RAF managed to keep straight faces, but not so the farmers, when the Air Marshal said, "But isn't that stealing my good man"? We all managed to re-adjust our slacks and the ACM was still there at the bitter end. Unlike his father, Tim was not to make a long term commitment to the RAF, and it was under slightly unusual circumstances when we eventually met up again. It came about when Arthur Gibson, arguably the best aviation photographer of his time, persuaded the Ministry of Defence to allow the pilot of his own private aircraft to formate on the RAF's last Lancaster bomber, which I was flying for the BBMF at the time, whilst he took film for a picture entitled "Force ten from Navarone". The flight itself was due to be direct from RAF Coningsby to Jersey for their annual Battle of Britain week, but Arthur talked me into a detour over the mountains of South Wales so that his shots would be a good simulation of the Yugoslav countryside. No face to face briefing was arranged, just a few phone calls. His chase aircraft would arrive over Coningsby at our proposed take of time and we would take it from there. Everything worked out just fine, and not only did Arthur manage good footage for the film company, he also took some magnificent still pictures of the BBMF over the English Channel and approaching Jersey. During the flight I had been impressed by the piloting of Arthur's Aztec pilot and naturally went over to his aircraft on the tarmac at Jersey to see if they had everything they needed. Yes, it was Tim Mills who had been at the controls throughout, and he was more than happy to be away from the constraints of Service flying- I knew exactly how he flt. Later we learnt that the film company were, indeed, pleased with Arthur's efforts and invited Sqdn Ldr Pete Edge, one of our navigators, and myself down to their Elstree studios to watch film crews completing the production during which we had the pleasure of meeting Edward Fox, one of the stars of that film.

I was to use up yet one more of my nine lives during my three years at Swinderby and, yet again, it was a spinning Vampire that was not responding to normal recovery action. My student was a young Scottish officer by the name of Robertson and the spin had been deliberately induced from the straight and level position. I knew full well that it was not an inverted one this time, but took the precaution of confirming it by reference to the turn and slip indicator. I also checked that the white mark on the control column was aligned with the one on the dashboard, which it was, and as the altimeter indicator was unwinding towards the lowest ejection height I told Robertson that he had better stand by for a bang out and place both his hands on the ejector handle while I had a final try at spin recovery. I needn't have said the last bit, because as soon as he let go of his stick the Vampire stopped rotating. Like myself, Robertson followed me into the transport world as a Hastings pilot. Twenty five years later, I was to pass through the hands of CFS for the third and final time, then based at Leeming, to be assessed as fit to instruct on Chipmunks, to play out my 44 years in the RAF. It was at that station during a coffee break between details, that I chanced upon one of the numerous air publications left around for general consumption. Guess what? I came across one which was devoted entirely to the spinning problems of the Vampire aircraft during it's RAF service. Part of the booklet stated what had been found out very early on in the life of the Vampire in RAF service, but only after a pilot had managed to bail out of a spinning Vampire, although many before him had been killed. He was adamant that after inducing a deliberate spin by bringing the aircraft to near the stall and then applying full rudder and bringing the stick fully back he had found recovery impossible because he could not move the rudders one iota when attempting to apply full opposite rudder. No one had believed him at first, but after the boffins at Farnborough had become involved, the problem was soon resolved. I don't know if they used their wind tunnel or not, but they concluded that the twin booms on the Vampire had probably flexed enough in the spin to prevent the rudders being moved because the elevator was, in that state, blocking any movement. The solution was simple, cost nothing, and could be achieved in minutes. Just cut a small bit of metal off each rudder. Next time you visit an air museum with a Vampire in it, don't forget to have a quick look.

Having solved the problem of rudder movement restriction, other incidents continued to occur and I was absolutely staggered at the sheer number, many fatal, over that type's life span in the Service. My mind obviously went back over the years and I thought that having had two incidents, one with a CFS instructor, I had just been unlucky, but obviously I was not alone. I also recalled that another type, the Bulldog, had also suffered a number of spinning incidents, to such an extent that a Sqdn Ldr on one of the University Air Squadrons flying that type had written to the RAF's house mag, "Airclues", stating that he personally could not understand the problem, because if the correct recovery action was taken, they always came out of the spin in his experience. A short time later it was reported in the national news papers that an RAF pilot and his student had been forced to bail out of their spinning Bulldog. Yes, the pilot was the author of the letter to Airclues.

It was during this last time at CFS that an interesting exchange took place between myself and my instructor. His name was "Paddy" Cullen, and knowing that I had just finished my time on the BBMF, proudly announced that in his time he had flown Spitfires and Hurricanes to which, looking at his age, I asked "and when were you on the BBMF"?, knowing that he had his fish well and truly hooked, he just replied "I never was". My mind was now in overdrive and I said in a quizzical voice, "In the Royal Air Force"? "No, of course not, I'm not that old, it was another

Air Force", was his response. His nickname of Paddy should have given me the clue, but I had never before met anyone who had served in both the Irish Air Force and the RAF. Before he put me out of my misery my mind had been more than half way round the world thinking which Air Forces he might have served with. Historically I think I'm right in saying it was the Irish Air Force who insisted on the British building a dual control version of the Spitfire before committing themselves to ordering the fighter version. If only the RAF had also taken that path after the pressure was off when the Battle of Britain had been well and truly won. Not only would it have cut down the alarming accident rate on that type but, more importantly, it would have produced far better fighter pilots. Just imagine if pilots like Ginger Lacey or Frank Carey had been sitting in the back seat telling you just how it should be done!

It had now been some little time since our Iraqi course had passed out and, as usual, they had progressed to RAF Chivenor for a bombing and gunnery course. My flight commander, Derek Atkinson and an excellent Cranwell product, suggested that we should take a day off and fly down to Chivenor to see how our ex-Iraqi students were getting on. I was particularly interested in one of my own ex-students by the name of Sinjackley. He was one of my better products at Swinderby, and I knew him well enough to know that he was the son of one of the top men in the telecommunications world back in his own country. Over the usual cup of coffee in the crewroom, both Derek and I noted some unease among our ex-brood. Eventually Sinjackley managed to take me to one side and said "I suppose you and the Flight Commander have come down here because of the revolution, haven't you"? "Certainly not", I replied, "we just wanted to know how you are all getting on, but what revolution are you talking about anyway"? "In our country, of course, the King is dead and we all want to know what will happen to us when we go back" was his sombre riposte. I always listened to the BBC news over breakfast in those days, and there had not been any mention of an uprising in Iraq. In fact, the news broke after our return to base which left the big question of how had Sinjackley found out about it? With his father being in telecoms, perhaps he had managed a phone call that morning. One rumour that did surface years later, was that Sinjackley had been put to death by his own people after his return, but how I wish someone could disprove that rumour. Before our unhappy departure from Chivoner, Khadom managed to put his mind at rest on one point, and it had absolutely nothing to do with flying, far from it, in fact. One of my favourite sayings in those days was "let the dog see the rabbit", which I might well have over used at times because Khadhom asked quite seriously, "Have you still got that dog, sir"? "Which dog are you talking about", was all I could think of saying. "You know, Sir, the one you let chase rabbits, very naughty". That put a smile back on my face for a time. Although I myself never instructed Iraqi students ever again, we still had one or two more passing through despite the revolution, and it was due to a most tragic accident involving two of them that I had an extension to my flying career in the RAF, right up to the age of 60, which at that time was still more than 25 years away.

The accident was a mid air collision between two of our Vampires which had resulted in the deaths of two instructors, two Iraqi students and a lady factory worker on the ground. Needless to say, the accident really hit the headlines and virtually every national newspaper in the land rang the Station for details. The WRAF officer adjutant seemed to be coping with all this until the Iraqi Embassy in London rang to tell her that it was customary in their country to view all bodies before burial which normally took place on the day of death. The poor WRAF officer probably knew as well as anyone, that what went into a coffin after an air crash was rarely what it was supposed to be. She was so upset that she was sent on a few weeks leave and I don't know to this day if I had upset anyone in high places, or it had been a Fred Symmond's type joke, but I was "specially selected" to take over during her absence. I pointed out to W C Symmonds, before setting off for SHQ, that I had no experience of admin work whatsoever. He merely said that the job was nothing like it was cracked up to be, and the main thing was to open the mail in the mornings and pass on any letters to the Station Commander that concerned him, and send the rest into orbit around the Station. "And how do I know which will interest him and which ones do I send around the Station"? was my obvious question. "Oh, that's simple, you know that all letters have Air/ Eng or Admin after the reference number, well just send air letters to the Station Commander and send the others to OC Admin or OC Tech". That sounded too good to be true and so it proved because, as Fred related after my stint as Station Adjutant had finished, he had asked Group Captain Ken Batchelor, by far the best Station Commander I ever served under, "how was Jackson making out"? The Station Commander replied that everything seemed to be fine except that service mail had suddenly dried up. In fact, he said, he had only received one official letter in the last four days, and that had been about the colour of French Letters.

Even the jokey Fred Symmonds admitted to having been taken aback and had queried "colour of French letters, Sir? Who would send you a letter about them"? "Yes", replied the Stn Cmdr, "they want to make them a darker red so they will not fade so quickly, those things that you hang on a pole on the landing strip, we used to call them wind sleeves on the Frontier in my day, what are they now, Windsocks"?

The tragedy of the accident was made worse by the fact that one of the instructors, Johnny Williams, born and bred in my home town of Southport, had become a father for the first time a day before his death. The other instructor, a New Zealander called Barry Kirkpatrick, was expecting his second child any day. In fact, later during the night of the crash, my wife was called out to rush his wife, Pat, into the RAF hospital at Nocton Hall, near Lincoln, to be delivered of a baby son, so his name lives on. His first child, Jane, became a doctor, but I discovered that in unusual circumstances. It was during my first week of work in civvy street, starting what was to become a twelve year stint as an instructor at Sherburn-in-Elmet Flying Club in Yorkshire, that I was checking the log book of a civilian pilot for currency, and noting his surname of Kirkpatrick, I asked if he had any Air Force connections. After a long pause he said, "Kind of, my father was an RAF pilot, but I never knew him". His mother's father, I well remembered, was a retired Army Major who lived in York, so it all fitted. The retired Major was well remembered because he had organised the funeral of his late son in law with military precision, and saw fit to have his daughter Pat removed to York from Swinderby in double quick time before the funeral, which was almost certainly the right decision. The widow of Johnny Williams, on the other hand, insisted on staying in her married quarters for quite a few weeks because, as she told her close friends, she was quite certain that Johnny would come back to visit her one night. Pat Kirkpatrick, whose son was a fireman in Selby, never re-married and agreed, via her son, to come down to the flying club one Sunday night, but became too emotional by the time that they reached the lane leading down to it and was forced to turn back, so we never did see her again, a big regret of my wife's life, and mine too.

There was, of course, a full inquiry into the accident but I have often wondered if one fact that was known to me, and a few others on our flight who knew Barry and Johnny particularly well, was considered. Both had served on the same fighter squadron together in the Far East, flying Hornets out of Butterworth in Malaya. It is just possible that they had arranged their take off times to coincide so that they could show their students what dog-fighting was all about- we will never know, of course.

Barry and Pat had had a very wretched life in their early days of marriage in the RAF and it was all down to one of the most stupid rules that had survived well into the post war years. No officer could draw a marriage allowance until he was 26 years of age and, if he was married before that age, and had the misfortune to be posted overseas, he could not even draw the local overseas allowance which was paid to others to take account of the extra money that was needed to maintain a reasonable standard of living in certain countries. Why post these unfortunate officers overseas in the first place, when many older married officers would have jumped at the chance of an overseas posting? It did not enhance the standing of British service personnel with the local populous to see British families living like paupers. This very stupid rule was eventually scrapped, but not until long after it should have been.

I was getting used to the well ordered life in SHQ and soon realised that I could leave most of the work to a highly qualified WRAF Corporal at my disposal. She bobbed in and out of the office like a jack in the box at times, often just pointing at the signature block with pen in hand, and after I had appended my signature was off like a flash. I well remember one letter I was about to sign when I caught sight of a list of names which contained many of my colleagues and, surprise, surprise, included my own. "What's this one all about"? I enquired. "Oh, just routine, Sir", was her reply, "we have to send off a list of all pilots who have flown for more than eight years without a ground tour to Group HQs every six months, so they can arrange an air traffic course for them, or even photographic interpretation or something like that. It looks like your number's up, Sir. According to our records you've been flying since April 1951. April 1951 kept going through my mind until the penny finally dropped. Another stupid rule in the forces of those days was that anybody being commissioned from the ranks was discharged from the service one minute before midnight and re-enlisted as an officer a minute after midnight. What a performance! Having already completed 12 years service by 1951 it had been wiped out at a stroke. Anyway, I looked long and hard at the letter, so long in fact that the WRAF corporal was getting decidedly fidgety. I could not possibly ask her to leave my name off the list, it would have placed her in a most invidious position, so I said, "it's a pity that with fifteen names being an odd number you have printed one long list. If it only had fourteen names you could have had two columns of seven side by side, have you got time to re-type it"? She gave me one of the most withering looks I have ever experienced and made off with the letter. About twenty minutes later she duly returned with it and said, "yes you are quite right, Sir, it looks a lot better with two columns". Needless to say, my name had disappeared and so I was in the clear for more flying tours, but only because of an act of God. Five people dead and a WRAF officer who had been on the brink was the only reason, of course.

The WRAF Corporal was in fine fettle the next day when she bounded into the office and said, "this is a job that only you can do, Sir. You are supposed to check all these forms to make sure they are correct and then ask the Station Commander to sign them before I send them off". She had a twinkle in her eye and before departing just had time to say, "I think you will find them quite interesting". The forms in question were called 1369s and made out on an officer's posting or once a year as the case may be and called "confidential reports". Those relating to pilots were certainly interesting in that they painted a fair picture, but one or two of them left me thinking that some squadron leaders knew precious little about the officer concerned. However, Wing Commander Symmonds injected some light relief by adding some details in pencil which, of course, could be easily rubbed out. One set of boxes on the form required an X to be placed in one of them indicating if the officer concerned drank wisely or drank unwisely or did not drink at all. For one of my friends who spent a great deal of time in the bar, Fred had turned a normal X into a far bigger one and drawn a fish alongside it. For the only officer reported upon in the batch in question with a "does not drink" X in the box, Fred had added in brackets "and he is the dullest bastard in the Mess". The last report that could need the attention of a rubber was about a real loner who made off to London every Friday afternoon and returned just before work on the Monday morning. Fred's assessment was that "this officer thinks that his d--- is his compass, but it is always pointing towards London and not due North". Before sending them into the CO I thought that I had better seek some advice from higher authority, my WRAF Corporal in this case, and ask if I should delete the various remarks before the CO saw them. "Good God, no Sir" was her immediate reaction, "you'd spoil his day, he loves reading them and it's my job anyway to see to that".

I liked certain continental countries outlook on confidential reports which only required an assessment of A,B, C, or D in one section. Apparently this stood for;

A. Highly professional, but lazy. (knows what should be done and makes sure everybody under his command is hard at work)

B. Not particularly well equipped for the post but is lazy (things tend to carry on as normal)

C. Highly professional but also hyperactive. (Does most of the work himself while everybody else sits back doing nothing)

D. Not up to the job and hyperactive. (Rushes around making a cock up of everything in sight while everybody looks on in dismay).

Three years later, when I became a Transport Command Captain, I was looking around Aden on a stop over, when I spotted the WRAF Corporal out shopping. She was now based there and seemed genuinely pleased to see me again and quipped, "still flying then, Sir"? "Yes, thanks to you dear lady", was my reply. After more chit chat our crew moved on, but the co-pilot eventually asked outright, "what was that all about, you are still flying because of her"? "Yes, quite true, but it's a long story, I'll tell you all about it one day", but I never did.

Another chance encounter, or nearly so, was that I caught sight of the WRAF officer who I had replaced as Station Adjutant for those three weeks. It occurred in Gibraltar when, after leaving my Hastings aircraft, I spotted her disembarking from an RAF Britannia parked next to us. We only had time for a nod of recognition and a smile before she disappeared up the passenger steps and into the Brit. I don't suppose she would have wanted to talk about those dreadful few days at Swinderby anyway.

I don't believe in million to one chances, but another WRAF officer who arrived on the station after the tragic accident, not only came from Southport, but had lived in the same road as the late Johnny Williams. We lost quite a few more students in flying accidents but one loss, through natural causes, hit me a little harder than it might otherwise have done. It occurred when Johnny Tayleur, who had fixed my transfer to XI Squadron for the occupation of Japan, was rushing across the front lawn of his married quarter to his car one morning when he suffered a massive heart attack and died instantly. He was badly missed but his widow, who I had only met once or twice because the Tayleur's married quarters were off the main patch and across the A46 at Morton Hall, gave invaluable service to the RAF in Germany, having taken up a post with the Malcolm Clubs- those Clubs being a marvelous legacy of Lord and Lady Tedder.

Our married quarter, luckily, was on the main patch, and just across the playing field from the Mess. The Officers' Mess in those days, unlike today, was a real hive of activity and although it was built before WWII and, therefore, had no bar on initial construction, one was added during the war, constructed by German POWs as an addition to the dining room. The Germans, being what they are as regards beer halls, built the best mess bar that I ever came across. One of the few things that I was looking forward to on my last RAF tour, was having a few pints in it for old times sake, but some purist had had it demolished.

On one particular "Battle of Britain" day, when for the first time, Swinderby was not putting on a show for the public, Betty and I wondered if we should visit RAF Syerston for a spot of nostalgia, but decided against this after receiving reports of massive traffic jams in Newark. During car cleaning on the Saturday afternoon in question we both looked up as the mighty roar of a Vulcan V bomber was heard approaching. It's delta shape at low level looked absolutely magnificent. Perhaps we should have made a more determined effort to get to Syerston after all was our thinking as it was obviously heading towards that station. How could anyone have thought that the entire crew had only minutes to live, because that aircraft broke up in mid-air shortly after finishing it's display with a high speed run. The aircraft was from the Rolls Royce engine test airfield of Hucknall, with an all civilian crew. The two airfields were only a few miles apart so the crew were nearly home and dry, but not quite as is so often the case.

As always, I picked up my share of secondary duties, one particularly mundane, Officer I/c the NAAFI, but another that I actually revelled in, was being in charge of the Station football team. Football had become something of an obsession with me over the years, and now here I was actually in charge of a team. During my time in the RAF the only other team activity I had even remotely been involved with was when I, and another NCO pilot by the name of Rod Burners, had been roped into the station tug of war team at Tern Hill. That had come about because our Flight Commander, Flt lt Mike Earland, Officer I/C of that sport had become quite desperate to find a full team. Very unexpectedly, we had taken all before us until being beaten in the inter services final in front of a madly cheering crowd at the Royal Tournament, Earls Court. The only crowd that we performed before, in fact. I never saw Mike Earland after leaving Tern Hill, but have seen letters written by him to the British Airline Pilots Association (BALPA) house mag called "the Log", from time to time. As for our soccer team, things could not have been better. With national service still being the order of the day, all Stations had a vast pool of 18 to 20 year olds to pick from, and at Swinderby we seemed to have been particularly well blessed with some excellent up and coming young players. One even claimed to have already played in an FA Cup semi-final, which took quite a bit of believing, but it turned out to be quite true. He was in the reserves as a centre half for one of the Sheffield clubs, when their first team had been forced into a replay, following a draw in that round. With the first team centre half having been injured, our young lad had taken his place for the replay. On demob he was transferred to Norwich City, but he was tragically killed in a car accident before he had established himself there. We certainly trained hard, with two long night sessions per week in the gym, which I well remember as one night a late comer brought the tragic news of the Munich Air disaster, which had wiped out many of Manchester United's team. So many talented players lost forever.

RAF Swinderby's team almost picked itself with talented players available for all positions. We won the inter services league for the Lincolnshire area and also reached the semi-finals of the RAF cup, being pipped in the semi finals by RAF Swanton Morely. We think that particular RAF station may have taken a leaf out of the British Army's books. It was well known that, for instance, the Army Corps of Signals, with outposts all over the country, could, by internal postings, arrange for all good players to be based in one particular barracks. It was well known that Signal Corps's best football players had been posted to Catterick, but our Station team managed to beat them in a friendly. One interesting game occurred at RAF Cranwell, when Doncaster Rovers asked if our Lincolnshire Services League could produce a team from the best players available in our organisation to play against their second eleven for a pre-season work out. It turned out to be great fun and an even handed match, possibly because one of the budding Doncaster players is now better known as a comedian; Charlie Williams. One player from the RAF Hemswell team, however, was known to be rather too robust for the likings of opposing players, be they footballers or cricketers. It was the one and only Fred Trueman doing his national service in the RAF.

Ever since being called on for armed guard duties during the war at both RAF Pershore and Warmwell, before becoming aircrew, I had always wanted to see what shooting over longer ranges than the standard 25 yard range on every RAF camp, was like. Now was my chance, because a fellow instructor, John Collins, was in charge of that sport. It was educational going down to Bisley, although it was tented accommodation, yet again, to fire over distances up to 600 yards or more. It was there that I was introduced to the art of sitting on ammo boxes to view bullets passing down the range. At the risk of repeating myself, I still think all budding fighter pilots would have benefitted from that experience during the war.

The mundane secondary duty of I/C the NAAFI was boring in the extreme, and the fielding of complaining phone calls from the two civilian cleaning ladies was driving me to distraction. I finally snapped when one of them, in a high state of excitement, rang one morning to report that she had found two disgusting objects under one of the billiard tables. It being early May she was not amused when I said "it sounds as if Spring is sprung". I could well imagine that young airmen and airwomen would find it a little difficult in locating a place to be alone in an RAF camp, but the top of the billiard table sounded disgusting to my mind. Leaving disgusting objects as a trade mark made it even worse. I did get my just deserts later that year during our annual Air Officers' Inspection. The NAAFI building was on the inspection list, and with the rear of that building being close to a wooded area keeping the courtyard clear of fallen leaves was our main worry. Everything went well on the numerous dummy runs, the NAAFI manageress having ensured that one of her girls had given it a good going over each time. Come the big day, of course, it turned into a right can of worms. The rear area was a complete mess, the AOC prodded every pile of leaves with his stick of office and, although he never said a word, the looks on the Station Commander's face was fit to kill. Needless to say, I did not know how quick to seek out the manageress when it was all over, to find out what on earth had gone wrong. She was very sorry but she, and all her living in staff, had been up all night because the girl who normally cleaned the back area each morning had become ill, and they had rushed her to the nearest hospital in the small hours. A fit of compassion came over me and I asked if it was anything serious. "Oh no", she replied, "It was a baby boy". Talk about being gob smacked! "Surely you knew she was pregnant, didn't you"? I managed to ask. "No, we didn't, never even suspected it for one moment", was her reply.

My interest in Flight Safety had not abated one little bit and I think that I managed to put the world to rights on two occasions, one which, in my opinion, applied to all RAF aircraft and not just the Vampire. It was after a report by a pilot that on a night detail he had virtually lost all his electrics, even the low voltage cockpit lighting which illuminated the all important blind flying panel. It was towards the end of his one hour detail that things had become really nasty. The engineering staff, and I concluded that the pilot must have failed to notice that the generator failure warning light had been on from shortly after engine start up. The pilot concerned said he would certainly have noticed such a light being on. I will just point out that all such lights had a dimmer device which was a simple glass coloured lid which reduced the intensity of warning lights so as not to distract the pilot in a power failure emergency at night. This was a standard fit to all RAF aircraft during the 1940s and 50s and being on night flying details myself at the time of the incident, I decided on a little experiment of my own. Before starting the engine which would extinguish the red warning light, I flicked the dimmer device over it and was amazed at the reduction in intensity of the red light. The light's position in the cockpit did not help either. I reasoned that the pilot concerned had failed to notice that, at some time or other, the dimmer device had been knocked to the on position. Concluding that the chances of seeing the warning light on during day trips with the dimmer on would have been impossible, so why should they not all be removed from important warning lights. Although everyone agreed with this, some noting that at night a warning light without a generator working would not remain a distraction for very long with so much battery juice being used in the aircraft anyway, all pilots worth their salt should be able to cope with that inconvenience during a rapid return to base. The recommendation to remove plastic type dimmers was passed up the line and with nothing happening over the next few months, I steadily removed them myself and nobody seemed to notice, not even on major servicing.

The other problem I dealt with after a few pilots had reported oxygen failure in flight only required a simple remedy. But nothing is simple, is it? For the ground staff, looking into the reported failures on each occasion found the oxygen supply tube was disconnected at a point in the bottom of the cockpit, where a quick release point had been introduced with the phasing in of ejector seats. All they had to do was reconnect and confirm that the disconnect point was not too loose, and that was it, the problem was then recorded as rectified. Needless to say, I certainly checked the length of the Oxygen tubes during my next few flights and concluded that although I was 6' tall and on the tubby side the length of tube was just about adequate. At first, I had missed one vital point and that was that height of the pilot worked in an inverse way. That is to say a tall pilot would lower his seat and a smallish one lift his seat before strapping in. So it turned out that the few smallish, and tubby, pilots had stretched the oxygen tube beyond it's limits. I obviously put into writing my observations and suggested that a 4" increase in tube length would solve the pilot height problem.

On the flying side we took turns in going over to RAF Strubby, a satellite airfield of the RAF flying college at RAF Manby, for a weeks flying of Meteor two seat T7s and also the single seat Mk 8s, both superb aircraft. One well remembered feature of the Meteor by all who had flown it was it's super suspension during taxying which was like riding in a Rolls Royce, or as near to it as you will ever get in an aircraft. The undercarriage was also well remembered for very different reasons which could prove fatal under certain conditions. If you lowered the undercarriage, which was, of course, normally carried out at circuit height, with the air brakes still out you could finish up in what was called a "phantom dive", particularly so if on asymetric power, simulated or for real. This phenomena was caused by the fact that in the Meteor aircraft one undercarriage leg always lowered before the other, and the extra drag on that side caused the aircraft to yaw and enter a spiral dive if the air brakes had not been selected in. This feature had been talked about by generations of pilots, but did the vintage pair (Vampire/ Meteor duo) pilot know about it when he was killed at a Coventry air display long after all other Meteors had passed out of service?

The other flying treat for me came about because our Flight

Gloster Meteor

Commander, Derek Atkinson, was a gliding fanatic who had persuaded the RAF to allow the East Midlands Gliding Club to use our field at weekends. Having shown some interest, he had me off solo after a couple of launches. It was pure heaven to be up there without any engine noise whatsoever but, unfortunately, I never chanced upon another RAF airfield operating gliders ever again, although Derek was still going strong on them as late as 1983 at RAF Syerston, and probably still is!

Students still came and went and two of mine I will never forget. They both came from New Zealand and went by the names of Mangin and Dywer. As it was approaching Christmas, many of us wondered what would happen to them over the festive season, as the Mess would close down as usual. They both opted for London, and we need not have worried because one night after their Christmas leave had started, they both appeared on TV being interviewed by a prim and proper lady reporter on a street in London who started the ball rolling by saying "I understand that you are both New Zealanders, what do you intend doing over Christmas in London then"? One of them then held up a dead turkey by it's neck and said "We'll give this a good stuffing to start with, and...' needless to say, the interview did not last much longer, with the lady with the microphone interrupting to say she hoped their first Christmas in England was a happy one; no doubt it was! For those watching at Swinderby, who knew the terrible twins well, concluded that they were both drunk as skunks. After Mangin had left the RAF to join Air New Zealand he worked his way up to the very top of that airline on the piloting side. I never heard much about Dwyer again, but his brother led a flight of Royal New Zealand flying boats through Singapore during my time there, on a final goodwill flight but, sad to say, died of natural causes shortly after that.

One particular course of specialists who passed through our training organisation before my time was up was a full house of RAF engineering officers. Some took to flying like ducks to water. A few others however, were just a little too pedantic, especially in mechanical matters, which was natural enough, but pilots must play their cards as they come, and flexibility is no bad thing in aviation. However, one was particularly helpful to me in my flying life when I had taken over the RAF's last flying Lancaster, but more of that later. In addition to students on the second phase of their wings course, we had others who had just graduated from the RAF college at Cranwell and, because the Station was still using the piston powered Balliol, had not yet received any jet training at all.

Obviously these young officers had decided to make the RAF a full career commitment and it showed a little at times. Although their flying was probably of a higher standard than the here today, gone tomorrow attitude of some short service students. I met many of the ex-Cranwell lads over the years and I was particularly pleased to see Hugh Rigg again when he was Wing Commander in charge of flying at an air display at RAF Duxford which I was involved in. Just in case anybody is wondering, yes, Hugh was the brother of the actress Diana Rigg.

In the case of instructors, a divide was beginning to set in as regards age groups. Although the majority still came from the wartime intakes, a growing number were eager beavers in their middle 20s. A few of these let it be known from time to time that perhaps some of the WWII wallahs had peaked and new blood was what the RAF now required. Having noted that most of them, although ex-fighter pilots had, after completing tours on Venoms or Meteors, passed through CFS before the introduction of the Hawker Hunter, I let it slip to one or two of the young is beautiful brigade that one had not really lived until you had flown a supersonic Hunter. Mutter, mutter, but it kept them quiet for a bit!

However, it was among the younger generation that I mostly mixed with when not on duty, and I will always remember Chips Carpenter, not only an ex-Halton apprentice like myself, but also the son of an apprentice. Then there was Pete Riley and Gordon Blagborough, both of whom were always ready for a night on the town. In our case a night on the town meant a trip to a village pub the Lord Nelson in Winthorpe or the Fox at Kelham, and sometimes both, each of these two public houses being just outside Newark. The wives of the two landlords were, in fact, sisters. The only daughter of the house at the Lord Nelson was named Pat, forty years later, my wife and I often made a trip over to Newark to see her, she was very popular.

Our little drinking group was soon split asunder by the fall of the Duncan Sandys axe of 1957 and the planned ending of National Service by 1960, which meant a reduction in RAF numbers of about 50% from 300,000. The politicians were now coming around to the thought long held by anyone who had seen Hiroshima, that prevention was better than cure, and in that context an atomic deterrent was essential. For the time being, at least, the RAF would rely on three new V bombers, the Vulvan, Victor and Valiant, but it was only a matter of time before delivery would be possible by intercontinental ballistic missiles and cruise missiles, the logical successors to the V1 and V2 of WWII. When that arrived, the strategic bomber would have had it's day and, along with it, at least two thirds of the interceptor fighter force. All that would remain for them would be the interception of spy planes intruding into friendly air space, because the chances of shooting down low level high speed attacking aircraft from the air had all but gone. However, the WWII fighter type aircraft had really come into their own as ground attack aircraft in support of the army in the Western Desert and during and after D Day. So, the fighter type aircraft would live on for ground attack missions, but medium and high level bombers would gradually pass into the history books. Although the anger about the Sandys axe still lingered on for many years in the RAF who, now, can gainsay he was not right? Back in the mid 1950s, the impact of cutting the interceptor force by such a vast amount resulted in a sudden surplus of young fighter pilots. Most of us fast approaching middle age, particularly so in the flying sense, naturally thought we would soon be shown the door, but it was quite the reverse in the event. I think the old military principle of only having so many people in a particular age group, the pyramid concept, held sway, and so it came about that it was pilots and others in their mid twenties that were made redundant.

As regards RAF Swinderby, it meant that Chips, Pete and Gordon all left within weeks of each other but, by a remarkable coincidence, they each joined BOAC, or British Airways as it is now. I was very sorry to see them go and, in particular, Chips with his RAF background. However, Betty and I often saw Chips staging through Singapore in the sixties and I met Gordon again at JFK airport in New York when I was on a night stop flying Belfasts. Looking back to those days, I'm startled when I think of those that lost their lives in later RAF accidents which included one in a Canberra, two in Helicopters, one in a Javelin and, of course, the crash in the King's Cup race. All particularly sad and one, for me, because I had been involved in a night search off Singapore Island for a Javelin aircraft which had disappeared from ground radar screens one evening. Being on a night circuits and bumps detail in a Hastings at the time we had been called upon to join the search, but it had been mission impossible under the night conditions but one can but try in certain cases such as that. The wreckage was found early the next morning and the name of the dead pilot announced as Flt Lt Peter Poppy. Peter had served as an instructor on the same flight as myself at Swinderby, but I did not even know that he was in the Far East at that time, with the night fighters being based at RAF Tengah. The wreckage was, in fact, found in shallow waters at about the mid point of the downwind leg that we had been flying on and, for the rest of my time at Changi, I always gave a quick look down to the sea at that point. About six months later, I saw a massive black "sting ray" near the point of the Javelin's impact. What a reminder! I well remember that at Swinderby, Peter's dress was always immaculate except for his service shoes which left a lot to be desired and were sometimes commented upon by our superiors. Being a friend of his, he confided one day that he would never dream of flying without them, although we were supposed to wear boots, particularly so after the introduction of ejector seats. It appeared that during his time on the first Vampire Squadron in the canal zone of Egypt he had crash landed in the desert after engine failure. After a day in the shade of his wrecked aircraft, and with no sign of a rescue party, he had set off due north to intercept the Western Desert coastal road to seek help and eventually made it. It was confirmed later that he had travelled all of seventy miles with his shoes almost in tatters by the end of his epic journey. The camp Arabs, needless to say, made an excellent job of repairing them.

Other names come thick and fast from those days and on our Squadron we had a WWII ground attack pilot by the name of Pat Courtney, who had a mention in the "Official History of the RAF during WWII", along with his brother Buck. They had served alongside each other on the same squadron in Burma and it recorded that on one occasion, during a ground attack mission against a Japanese strong point, both brothers had hit the same tree and each had managed to bring back their damaged Hurricane to a safe landing. Their unlikely story was later confirmed by an army forward air controller. I completely lost touch with Pat, but met his brother, Buck, for the first time after he had left the service as a Group Captain. It was after landing with the BBMF at Norwich Airport, my old stamping ground of Horsham-St-Faith's, that I learnt that the airport director was, indeed, Buck Courtney. After introduction, he kindly took us all down to their Workers Club, which I instantly recognised as being the old Station Commander's residence, it being set some distance away from all other quarters! It was sad to see in later years that the names of the brothers both appeared in the obituary columns of the Daily Telegraph. Another fellow instructor at Swinderby was Flt Lt Dave Court. After moving into married quarters he became the proud father of triplets, all girls, and the only set that I ever came across in the RAF. After deciding that civil flying was probably better than the RAF at that time, Dave took up an airline appointment and rapidly shot up the ladder with British Midland Airways. I seem to recall that, after becoming their senior pilot, he was later a director of that splendid airline. In the RAF, meanwhile, not many of the Swinderby staff made much impression as regards promotion, although Flight Lieutenants "Mo" Short and Gordon Gilbert of our flight, became Group Captains, another Gilbert, Joe, became an Air Chief Marshal.

In the time and place concept it is often difficult to place people who you have not seen for a quarter of a century or so, but one person I really should have picked up during my third and final passage through CFS at RAF Leeming in 1981, was Tom Lecky-Thompson who had made a name for himself by taking off his Harrier jump jet from a coal yard, near St Pancras Station in London, and flying non stop to New York in 6 hours and 11 minutes. He had, of course, been refuelled in mid air over the Atlantic by Victor tankers of No 57 and 214 Squadrons. The flight had taken place in May of 1969 and earned Tom the winners award in the East/ West section of the Daily Mail's Transatlantic air race. However, I should have remembered him also for his robust style of soccer play at Swinderby, if nothing else, even outshining Freddie Trueman in that department.

It was in the Mess bar one night I noted a stranger who looked vaguely familiar but I just couldn't put a name to him at first, but eventually I decided that it could possibly be Tom Lechy -Thompson except that Tom had left the service in the 1970s. Later that evening when, as usual the late drinkers tended to join company, I eventually said to the stranger that he looked a bit like a chap I had met in the 1950s. "And who might that be"? was his very obvious reply. "Oh, an officer called Lecky-Thompson, but I understand he left the service some time ago". "But I am Lecky-Thompson", came the excited riposte, "I've just re-joined". I was happy to tell him that in my local village of Woodhall Spa, near RAF Coningsby, one pub by the name of the Abbey Lodge had, amongst it's display of ten or so aviation prints and photographs, one showing his take off from St Pancras and another of myself flying the BBMF's Lancaster over Trafalgar square which had occurred as part of the build up to one year's Royal Tournament, when the RAF's turn came around to be the organiser for that event.

It might be worth pointing out that in the aftermath of the cutbacks in the strength of the RAF in 1957, 1968 and 1975, the RAF had on each occasion found themselves short of pilots soon afterwards, and with a training bill then approaching £4 million per pilot in today's money, they had to almost beg pilots to return to the colours. After leaving Leeming to finish my time at Swinderby, I came across one such pilot flying Chipmunks there, who told me quite a funny story about his own return. Flt Lt George Smith had served in both the Royal Navy and RAF as a pilot but, now well into his fifties, about 56 in fact, he thought, having heard about the shortage, that he might well chance his arm and drop into the RAF recruiting office in Nottingham to see if they might just take him back. The Officer I/C was away on business, but the usual two young WRAF dolly birds, bait to catch unsuspecting young male recruits no doubt, were sitting behind their desk and looked with curiosity more than anything else when George entered and gave the various recruiting displays a quick glance. One of the girls said, "and what can we do for you, Sir"? "I'd like to know something about joining the RAF", was George's reply, when he really meant to say re-joining. "For yourself, Sir, or perhaps one of your young sons"? was the young lady's next one. The two girls gave each other a quick knowing glance when George said, "No, it's for me all right". No doubt they had dealt with cranks before, and the name of the game was to play along with such people, so one of them said, "and what have you got in mind, Sir, there are upper age limits you know"? "Oh, flying, as a pilot of course". That really was too much for the two WRAFs who both had smirks on their faces as they advised him that perhaps he should return the next day when their Flight Lieutenant would be pleased to deal with him, and thinking, no doubt, that would be the last of him, with a couple of chaps in white coats as well, was George's thought as he left the premises. He did have the last laugh, of course, the next day, when he saw the flight Lieutenant who welcomed him with open arms and said in view of the fact that George was a QFI he would almost certainly be taken on again to the age of sixty, like myself, with a good chance of a posting not far from his home, to RAF Swinderby, which had just started flying operations again as a grading school. The two young WRAFs looked a little sheepish as George made his exit with a very big smile on his face.

My time was fast running out at RAF Swinderby and I had an inkling of what might be on the cards when Wing Commander Fred Symmonds rang one day and said "I seem to remember that under types flown in your log book a number of multi piston types get a mention, could you just run over them"? Even I thought it sounded as if I'd been around a bit in that world when I reeled off, Oxford, Anson, Wellington, Mosquito, Lancaster, Valetta, Meteor, and Lincoln, but, on reflection, it was just as well that he had not asked for total multi engined hours, which did not amount to all that much at that time. Another point was that many people assumed in those days that you must have trained on Oxfords up to Wings standard if you had flown some of the types I have mentioned, which was not so in my case. Fred told me to hang around the flights at the end of my flying details, he might just have some news for me. Talk about "the Longest Day"; I thought it was never going to end. Eventually, he rang to say he had found a niche for me, but what a niche! It turned out that Transport Command had fallen for the idea that all instructors on their long range Transport OCU should be QFIs, and both RAF Oakington and RAF Swinderby were to produce one each for direct entry Captaincy on Hastings. The very likeable "Cobber" Kane was selected from Oakington, and I was the lucky one from Swinderby.

I had two very emotional send off parties, and each with a presentational tankard to mark my departure. The first one was given by the Station football team during a party at a pub called "the Halfway House" on the A46 Newark-Lincoln road. The second was hosted by our Squadron CO, "Boss" Blair, at the Fox, at Kelham and it was most fortuitous the night he picked and not the previous one. I expect that it is only older readers that will recall that in the heyday of the cinema, one film company always showed a strapping figure of a man striking a massive gong at the start of all their productions. He was known to all as Bombardier Billy Wells. By the 1950s he must have fallen on hard times because he was touring the pubs, that would have him, with a performing donkey! Those present at the Fox the night before all enjoyed it, but I doubt if it would have fitted in with a farewell party.

Just before I left for pastures new, the RAF, with the end of national service in sight and, therefore, the end of unlimited cheap labour, had decided to give civilian catering a trial run at three stations. Namely, RAF Dishforth, Northolt, and Swinderby. The diehards thought that their world had come to an end because, with civilian caterers, any extra work, beyond normal hours, would call for extra money, probably the usual double for overtime, and the number of dining in nights would reduce dramatically, and so it came to pass. With moving from Swinderby to Dishforth I was probably one of the first to sample two out of the three and, I must say, that I thought that both firms were first class. Contracting out has spread far beyond catering in the years since, and although flying squadrons might come and go, with their supporting staff, the basic structure of any permanent RAF base in the UK is going nowhere, so why should not locally employed civilians gain some benefit from defence spending? At the end of the day, we are all paying for it.

When I look back over the time I spent in the Service, I always recall that the four month Hastings course at RAF Dishforth was by far the best I ever undertook. It consisted of two months of ground school and two months of flying. Both ground and air instruction was of the highest standard, carried out by dedicated staff. One of the most professional was the chief civilian meteorologist who ploughed through 50 hours of meticulous in depth tuition of meteorology worldwide; which left me with an abiding interest in that subject over the years.

Having served in Egypt, I was well aware that sandstorms could appear from nowhere and reduce visibility to nil in no time at all, during the winter months. Until listening to Mike giving one of his lectures, I had never realised that it's official name was not only Arabic but had three different spellings depending in which part of the world you landed in. He confirmed that we might come across Khamsin, Kamsin or Khamseen, but all meaning southerly sandstorm. He also told us that when dealing with very senior officers who had, obviously, been trained before WWII, to accept that their knowledge of meteorology was more than likely to be rudimentary in the extreme. He underlined this by a short funny story. It was about an Air Marshal who was due to fly from an airfield near Cairo to Khartoum, via a refuelling stop at Wadi Halfa. The VIP aircraft was to be flown by a junior officer, who was only informed at the very last minute that a Khamseen had suddenly set in at Wadi Halfa, and that airfield was closed until further notice. He knew full well that this late cancellation was not likely to best please the Air Marshal, and was certainly not looking forward to his arrival. When the staff car duly arrived, with the flag of rank well to the fore, the pilot stepped forward and, after an immaculate salute, said, "I'm terribly sorry, Sir, but we can't go today, there's a Khamseen on down south", to which the Air Marshal replied, "those bloody natives and their religious festivals". Before the pilot could enlarge, the very important person had jumped back into the staff car and was last seen disappearing at high speed into the distance. The pilot stood with his mouth open, but the ground crew obviously thought it hilarious.

I came under the wing of a first rate instructor when allocated to Flt Lt Jim Collyer, who was then the Deputy Flight Commander. The first experience of another type of aircraft is always significant to a student, but I really took to the dear old Hastings. It seemed to have something

Handley Page Hastings

special about it and the only thing that I had to try and get used to during the first few trips was, compared with the Vampire, a very large circuit, the downwind legs seemed to go on for ever and ever. One aspect that all ex-Hastings pilots will always remember is the superb seating arrangements. Not only very well upholstered with the usual backwards and forwards movement, but also arm rests, inclining backrests, and a headrest which could be reversed according to a pilot's liking. Unfortunately, like almost all other twin railed seats, it could slip back if not properly locked, particularly at one of the most critical phases of flight, that is the take off run, and with the Hastings being a tail dragger this was more likely to happen than on a nose wheeled aircraft. It is thought that a fatal accident on the Berlin airlift may have been caused by the Captain's seat slipping back at such a critical time. It was rumoured that when the makers of any later large aircraft for the RAF, other than those equipped with ejector seats of course, asked "What type of Pilot's seat do you require?", the answer came back, "the same as the Hastings of course". It never turned out like that, needless to say.

I was always keen to see the sharp end of any aircraft, even those that I was never likely to fly myself, at the first opportunity. The chance to inspect a Comet came about after a landing at RAF Lyneham when I found one which No 216 Squadron had been operating since 1956 parked nearby. I nipped up the front passenger steps to have a quick look and found everything looking just dandy except for the pilot's seats, they looked as if they had been copied from an old Austin Seven, rather than a Hastings. The sharpness of the nose had dictated that, and on the principle of nothing for nothing that nose shape was imperative if high speed flight was the name of the game. The jump from Vampire instructor to four engined transport Captain, with a total crew of six, had been a mighty leap but for Cobber Kane and myself it had many compensations such as no wearing of Bonedomes, flying boots or wearing of parachutes connected to ejector seats. Use of oxygen, although provided was most unlikely and although long hours between staging posts was now the order of the day we had automatic pilots at our disposal and eager, sometimes too eager, loadmasters to thrust cups of coffee into your hands. During these long legs the Hastings was mostly flown at the nearest quadrantal level to 10,000' and at an indicated airspeed of 173 knots which worked out at 200 knots true in standard temperature conditions. The flight engineer would calculate fuel used every hour for the benefit of the navigator and captain. It was quite something on the rare occasions when it dropped to 200 gallons/ hour, one nautical mile flown for each gallon of fuel used.

The flying was fairly intense with the emphasis, quite rightly, placed on instrument flying and various approach aids, such as the non-directional beacon and the wartime's BABS system of giving dots four or dashes three or whatever. All students, of course, looked forward to one of the final stages of the course which was the route trainer, this was a flight to one of the RAF's bases in the Mediterranean and back, two student crews were always carried under the supervision of a staff crew. In our case me and my crew would fly the outbound leg to Idris, twenty miles south of Tripoli, and return as passengers, while the other student crew would fly the return journey. It turned out that the name of Idris was at the request of the post war Libyan government and their head of state King Idris. All WWII airmen and soldiers will better remember it by the Italian name of Castel Benito when they first constructed it in the 1930s. For the many people who ask why it was built 20 miles south of Tripoli when so much desert land was available much closer to that city, the quick answer is that it was to protect it from the 18" guns of British battleships in the event of war in the Mediterranean. The same applies to El Adem, Tobruk and Benina Benghazi.

The day of the route trainer gave me a taste of things to come in the transport world. It was a leisurely jaunt down to RAF Lyneham on day one, the start point of many overseas departures and arrivals as they had a permanent staff of HM Customs and Excise based there. To say that accommodation for transitting crews was basic would be a massive understatement. Although Lyneham had been built on pre-war lines, it was visualised that it's use would be confined to MU work and, possibly, for basic flying training. However, WWII had changed all that and due, no doubt, to it's location in the south west of England, it became one of the first major RAF station used for both overseas transport and aircraft ferry operations. This was, of course, due to the fact that all such flights to Africa and the Middle and Far East had to be routed via the Bay of Biscay and Gibraltar, as long as France remained in German hands. Due to the almost nonexistent accommodation for passengers and transit aircrew, the old wartime grass airfield at Clyffe Pypard, on high ground a few miles to the south, had been taken over to try and solve the problem. The sleeping arrangements consisted of old wartime wooden huts with virtually no heating. Thank goodness it was only on outbound trips, when an early start was required, that we were to be subjected to such one night stands. The only saving grace was that there was a lovely village pub just one mile from the camp, but down a very steep hill. It was a pity that it wasn't the other way round and then it would have been downhill at closing time and not up. The station Warrant Officer (SWO) in charge of discipline visited the pub every other week, but he certainly wasn't there for the beer. He always came in a five ton lorry at midday to collect stolen bicycles which enterprising airmen had nicked for a free wheel down and a walk, or stagger back. Historically, the RAF eventually got it's long promised transit hotel, and new Officer's Mess, in 1967. That is to say, 22 years after the war ended, the same year that the British pulled out of Aden and only five years before the withdrawal from both the Far East and Persian Gulf. What planning, what timing.

I'm sure the money spent on keeping Cliffe Pypard open, even for just one year, would have paid for the new accommodation at Lyneham, penny wise pound foolish really, coming into it's own. RAF Brize Norton, after it became the main transit airfield, managed to achieve the same building programme in six years but even that was longer than it needed to have been according to some experts on the subject.

The trip itself went off quite well and the flying of the airways system over France was quite interesting for first timers like ourselves. We were made more than welcome at Idris by the movements staff who seemed genuinely pleased to be dealing with a dedicated transport aircraft for a change because the main staging post for such aircraft was now at El Adem for those who were en route to Aden and the Far East. Idris seemed to be used mostly for Squadron detachments and also experimental aircraft from Boscombe Down needing a hot climate for certain trials. One interesting story from our hosts at Idris, that underlined what we had already been taught during our course, was regarding the only ditching that was ever to take place in a Hastings aircraft. It had been stressed time and time again that if and when we needed an uplift of engine oil at any other airfield we must double check that it was of the non-detergent variety and not detergent. Apparently, there had been a number of cases of ground crew working on the principle that engine oil is engine oil, and had replenished the rather thirsty Hercules engines with what turned out to be detergent oil, the nearest to hand in most cases. Detergent oil led to a phenomena known as gulping which led to all the engine oil being dumped overboard. Transport command became so alarmed at the situation, which seemed to occur mainly in the Near and Middle east, that they decided to send a small team of technical officers down the route to check and, if necessary, educate all concerned with the replenishment of engine oil for staging transport aircraft. It was on their flight into Idris from another Mediterranean airfield, when still over the sea, that the Captain was forced to ditch after losing three of his four engines. I suppose that is what is called first hand experience. All crew and passengers survived, by the way. After arrival back at Dishforth all that remained was a number of category tests. In the transport world you could hold a cat "D" which limited you to cargo only flights, a "C" which would allow you to carry passengers, a "B" which was above average and essential for VIP work, and "A" which was as rare as hens teeth. I managed to get a "D" REC "C" which meant I was up to passenger carrying standard but lacked the number of hours on type for me to do so. The upshot of this was that on arrival at the main Hastings base of RAF Colerne, near Bath, I carried out many non-passenger trips purely to build up the necessary hours required. The odd freight only detail proved to be quite productive and one, in particular, highlighted the fact that it was not only the wrong type of oil that could cause major problems to the fading petrol driven transport force. My task was to take four Hercules engines to Germany, two at a time, and recover four that needed major overhauls in the UK. It had come about because jet fuel had been used by re-fuellers instead of petrol. Quite naturally, the error had only surfaced after the four engines had been started up, and the petrol already in the fuel lines burnt off. Quite a shock for the crew when one engine after another failed, luckily well before take off. It was on the day of the first Germany return trip that I met the then CO of No XI Squadron, and the less than fruitful chat about squadron silver.

The only item that I was not happy with on the dear old Hastings from a flight safety point of view was similar to the generator warning light problem on the Vampire, only in this case, it was the four engine fire warning lights which were incorporated into the individual engine feathering buttons. I was glad to see that the night dimmer gadget device, this time a slide and not of the lid type, was wired in the off position so that the light would be seen even in sunlight conditions, but did anyone actually know if the red light bulb was in a serviceable condition? I thought a simple test switch that would activate all four bulbs for test purposes could have been fitted at very little cost. The suggestion that it should be done fell on deaf ears and I was only a new boy poking my nose in.

So, the first three phases of my time in the RAF had ended. From Halton, through pilot training and my time on fighters into the world of training, I had already gained a wide experience of both the world and the RAF. As we end this first volume of '52 Years in the Cockpit' I am about to embark upon a new phase in my career in the world of Transport Command. Volume 2 details my career from this point and includes my time as pilot of the BBMF Lancaster. I did not know then what lay ahead of me, in all its rich variety, and I hope you will be intrigued enough to read on.

RAF TYPES FLOWN

Tiger Moth
Cornell
Harvard
Spitfire
Master
Martinet
Oxford
Mosquito
Prentice
Vampire
Balliol
Seafire
Wellington
Anson
Chipmunk
Piston Provost
Hunter
Meteor
Hastings
Valetta
Varsity
Belfast
Lancaster
Auster
Lincoln
Devon
Twin-Pioneer
Canberra
Hercules
Argosy
Andover
Shackleton
Bulldog
Jet Provst

CIVILIAN AIRCRAFT FLOWN

Taylorcraft 'D'
Cessna 120/140/152/172
PA 28 Archer/Cherokee/Arrow/Cadet
Beagle Pup 121
TB10 Tobago
TB20 Trinidad
PA23 Aztec
Falco
Cap 21
Trago Mills
PA38 Tomahawk
Mooney M20A
Pitts Special (Single Seat)
Beech Duchess
Jodel 117A
AA5B Tiger
Bucker Jungmann
Sundowner
Bolko
Zlin
Rallye
PA22 Tri-Pacer
PA32 Cherokee Six
Miles Magister
PA18 Super Club
Robin 180
Antonov AN2
GY80 Horizon
Auster
Cessna 310
Bijou
Wacco
ME108
Cambodian Gunship
PT17 Stearman
Fairchild Argus
PA39 Twin Commanche
Slingsby Firefly